Electronic Literacies
Language, Culture, and Power
in Online Education

෪•෫

Electronic Literacies
Language, Culture, and Power in Online Education

ॐ•ॐ

Mark Warschauer
University of Hawaiʻi

LEA LAWRENCE ERLBAUM ASSOCIATES, PUBLISHERS
1999 Mahwah, New Jersey   London

Lawrence Erlbaum Associates, Inc., Publishers
10 Industrial Avenue
Mahwah, NJ 07430

Cover design by Kathryn Houghtaling Lacey

Library of Congress Cataloging-in-Publication Data

Electronic liliteracies : language, culture, and power in
online education / Mark Warschauer.
　　　p. cm.
Includes bibliographical references and indexes.
ISBN 0–8058–3118–5 (cloth : alk. paper). —
ISBN 0–8058–3119–3 (pbk. : alk. paper)
　　1. Computers and Literacy—Social aspects—Hawaii—Oahu—Case studies. 2. Education, Higher—Hawaii—Oahu—Data processing—Case studies.　　3.
Computer-assisted instruction—Social aspects—Hawaii—Oahu—Case studies. 4. English language—Hawaii—Oahu—Rhetoric—Case studies. 5.　　English
language—Study and teaching—Hawaii—Oahu—Foreign speakers—Case studies. 6.　Multicultural education—Hawaii—Oahu—Case studies. I. Title
　　LC149.5.W37　　　1998
　　371.33'4—dc21
　　　　　　　　　　　　　　　　　　　98–23392
　　　　　　　　　　　　　　　　　　　CIP

Books published by Lawrence Erlbaum Associates are printed
on acid-free paper, and their bindings are chosen for strength
and durability.

Printed in the United States of America
10　9　8　7　6　5　4　3

Contents

༄·༖

Preface

ᘛ•ᘚ

I planned and conducted the research for this book from 1995 to 1997, years when the Internet emerged from a convenient communications tool for a small number of scholars and hackers to a full-blown mass medium affecting many aspects of American life. It was during these years as well that the U.S. educational system began to confront the necessity of developing electronic literacies as an important part of the school curriculum.

In this book, I look at how the nature of reading and writing is changing and how those changes are addressed in the classroom. I focus on the experiences of culturally and linguistically diverse learners who are at special risk of being marginalized from the information society: immigrant students, indigenous students, learners of second languages, and speakers of second dialects.

I provide an in-depth view of four language and writing classes that I investigated in 1996 and 1997: an undergraduate English as a second language (ESL) writing class at a small Christian college, a graduate ESL writing class at a large public university, an undergraduate writing-intensive Hawaiian language class at the same public university, and an English writing class at a community college. All four classes took place in Hawai'i, on the island of O'ahu. Hawai'i is an exceptional place for learning about interaction across cultures. Its population includes large numbers of indigenous people and immigrants from many countries. It is the only U.S. state that has two official languages (English and Hawaiian) and where the majority of residents speak a creole (Hawai'i Creole English, commonly referred to as Pidgin). The state's colleges and universities enroll numerous international students, especially from the Asia-Pacific Region.

Although Hawai'i is a special place, the issues confronted here are similar in many ways to those that exist throughout the United States and many other countries: how to provide culturally and linguistically diverse students with the literacies needed to allow them to fully participate in public, community, and economic life in the 21st century.

In this book, I discuss these issues in the following manner. In chapter 1, I provide a brief historical analysis of the socio-economic and technological bases of literacy and introduce contentious issues related to the emergence of electronic literacies today. In chapters 2 through 5, I report in depth on each of the four classes I researched. In chapter 6, I interpret this research to draw conclusions about the relation of new online technologies to literacy, education, and culture. In the epilogue, I revisit the teachers of the four classes to see how their perspectives and practices continued to develop following the semester that I worked with them. Finally, in the appendix, I introduce the ethnographic approach and methods I used for researching the online classroom.

ACKNOWLEDGMENTS

I am extremely grateful to the teachers and students who welcomed me into their classrooms for this project. I will not soon forget their generosity of spirit.

This book represents a revised version of my doctoral dissertation at the University of Hawai'i. It would not have been possible without the guidance and support offered by the faculty members of the university's Department of English as a Second Language and doctoral program in Second Language Acquisition, and particularly the members of my dissertation committee: Kathryn Davis, Graham Crookes, Gabriele Kasper, and Richard Schmidt of the Department of English as a Second Language; Lois Yamauchi of the Department of Educational Psychology; and Jim Cummins of the Ontario Institute for Studies in Education. Jim Cummins later provided very helpful guidance as I developed the book that grew out of the dissertation.

Lourdes Ortega of the University of Hawai'i assisted with much of the data analysis included in chapter 3, and I appreciate her collaboration and insights. Richard Kern, Paul Lyons, and Cynthia Selfe read previous versions of the manuscript and offered numerous helpful comments and suggestions. Denise Murray of San Jose State University reviewed the book for Lawrence Erlbaum Associates and provided very helpful comments.

Special thanks go to my wife, Keiko Hirata, whose personal support and encouragement helped make this book possible.

Finally, I acknowledge other places where some of this research has been previously published or reported. Another version of chapter 2 was published as "Online Learning in Sociocultural Context" in volume 29, number 1 of *Anthropology & Education Quarterly* (March, 1998). Parts of chapter 3 were reported on in papers delivered at the 1997 Annual Conference of Teachers of English to Speakers of Other Languages in Orlando, Florida

(with Lourdes Ortega); the 1997 Annual Conference of the American Association for Applied Linguistics in Orlando, Florida; and the 1997 Annual
Computers & Writing Conference in Honolulu, Hawai'i. Parts of chapter 4
were reported on in a paper delivered at the 1997 Annual Conference of the
American Association for Applied Linguistics in Orlando, Florida.

Although many people provided generous assistance and collaboration,
all faults and errors in the book are mine and mine alone.

1
Introduction: Surveying the Terrain of Literacy

༄•༅

As what we mean by *literacy* changes (as it will), specific arguments about progress and decline will prove less instructive than an historical understanding of the process itself—an understanding of where our notions of being literate, or reading, and of writing come from, and how and why they are likely to evolve. Only such an understanding can provide an adequate basis for discussing the larger issues of language and public policy. To argue about the impact of computers on literacy otherwise is akin to designing buildings and bridges without a concern for the geological forces actively reshaping the earth's crust. As educators and citizens, we may not be able to alter the course of history by our own efforts, but like prudent architects and engineers we can survey the terrain, locating the bedrock that can provide the foundation of sound pedagogic practices and social structures.
—Myron C. Tuman (1992, p.22)

Literacy is frequently viewed as a set of context-neutral, value-free skills that can be imparted to individuals. A study of history, though, shows this model of literacy to be off the mark. Rather, being literate has always depended on mastering processes that are deemed valuable in particular societies, cultures, and contexts. Changes in the technologies available for reading and writing have an important impact on how we experience and think of literacy, but technology alone is not all-powerful. Rather, technological change intersects with other social, economic, cultural, and political factors to help determine how literacy is practiced.

A historical perspective can illustrate how concepts of literacy change. Looking back on the development of the printing press, Marshall McLuhan (1962) commented:

Had any of our current testers of media and various educational aids been available to the harassed sixteenth century administrator they would have been asked to find out whether the new teaching machine, the printed book, could do the full educational job. Could a portable, private instrument like the new book take the place of the book one made by hand and memorized as one made it? Could a book which could be read quickly and even silently take the place of a book read slowly? Could students trained by such printed books measure up to the skilled orators and disputants produced by manuscript means? (p. 145)

McLuhan's wry questions suggest some of the ways that notions of literacy began to change after the introduction of the printing press in Europe. In the pre-Gutenberg era, most thinkers did their composing orally and publicly as speeches and sermons (Olson, 1996; Ong, 1982). Writing in that era principally involved memorizing and transcribing oral speech or carefully and accurately copying classical manuscripts (McLuhan, 1962). A skilled writer thus had outstanding mnemonic and penmanship abilities. Reading was often done publicly, with an orator slowly reading a manuscript out loud. Whether done publicly or privately, though, the purpose of reading was to interpret a small number of classical and religious texts in order to achieve "a new consciousness of what a text *could have meant* or *could mean* to a putative reader" (Olson, 1994, p. 157, emphasis in original).

These notions of reading and writing started to change as early as the 12th century (Olson, 1994) but changed much more rapidly following the introduction of the printing press in the mid-15th century. In the new print era, scholarly writing came to be viewed as authorship of original material, and scholarly reading came to mean the gathering, comprehending, and making use of information from a variety of sources, thus laying the basis for modern scholarship (Eisenstein, 1979a; 1979b).

In analyzing this history, it is important to consider the changes that were brought about by the introduction of new technology and the changes that resulted from broader social, political, and economic transformation. Eisenstein's (1979a, 1979b) two-volume history makes a convincing case that the availability of printed material had a major impact on society in the 15th and 16th centuries, although relatively few people knew how to read. Modern science was unleashed, as researchers were for the first time able to build systematically from previous knowledge that began to be available in print form (Ziman, 1968). Education was transformed as teachers and students were eased of the burden of slavish copying, and "students who took full advantage of technical texts which served as silent instructors were less likely to defer to traditional authority and more receptive to innovating trends" (Eisenstein, 1979a, p. 689). The very format of the printed book—with tables, figures, footnotes, and indexes—contributed to new ways of categorizing and conceptualizing information (Eisenstein, 1979b; McLuhan, 1962).

At the same time, it should be clear that neither the printing press nor any technology operates as an autonomous agent bringing about change independent of broader social circumstances. As Eisenstein pointed out, movable type was developed in Asia earlier than in Europe but had much less impact. Its impact in Europe was dependent on other changes already underway there, including the emergence of a capitalist class, colonialism, and "a heightened sense of individuality and personality, of nationalism and secularism" (Murray, 1995, p. 28). Nor can the printing press be seen to have caused the spread of mass literacy in Europe, because that did not occur until several centuries later. It was the industrial revolution, not the industry of printing, that brought about mass print literacy and helped shape its current characteristics (see discussion in Tuman, 1992).

Notions of literacy have continued to change in the last 100 years. De Castell and Luke (1986) identified three distinct paradigms of school-based literacy in recent U.S. history, each highly dependent on the social, economic, and cultural norms of particular epochs. In the 19th-century classical period, literacy was viewed as knowledge of literature and attention to rhetorical appropriateness. Literacy pedagogy involved rote learning, oral recitation, copying, and imitation of so-called correct speech and writing. The literacy curriculum was based on exemplary texts such as the Bible, a narrow selection from Greek and Roman literature, and handwriting primers. This paradigm corresponded to the needs of an aristocratic social structure, in which land, power, and knowledge were concentrated in few hands and education involved obedience to tradition and power.

Following the mass industrialization of the early 20th century, a Deweyan progressive paradigm of literacy emerged as a "self-conscious attempt ... to provide the skills, knowledge, and social attitudes required for urbanized commercial and industrial society" (de Castell & Luke, 1986, p. 103). In this paradigm, literacy was viewed as a form of self-expression. Literacy pedagogy involved teacher–pupil interaction and the discovery method. The literacy curriculum included civics, adventure stories, and self-generated texts.

However, the progressive model never fully took hold; rather, it was in constant struggle with a more technocratic paradigm that eventually won out (Cuban, 1993). In this technocratic paradigm, literacy was viewed as survival skills necessary to function in society. Literacy pedagogy involved programmed instruction, learning packages with teacher as facilitator, and mastery learning of a common set of objectives. The literacy curriculum was based on decontextualized subskills of literate competence.

The technocratic paradigm that emerged in the 1940s both mimicked and served the needs of the dominant Fordist industrial structure of the era.[1] Just as employees were required to carry out carefully programmed, narrowly defined tasks in the workplace, students were taught to do so in the schools. This approach won out not only because it trained students for the types of relationships and attitudes expected in the workplace but also because it was believed to be the most advanced method of production—whether of cars or of functionally literate citizens. Today, this technocratic notion of literacy is itself being undermined as further changes in technology and society point to the need for new concepts of literacy.

From this brief historical sketch, we can conclude two points. First, literacies are not context-free, value-neutral sets of skills; rather, being literate "has always referred to having mastery over the processes by means of which culturally significant information is coded" (de Castell & Luke, 1986, p. 374).[2] Second, technologies can contribute to altering conceptions of literacies, but the extent to which they do so depends on the broader social and economic contexts in which they emerge.

THE ONLINE ERA

As we look toward the 21st century, what changes are now taking place in technology and in society that are affecting notions of literacy? As for technology, the most important current development affecting reading and writing is the development and spread of the Internet.

Started as a U.S. government experiment connecting a few defense agencies in 1969, the Internet has developed within three decades into a mass information and communications medium.[3] Few doubt that within another three decades it will have reached into virtually every school and library and most homes in the United States and other developed countries, dramatically affecting business, education, and entertainment in the process. Developing countries are also placing emphasis, within their more limited capacity, on joining global information networks, and their ability

---

[1]Referring to the industrial management practices of Henry Ford, one of the first to organize mass production based on the assembly line.

[2]Because literacy consists of many types of practices depending on social context, I use the plural form *literacies* both in this sentence and throughout this book.

[3]For an in-depth history of the development of the Internet, see Hafner and Lyon (1996).

to do so may be an important factor in their overall economic development (Carnoy, Castells, Cohen, & Cardoso, 1993).

In examining the technology of the Internet, it is worthwhile to distinguish between two related developments, computer-mediated communication, and hypermedia and the World Wide Web.

Computer-Mediated Communication

Computer-mediated communication combines several features that together make it a powerful new medium of human interaction. Specifically, the online environment allows interaction that is text-based, many-to-many, and time- and place-independent.

Text-based interaction brings into one medium the two main functions of language: It allows us to interact communicatively and "interpret experience by organizing it into meaning" (Halliday, 1993, p. 95). Historically, the interactive role has principally been fulfilled by speech, whereas the permanence of written texts has made them better vehicles for interpretation and reflection (Bruner, 1972). Writing can be accessed and analyzed again and again by a different people at different times. Print extended this advantage to limitless numbers of people around the globe. This is why the development of writing and print are viewed as having fostered revolutions in the production of knowledge and cognition (Harnad, 1991). Unfortunately, though, "the real strength of writing ... was purchased at the price of becoming a much less interactive medium than speech" (p. 42).

It is precisely the intersection between interaction and reflection that is of critical importance in cognition. Heath (1983), in her classic ethnographic study of language use in three communities, pointed this out well as she illustrated the way the middle-class townspeople use language to educate their children:

> It is as though in the drama of life, townspeople parents freeze scenes and parts of scenes at certain points along the way. Within the single frame of a scene, they focus the child's attention on objects or events in the frame, sort out referents for the child to name, give the child ordered turns for sharing talk about this referent, and then narrate a description of the scene. Through their focused language, adults make the potential stimuli in the child's environment stand still for a cooperative examination and narration between parent and child. The child learns to focus attention on a preselected referent, masters the relationships between the signifier and the signified, develops turn-taking skills in a focused conversation on the referent, and is subsequently expected to listen to, benefit from, and eventually to create narratives placing the referent in different contextual situations. (p. 351)

A rereading of this paragraph gives a glimpse of why computer-mediated communication is considered to be a potential intellectual amplifier (Harasim,1990; Harnad, 1991). For the first time in history, fast-paced human interaction now takes place in a text-based form—what's more, a computer-mediated form is easily transmitted, stored, archived, reevaluated, edited, and rewritten. The opportunities to freeze a single frame and focus attention on it are thus multiplied greatly. Individuals' own interactions can now become a basis for epistemic engagement. The historical divide between speech and writing has been overcome with the interactional and reflective aspects of language merged in a single medium. It is precisely this feature, the combination of writing and speech, that led one prominent cognitive scientist to describe the Internet as bringing about "the fourth revolution in the means of production of knowledge," on par with the "three prior revolutions in the evolution of human communication and cognition: language, writing and print" (Harnad, 1991, p. 39).

The advantages of text-based interaction increase when they are combined with many-to-many communication. Any participant in a discussion can communicate with all the other participants in the discussion. Combined with the time- and place-independent attributes of electronic mail (i.e., e-mail), this interaction creates an unparalleled opportunity for grassroots global interaction. Indeed, even Theodore Roszak (1994), one of new technology's harshest critics, conceded that

> Computer networks are in many ways a unique form of communication.... There is no other way in which a great number of people over an area as large as the world's telephone system can exchange ideas in so unstructured a way at all hours of the day and night, and even preserve a transcript in the form of hard copy. (p. 169)

Many different forms have been devised for carrying out computer-mediated communication, including e-mail, bulletin boards, and various kinds of conferencing systems. Probably the most important distinction is between forms that are asynchronous, such as e-mail, and forms that are synchronous or "real-time," such as chat groups. This book discusses the uses of both in the classroom.

None of the previous discussion is meant to imply that computer-mediated communication automatically has any particular impact on its users. As Roszak (1994) pointed out, computer networks can be used for hateful propagandizing or insipid chat as easily as they can be used for collaborative development of knowledge. The advantages and disadvantages of using e-mail and other new communications media depend in large part on the way that they are used. Nevertheless, the features of this new medium are quite powerful, which explains in part why the Internet has been such a fast-growing technology.

Hypermedia and the World Wide Web

Computer-mediated communication alone could be expected to have a dramatic impact. However, users around the world can do more than send out messages to individuals or groups. They can also create multimedia documents that are linked together in a worldwide database.

A hyperlinked database was first proposed by Vannevar Bush (1945), who saw in it the potential to manage the amount of scientific information that, even then, was starting to expand rapidly. Though Bush's particular proposal, which involved the use of microfilm, was never developed, his vision finally reached fruition in the 1980s and 1990s with the development of hypertext and the World Wide Web. Hypertext creates a very different way of storing and presenting information than earlier forms of writing, even if only within a single user's pages; pieces of texts are connected through associative links rather than included in a single linear document. George Landow (1992) and Jay David Bolter (1991) wrote and taught hypertext fiction years before the development of the World Wide Web. Landow and Bolter were thus working with individual hypertexts, which may have had a number of links to other work archived on the same computer but were not yet linked to computers around the world. Nevertheless, even in this more limited form, they found that the associative nature of hypertext helped create for their students a very different sense of the meaning of author, reader, narrative, and text. Without a single linearity imposed on the text, readers are forced to take a much more active role in aspects traditionally viewed as authoring, such as deciding in what order a story should proceed (Landow, 1992).

The impact of hypertext becomes more profound when a single computer's files are linked with other files around the world, as on the World Wide Web. First, the Web places an unprecedented amount of information at the hands of individual users around the globe. Second, it makes any computer user around the world a potential international author, without having to go through the costly expense of printing and distributing information on paper. Third, the Web further complicates the process of both writing and reading by allowing the author to make links (and the reader to thus pursue links) to any other work created anywhere in the world on the Web. The Web can thus be expected to have a deep impact not only on how we gather and share information but also on how we conceptualize reading and writing (Burbules & Callister, 1996; Gibson, 1996; Tuman, 1992).

Finally, and worthy of consideration as a revolutionary development in its own right, hypertext systems such as the Web allow for the inclusion not only of texts but also of graphics, sound files, and full-motion video.[4] Whereas print has some graphical features, the ability to include a broad range of media is greatly expanded on the Web, thus potentially challenging the textual emphasis of print literacy. The emphasis on multimedia is not a new development but stems from a century of changes in mass media, including the invention and diffusion of radio, film, and television, which have drastically altered patterns of information exchange and entertainment. The turn to audiovisual media has also greatly influenced education, not so much in schools (Cuban, 1986) but rather in applied educational training that take place in business, government, and the military (Lanham, 1993). Although the development of multimedia has no doubt influenced print media (as evidenced by magazines and newspapers ranging from *Wired* to *USA Today*), it is in the computer-based multimedia on CD-ROMs and on the World Wide Web that the integration of text and audiovisual material is most complete, with the processes of reading and writing transformed into multimedia interpretation and authoring. Whether this development toward multimedia communication should be welcomed or abhorred is discussed later in this chapter and throughout the book.

These features of computer-mediated communication and the World Wide Web combine to potentially transform our notions of reading and writing. Indeed, already in the United States and other developed countries, the vast majority of writing in academia, business, and government takes place at a computer screen, and much of that writing is posted via computer rather than printed on paper. An increasing proportion of reading is done at the screen as well, including e-mail, Web browsing, and other forms of Internet use. The screen has not yet supplanted the page, but it has already joined it as an important medium of literate activity in modern society.

However, as discussed earlier, technological developments alone cannot account for changing conceptions of literacy. Rather, we must also take into account the broader social, economic, and political context. What changes

---

[4]For this reason, such systems might more appropriately be called *hypermedia* instead of *hypertext*. However, the word hypertext has now been popularized to mean the inclusion of a variety of media rather than only texts. For that reason, I use hypertext and hypermedia interchangeably in this book.

are taking place in society that help shape the emergence of new screen-based literacies?

THE AGE OF INFORMATION
AND THE NETWORK SOCIETY

Just as the Gutenberg era achieved its maximum impact only in the context of an industrial revolution, the online era is also shaped by a new industrial revolution. Whereas the first industrial revolution was based on the harnessing of steam power, the newest industrial revolution is based on the harnessing of information, knowledge, and networks. This information-based revolution, which began in the post-war period and is accelerating today, is viewed by many as bringing about a new postmodern world based on radically different production methods and accompanying changes in lifestyle.

There is broad consensus of political economists (e.g., Carnoy et al., 1993; Castells, 1996; Reich, 1991; Rifkin, 1995), management specialists (e.g., Senge, 1991), post-modern theorists (e.g., Lyotard, 1984), and critical literacy scholars (e.g., Gee, Hull, & Lankshear, 1996; New London Group, 1996) on the main features of the informational revolution. First, productivity and economic growth are "increasingly dependent upon the application of science and technology, as well as upon the quality of information and management, in the process of production, consumption, distribution, and trade" (Carnoy et al., 1993, p.2). This is in contrast to the pre-information era, when advanced economies increased their productivity due principally to the amount of capital or labor added to the productive process. Second, in advanced capitalist countries there has been a shift from material production to information-processing activities; this change entails not only a shift from manufacturing to service but also a shift within the service sector from non-information activities (e.g., cleaning floors) to information-processing activities (e.g., writing computer software; Castells, 1996).

A shift from the standardized mass production and vertically integrated large-scale organization of the Fordist era to flexible customized production and horizontal networks of economic units has also occurred. In order to be able to develop, interpret, and make use of new information and knowledge as quickly and as flexibly as possible, new post-Fordist management techniques are used, which emphasize a flattened hierarchy, multiskilled labor, team-based work, and just-in-time production and distribution (Castells, 1993; Gee et al., 1996; Reich, 1991). Also, the new economy is a global one, in which capital, production, management, labor, markets, technology, and information are organized across national boundaries (Reich, 1991). Finally, all of these changes are directly dependent on ongoing revolutions in science and technology, especially in the development of information technologies and telecommunications (Castells, 1993).

An example of the nature and impact of the informational revolution is seen in the automobile industry. In 1977, about 35 person-hours of labor were required to assemble an automobile in the United States. New Japanese production techniques, based on technological developments and multiskilled teamwork, brought that number down to 19.1 hours by 1988, and it is estimated that Japanese automobiles assembled in the United States will require 8 person-hours of labor by the end of the 1990s (Reich,1991). Just-in-time production and distribution techniques allow car manufacturers to save money on inventory and warehousing, and customized, flexible global production and distribution have given Japanese companies a big advantage over slower, more cumbersome U.S. companies (although U.S. companies are now catching up). In the future, new scientific developments are expected to reduce the weight and thus engine size of cars dramatically, and increased computing power will make combustion and driving more intelligent, to the point where the value of a car will be better understood by seeing it as "chip with wheels" rather than wheels with chips (Kelly, 1997, p. 194). The ability to competitively design, manufacture, market, and distribute such a product internationally will be—already is—dependent on modern telecommunications, with executives, designers, managers, and sales people around the world consulting, collaborating, communicating, and sharing information via computer networks.

Castells (1996) analyzed in depth what he called the new informational mode of development and its impact on everything from media to culture to architecture to warfare. Castells concluded that the same network-based structural changes occurring in the world economy are emerging in cultural and social spheres as well, resulting in what he termed a *network society*:

> Networks are appropriate instruments for a capitalist economy based on innovation, globalization, and decentralized concentration; for work, workers, and firms based on flexibility, and adaptability; for a culture of endless deconstruction and reconstruction; for a polity geared towards the instant processing of new values and public moods; and for a social organization aiming at the supersession of space and the annihilation of time. Yet the network morphology is also a source of dramatic reorganization of power relationships. (pp. 470–471)

Just what that reorganization of power relationships may be is discussed at the end of this chapter. It is the final and perhaps most important issue I explore regarding the impact of the informational revolution on the development of new literacies.

ELECTRONIC LITERACIES:
ISSUES AND CHALLENGES

The development of new communications technologies described earlier, in the context of the broader economic and social changes, set the stage for a major and rapid paradigm shift in notions of literacy. Whereas it took several hundred years after the Gutenberg revolution before large numbers of people had access to printed works (Eisenstein, 1979b), tens of millions of people have achieved access to the Internet in only a matter of decades. As of July, 1997, the Internet connected 19.5 million host computers worldwide (Network Wizards, 1997) and an estimated 50 million users.[5] This 52% growth in Internet hosts over the previous 12 months indicates that the Internet continues to expand at a rapid rate.

Although there is little doubt that electronic literacies are going to become increasingly prominent in the coming years, there are several major controversies surrounding the development of these literacies. I briefly discuss three contentious issues: (1) the nature of electronic literacies, (2) electronic literacies and school reform, and (3) electronic literacies and (in)equality.

The Nature of Electronic Literacies

Scholars of new media are equally divided as to whether reading and writing on the screen are to be celebrated or abhorred. On the one hand, writers such as Richard Lanham (1993), Jay David Bolter (1991), and George Landow (1992) are celebratory of new electronic literacies, claiming that they represent much fuller and richer ways to present and access information. According to these scholars, the decentered, multimedia character of new electronic media facilitates reading and writing processes that are more democratic, learner-centered, holistic, and natural than the processes involved in working with precomputer, linear texts (Bolter, 1991; Lanham, 1993). In their view, hypertext facilitates a critical and dynamic approach to literacy that is an extension of the best traditions of the print world and finally fulfills the visions of critical literacy to reconfigure the text, author, and reader (Landow, 1992).

---

[5]This personal estimate is based on ratios of users to host computer used in previous studies by the Matrix Information and Directory Services, Inc. (see Quarterman, 1996).

The same future that tantalizes Landow is terrifying to media critics such as Theodore Roszak (1994), Neil Postman (1993, 1995), Clifford Stoll (1995), Stephen Talbott (1995), and Sven Birkerts (1994). These scholars see net-based reading and writing as fulfilling, not the best dreams of critical theory, but the worst nightmares of television, with readers surfing through catchy but vacuous material, never pausing long enough to read something from start to finish, much less critically analyze it. Writing, from such a perspective, would be reduced to searching for the snazziest graphics rather than attending to serious argument.

There are some who see positive potential in new communications media but just don't like the current manifestations, such as hypertext author Michael Joyce (1998), who wrote that "The web's become a zombie news-stand ... where lots of glossy things wave in the light" (p. 172). Others, criticize the prospects of hypertext as well as its current reality. Sven Birkerts argued that multimedia computing, following on the heels of other media such as television, will destroy young people's ability for serious, reflective reading. To the point that hypertext diminishes the elevated role of the author (see Landow, 1992), Birkets responded that

> This "domination by the author" has been, at least until now, the *point* of writing and reading. The author masters the resources of language to create a vision that will engage and in some way overpower the reader; the reader goes to the work to be subjected to the creative will of another. The premise behind the textual interchange is that the author possesses wisdom, an insight, a way of looking at experience, that the reader wants. A change in this relation is therefore not superficial. Once a reader is enabled to collaborate, participate, or in any way engage the text as an empowered player who has some say in the outcome of the game, the core assumptions of reading are called into question. The imagination is liberated from the constraint of being guided at every step by the author. Necessity is dethroned and arbitrariness is installed in its place. (p. 163)

Birkets fears that electronic postmodernity will bring about language erosion, a flattening of historical perspectives, and a shattered faith in institutions and grand explanatory narratives:

> My core fear is that we are, as a culture, as a species, becoming shallower; turned from depth—from the unfathomable mystery—and are adapting ourselves to the ersatz security of a vast lateral connectedness. That we are giving up on wisdom, the struggle for which has for millennia been central to the very idea of culture, and that we are pledging instead to a faith in the web. (p. 228)

Writing historian and hypertext author Jay David Bolter (1991) antici-pated such critiques and answered them by placing new ways of writing squarely within the realm of broader social changes.

> Our culture is itself a vast writing space, a complex of symbolic structures. Just as we write our minds, we can say that we write the culture in which we live. And just as our culture is moving from the printed book to the computer, it is also in the final stages of the transition from a hierarchical social order to what we might call a "network cul-ture." ... Our culture of interconnections both reflects and is reflected in our new technology of writing. With all these transitions, the making and breaking of social links, people are beginning to function as elements in a hypertextual network of affilia-tions. Our whole society is taking on the provisional character of a hypertext. (pp. 232–233)

Bolter admitted that reading will change dramatically but claimed that this change will serve the new society well:

> The computer is an ideal writing space for our networked society, because it permits every form of reading and writing from the most passive to the most active. A large group of users (perhaps the largest) will use the resources of the machine to shop, read the weather report, and play fantastic video games under the rubric of virtual reality. There will be a large market for the electronic equivalents of how-to books and inter-active romances, science fiction, and the other genres. Small groups will read and write "serious" interactive fiction and non-fiction. Tiny networks of scholars will con-duct esoteric studies in ancient and modern literature and languages. Hundreds or thousands of different interest groups from fundamentalist religion to space explora-tion will publish and read each other's messages and hypertexts—on commercial, aca-demic, or governmental communication networks. Government and business will produce electronic documents by the billions.... In the world of electronic writing, there will be no texts that everyone must read. There will only be texts that more or fewer readers choose to examine in more or less detail. The idea of the great, inescap-able book belongs to the age of print that is now passing. (pp. 238–240)

Although Birkerts and Bolter take difference stances—that of techno-pessimist and techno-optimist—their views share much in com-mon. They both agree, as do I, that the development of electronic literacy means a weakening of grand meta-narratives. Electronic literacy involves not only adapting our eyes to read from the screen instead of the page but also adapting our vision of the nature of literacy and the purposes of reading and writing.

Electronic Literacies and School Reform

Controversies over electronic literacies are taking place in the midst of broader societal struggles over the nature of literacy and schooling. In many

U.S. shools, the technocratic paradigm of literacy that emerged after World War II continues to dominate today. Literacy is viewed as a series of discrete functional skills that can be taught through isolated technocratic methods. Yet this skill-based approach has come under attack.

In a widely publicized critique of functional literacy, E. D. Hirsch (1987) noted that many students today neither read with much understanding nor have much general knowledge about important historical or current events. Hirsch issued a call for *cultural literacy* as a proposed alternative to functional literacy. Over the years he has published a series of books detailing the elements of cultural knowledge that students of particular grades should know, including names of particular historical figures and dates of historical events.

Though championed by conservative politicians such as William Bennet (Secretary of Education in the second Reagan administration), Hirsch's views have earned broad criticism from educators who see his perspective as out of date with the realities of the 20th century, let alone the 21st. As Tuman (1992) explained:

> The essential historical shift behind Hirsch's analysis was from a mercantile, pre-industrial world where wealth (and, by extension, culture) resulted from the accumulation of land and surplus goods (the economic equivalents of Hirsch's lists of cultural information) to a capitalist, industrial world where wealth (and culture) resulted from the systematic application of technological innovation. At the center of modern educational reform that Hirsch so opposes is the realization that, as industrial production replaced domestic economy in the nineteenth century, it was no longer enough to know what one's parents or one's fellow citizens knew. (p. 30)

The problems of both the functional literacy and cultural literacy approaches are illuminated by Reich's (1991) in-depth analysis of society and education in the informational era. Reich's research shows that the vast majority of jobs in developed countries today fall into three categories: *routine production services* (e.g., data processors, payroll clerks, factory workers), *in-person services* (e.g., janitors, hospital attendants, taxi drivers), and *symbolic analyst services* (e.g., software engineers, management consultants, strategic planners). The income, status, and opportunities for workers in the first two categories are continually diminishing, whereas symbolic analysts command a disproportionate and rising share of the wealth in the United States and other countries. What's more, symbolic analysts do work that is enjoyable and personally rewarding, whereas those in routine-production and in-person services do work that (post-Fordist management techniques notwithstanding) is too often dreary and dull.

Reich analyzed the educational experiences of symbolic analysts; these experiences usually take place in either elite private schools or high-quality suburban schools followed by good 4-year colleges. Such education focuses on neither the development of basic functional skills nor the accumulation of facts:

> Budding symbolic analysts learn to read, write, and do calculations, of course, but such basic skills are developed and focused in particular ways. They often accumulate a large number of facts along the way, yet these facts are not central to their education; they will live their adult lives in a world where most facts learned years before (even including some historical ones) will have changed or have been reinterpreted. In any event, whatever data they need will be available to them at the touch of a computer key. (p. 229)

Reich explained that in America's best schools and colleges, the curriculum is "fluid and interactive" (p. 230). Instead of emphasizing the transmission of information, the focus is on judgment and interpretation. Students are taught to get behind the data, to examine reality from many angles, and to visualize new possibilities and choices. The symbolic-analytic mind "is trained to be skeptical, curious, and creative" (p. 230). This training involves an education that is based on abstraction, system thinking, experimentation, and collaboration. Students learn to "articulate, clarify, and then restate for one another how they identify and find answers" (p. 233). They learn how to "seek and accept criticism from peers, solicit help, and give credit to others" (p. 233). They also learn to "negotiate—to explain their own needs, to discern what others need and view things from others' perspectives, and to discover mutually beneficial resolutions" (p. 233). All this training prepares them for their future careers, in which they will "spend much of their time communicating concepts—through oral presentations, reports, designs, memoranda, layouts, scripts, and projections—and then seeking a consensus to go forward with the plan" (p. 233). Reich's analysis lays bare the weaknesses of both the functional literacy and cultural literacy perspectives and indicates the types of literacy practices necessary to prepare students for full participation in society.

These three educational models naturally have different visions of the role of technology in the schools. In the functional literacy paradigm, the computer is a device for delivering instructional drills. The computer supplements the teacher and workbook by offering individualized lessons to help students develop basic competencies in areas such as grammar, spelling, and reading comprehension. These lessons are referred to as either drill-and-practice or, more pejoratively, as drill-and-kill. Thus, the computer becomes a vehicle for literacy (albeit of a limited scope) but does not itself become a medium of literacy practices. In some cases, computing itself becomes one of the skills to be taught. Students might be brought to the computer lab once a week and taught various computer skills, such as the operation of basic programs, but without reference to any other meaningful content, goals, purposes, or tasks, such computer literacy does little to enhance broader literacy skills. As Neil Postman (1992) put it, there are "no 'great computerers,' as there are great writers, painters, or musicians." (p. 118) Or, as Michael Bellino, another critic of school computing, stated, "Tools come and tools go.... The purpose of schools is to teach carpentry, not hammer" (Oppenheimer, 1997, p. 62).

Hirsch's vision of cultural literacy dismisses the role of the computer in education entirely. The only direct reference to computers in Hirsch's (1987) book suggests that literacy and technological change are opposing cultural forces: "The more computers we have, the more we need shared fairy tales, Greek myths, historical images, and so on" (p. 31). Thus, as Tuman (1992) noted, Hirsch sees computers as part of a more general movement in culture to increased specialization and therefore part of the disease for which broad cultural literacy training is the antidote. Hirsch ignored the role that computerized databases could play (and are playing) in providing the kinds of facts, figures, and linked background information that he feels is so important, and he of course didn't ponder the effects on cultural literacy of being bound in a print-based world when the rest of the culture is increasingly communicating in an electronic medium (see discussion in Bolter, 1991).

Finally, any educational program that seeks to implement Reich's educational goals of abstraction, system thinking, experimentation, and collaboration will clearly have modern technology integrated in as a central component. Unlike in the functional literacy approach, the computer will would not be relegated to imparting basic skills, nor will it be seen as a skill in itself. Rather it is one of a number of tools that students learn to use as they engage in authentic and collaborative experiments, projects, and analyses.

Although Reich has not put forward a detailed educational model, the kind of project-based interactive education that he proposes has been elaborated by other educators (e.g., Bayer, 1990; Tharp & Gallimore, 1988; Wells & Chang-Wells, 1992). In fact, such a model of collaborative learning is broadly promoted in U.S. colleges of education, but the extent that it is actually practiced in schools, especially outside of wealthy and upper-middle-class neighborhoods, is open to question (see discussion in Cummins & Sayers, 1995).

Electronic Literacies and (In)Equality

The last issue I look at, and one that is particularly important for this book, is the complex relation of electronic literacies to (in)equality in society and in education. This relation encompasses two contradictory factors. On the one hand, the Internet represents the most diversified mass medium the world has ever known, potentially allowing greater numbers of people than ever before to put forth their views and publish their messages. On the other hand, the cost of using personal computers, the language used on the Internet, and other exclusive factors mean that the medium is thus far dominated by a relatively wealthy elite, with most of the world's people shut out from using it at all.

Castells (1996) analyzed both sides of this contradiction, placing the development of the Internet within the more general trend of control and diversification of mass media. Thus while television, radio, and newspapers are coming under the control of smaller numbers of corporations and governments, they are also diversifying their programming over a plethora of channels, networks, and stations. There is an evolution from a mass society to a segmented society, with the audience increasingly fragmented by ideologies, values, tastes, and lifestyles. As Castells pointed out, "while the media have indeed globally intraconnected, and programs and messages circulate in the global network, we are not living in a global village, but in customized cottages globally produced and locally distributed" (p. 341).

This diversification of the media remained unidirectional—with individuals receiving more and more diverse raw material but not producing it—until the development of the Internet. The Internet is more exclusive than other media (such as television, radio, or newspapers) due to the cost, education, and language requirements necessary to access it. It is also more diversified than other media in that it allows for not dozens of communication channels but millions, as each individual user potentially becomes an author and producer.

The Internet had its initial roots among a small number of well-educated, relatively affluent, and mostly male computer users in the United States. It has branched out rapidly to larger numbers of users, but its usage still remains skewed by gender, wealth, and nationality. Within the United States, two 1995 surveys of Internet users found that 67% were male and that 65%

were affluent, with the median household income of all users at $62,000 (Castells, 1996). Internationally, the Internet remains dominated by users in the United States and, secondarily, other industrialized countries (see Table 1.1).

Access in developing countries remains rare. For example, Latin America and Africa each have less than 1% of all the world's Internet sites (see Table 1.1). Yet even these figures don't reveal the full inequality. For example,

TABLE 1.1

Geographic Distribution of Internet Host Computers

Country or Region	Percent of World's Internet Host Computers
United States	60.5%
Western Europe	20.7%
Japan	4.9%
Australia and New Zealand	4.4%
Canada	3.5%
Eastern Europe and former Soviet Union	2.1%
Asia and Pacific (excluding Japan, Australia, and New Zealand)	1.9%
Latin America	0.9%
Africa	0.6%
Middle East (excluding North Africa)	0.4%

Note. Based on Network Wizard's Internet host domain information for July, 1997 (http://www.nw.com/).

fully 98% of Africa's sites are located in a single country (South Africa), leaving the entire rest of the continent with fewer connections to the Internet than a single good-sized university in the United States. Similarly, 88% of the Internet sites in the Middle East are located in Israel.

The poor in developing countries are not likely to get online soon, as some 80% of the world's population lacks basic telecommunications facilities, let alone computers, (Panos Institute, 1995). The elite in developing countries will of course have better access, but they will still be confronted by a situation in which the overall content and direction of the Internet is largely shaped in California and New York rather than in their own country (Schiller, 1996; Wresch, 1996).

At the same time, the many millions who get online can experience a medium dramatically more democratic in many ways than other media or communication channels. First, the Internet allows instantaneous access to vast amounts of information. This point is particularly important in developing countries, where resources are scant for international journal subscriptions, newly published books, and other print resources. Scholars, students, and entrepeneurs in these countries can often get access to types of information online that would have been beyond their reach otherwise (see, for example, Rich & De Los Reyes, 1995). Second, and equally important, the Internet allows these millions of users to initiate communication and provide content, rather than just receive it, whether by sending a simple e-mail message or creating a web site.

This contradiction—between the Internet as a medium of exclusion or a voice of pluralism—is well illustrated by the use of languages on the Internet. On the one hand, a 1997 study showed that fully 82% of the Web pages in the world were in English (Cyberspeech, 1997). This skew is partly a result of the Internet's being born in the United States and still dominated by users in that country and partly a result of the general dominance of English as a language of international communication in academic, business, and entertainment spheres (Kachru & Nelson, 1996; Pennycook, 1995). Indeed, by creating more channels for global communication and thus a need for a lingua franca, the Internet is likely to strengthen the dominance of English as a global language (The Coming Global Tongue, 1996). At the same time, the narrowcasting multichannel feature of the Internet means that it can allow communication in hundreds or thousands of languages at the same time, as is already apparent by the amount of discussion on Internet bulletin boards in a great variety of languages (Paolilo, 1997). The result might be that people use English on the Internet for certain instrumental reasons and other languages or dialects to fulfill other social and cultural needs (Joseph Lo Bianco, personal communication, January 14, 1997). As a result, the main impact of the Internet "is likely to be to protect subsidiary languages" rather than to endanger them (The Coming Global Tongue, 1996, p. 78). Indeed, speakers of several Native American and other endangered indigenous languages have started to make use of the Internet's capacity to connect isolated groups of small numbers of speakers and to allow low-cost archiving and publishing of indigenous language materials as a way to promote language maintenance and revitalization.[6] Of course, the po-

---

[6]For reports on Native American uses of telecommunications and digital technology, see Office of Technology Assessment (1995) and Bernard (1992). For a discussion of a Māori bulletin board system, see Benton (1996). For reports on a Hawaiian bulletin board system, see Hale (1995) and Warschauer and Donaghy (1997).

tential of the Internet to protect minority languages is no guarantee that this will actually occur, because the fulfillment of that potential depends on access to technological resources that may or may not be available as well as on the commitment of a community to continue valuing its own language when more and more of the world's informational resources are available in English.

A recent article in the *Sydney Morning Herald* (Jopson, 1997) provided a concrete example of the contradictory nature of the Internet for economically and politically marginalized groups The article discusses ways that Aboriginal groups in Australia are using the Internet to promote their culture and express themselves politically. One Aboriginal spokesperson told a newspaper that in the past Aborigines "had been endlessly falsely interpreted" and that the Internet now allowed them "to cut out the middle people and ... to speak directly to their audiences" (n.p.). Yet the same leader complained that 85% of the information on the Internet described as Aboriginal had no input from the indigenous community and "should be pulled down" (n.p.). The potential of the Internet for supporting cultural pluralism is thus dependent on marginalized groups achieving equal access to help shape the content of the internet.

INTERACTING OR INTERACTED?

Currently, with Internet use concentrated disproportionately among educated, affluent people, most users of the Net have opportunities for a high degree of interaction. As the Internet becomes more widespread it may also become more commercialized, with a higher amount of prepackaged content supplementing (or replacing) user-defined content and with easy-to-use (but less interactive) machines such as Web TV finding their place along with personal computers. We can thus expect increasing social stratification among online users, as explained by Castells (1996):

> Not only will choice of multimedia be restrained to those with time and money to access, and to countries and regions with enough market potential, but cultural/educational differences will be decisive in using interaction to the advantage of each other. The information about what to look for and the knowledge about how to use the message will be essential to truly experience a system different from customized mass media. *Thus, the multimedia world will be populated by two essentially distinct populations: the interacting and the interacted,* meaning those who are able to select their multidirectional circuits of communication, and those who are provided with a restricted number of prepackaged choices. And who is what will be largely determined by class, race, gender, and country. The unifying cultural power of mass television (from which only a tiny cultural elite had escaped in the past) is now replaced by a socially stratified dif-

ferentiation, leading to the coexistence of a customized mass media culture and an interactive electronic communication network of self-selected communities. (p. 371, emphases in original)

Seen in this light, the three issues described previously—the nature of electronic literacies, school reform, and information inequality—are closely related. Electronic literacies can be either empowering or stultifying; people will use the Internet for everything from creative construction of knowledge to passive reception of multimedia glitz. Whether users fall on one end of this continuum or the other is likely to be highly influenced by class, race, gender, and country, but *highly influenced* does not mean *completely determined*. Literacy practices are influenced by day-to-day struggles of power (Street, 1993), as are uses of new technologies (Feenberg, 1991). Among the main sites of these struggles are schools (Giroux, 1993, 1988). To a large measure, it is in schools and colleges where people will become more or less knowledgeable users of electronic media, critical or less critical readers and writers in an electronic era. The nature of pedagogical practices and school reform will contribute to who becomes the *interacting* and who becomes the *interacted* in the network society.

The rest of this book examines in more detail this question—the relation among new literacies, pedagogical practices, and struggles for equality and power—by looking in depth at four classrooms of culturally and linguistically diverse students in the state of Hawai'i. Through this process, I hope to contribute to a better understanding of how the teaching and learning of electronic literacies in the schools helps or hinders diverse learners from becoming interacting members of the network society.

2

Computers, Composition, and Christianity

ফ·ঔ

Perhaps the greatest of all pedagogical fallacies is the notion that a person learns only the par-
ticular thing he is studying at the time.
—John Dewey (1938, p. 48)

I first met Mary Sanderson[1] in 1995 at a conference on new technologies
and language teaching. A wiry woman with an infectious smile, she exuded
enthusiasm and a tireless energy to learn and teach and share. I took a liking to her immediately. Later that year, when I began planning this study of
new technologies in college language and writing classes, it was only natural that I contact Mary. Not surprisingly, she was enthusiastic about the
possibility of my carrying out my study in her classroom.

Mary had been teaching English as a second language (ESL) for more
than 10 years at Miller College, a small Christian school on the island of
O'ahu. She had a long-time interest in technology and was director of the
college's multimedia language center. She started teaching special computer workshops for ESL students in 1993 and in 1994 began to bring her
own ESL classes to the computer lab on a regular basis. By 1995, computer
networking was thoroughly integrated into her ESL writing classes.

What most interested me about working with Mary was the population
of students she worked with. The majority of the ESL students at Miller
College were from Pacific Island nations such as Tonga, Tahiti, Samoa, and
the Cook Islands, with a scattering of students from other countries in
Asia and Latin America. Most students were using online computer tech-

---

[1]All names of teachers, students, and schools are pseudonyms, unless otherwise noted.

nologies for the first time. Because I was interested in investigating the electronic literacy experiences of students from a variety of cultures, I thought it could be especially interesting to work with these international students. That Mary taught in a conservative Christian college was not a factor in my decision to work with her. I realized at the time that the nature of the institution could have substantial influence on the class, but I did not set out with the goal of learning about Christian education.

Mary and I met a couple of times in fall 1995 to discuss the nature of her class and the research project. Mary's course was an advanced ESL composition class in the college's English Language Program. Mary explained that the students in this program have been admitted to the university but due to low test scores are required to complete some special ESL classes. I learned that the purpose of this particular class is for students to master the genres of U.S. academic writing to a sufficient degree to be able to succeed in regular college classes. She explained that the class would meet four times per week, twice in the computer lab and twice in regular classrooms, and that computer activities would involve a range of networked projects, including written e-mail communication in small groups, exchanges of letters with penpals, and e-mail contact between students and teachers. We discussed how some World Wide Web activities could be integrated later as well.

Mary and I agreed that I would be more than an outside researcher; rather, to the extent possible I would contribute my ideas to the teaching of the class and would also help the students during my visits. Mary and I began to talk generally about our ideas about writing, language learning, and technology. I offered some suggestions on how e-mail exchanges with outside classes could be handled, focusing on discussion and writing about various aspects of culture. Mary showed me a draft syllabus, and I offered some suggestions. There appeared to be some differences in our outlooks, but it became difficult to explore them as Mary left for a month-long trip to the Pacific to teach a winter course to some teachers in training. When she returned, the semester was about to begin. I next saw her in class during the first week of the semester.

The first day I arrived at her class the students were sitting sullenly outside the computer lab. The class started early in the morning, at 7:00 a.m., and apparently the lab monitors had not even arrived yet. Nobody looked very happy with the situation. This was the second day of class, but the first in the computer lab. The students were to meet twice a week in the lab and twice a week in a regular classroom. On this day, the students finally got into the lab some 20 minutes late, but because the computer system wasn't functioning well, most of the remaining half hour was spent trying to troubleshoot problems. The students filed out after the period having accomplished little.

One of the only students I made a personal connection with that day was Paulo. A bright, handsome 20-year-old from Brazil, Paulo was pretty quick on the computer. He seemed less fazed than others with difficulties and even took time out to help his classmates. In contrast to Paulo there was Jon, a tall, strong adult in his mid-20s from the Cook Islands. Jon was completely lost and had a pained, puzzled look on his face throughout most of the period.

After the class ended, I spent much of the rest of the day wandering around the Miller College campus. I was struck by how different Miller College was than other schools I was used to, such as my alma maters, the University of California at Santa Cruz and San Francisco State University. Miller College's well-manicured lawns, quiet and clean grounds, and polite, conservatively dressed students gave me the sensation of entering a small town in the 1950s. The college's strict dress code was prominently displayed on all buildings (e.g., "Sideburns should not be long or bushy, and should not extend below the bottom of the ear.") When I ate in the cafeteria, I was surrounded by signs urging "Stop legalized abortion" and "No to legalized gambling." A front-page headline on the school newspaper asked readers, "Judgment Day: Will you want justice or mercy?"

DISCIPLINE AND ORDER IN THE CLASSROOM

I continued to visit Mary's class on nearly a weekly basis, almost always during one of the days the class was in the computer lab. What I found was that the atmosphere of discipline and obedience that pervaded the college was apparent in Mary's class as well. The students worked quietly and in an orderly fashion, without getting out of their seats to work with classmates at other computers. They raised their hands politely when they wanted to ask a question or needed assistance. A wall display in the computer lab contained gold stars for students who had successfully completed their assignments.

Every class in the computer lab began with a 5-minute assignment or quiz, sent to the students over e-mail (for e.g., "Correct the following sentence: It was not until the 1970s that Waikiki become one of most popular visiting sites"). Students had to complete the quiz and send it back within the allotted 5 minutes or they received no credit. After the 5 minutes were up, Mary announced that no more credit would be given for the quiz. She later explained to me that "the class meets really early in the morning, and I'm worried about them coming late. This helps make sure they get here on time."

These quizzes were frustrating to many of the students, especially the ones who were new to computers and couldn't work very fast. Don, from Tonga, had never worked with computers before and was always a little bit behind in class. While other students were completing their quizzes, he was often still trying to figure out how to log in. Inevitably, when the time was up, he still had not completed the assignment, no matter how hard he tried. I never saw him smile in class.

The standards of discipline and hard work applied to the quantity of assignments as well. A handout students received the first day (which warned them twice to respect the dress code) explained in great detail an exhaustive list of assignments to be completed during the semester, including 60 grammatical exercises, 5 typing tests, 10 take-home essays, 5 in-class essays, 2 reading reports, 20 keypal letters, and a final research paper. Mary worked extremely hard correcting all these assignments, on occasion staying at her office all night in order to keep up with her work.

Mary's concern with rules and order also extended to her view of composition. She was not a proponent of free writing or discovery writing. Rather, her verbal instructions and handouts explained to students exactly what was expected in a composition, as can be seen in this handout:

> Remember that in *comparison* writing, you are presenting similarities (NOT DIF-FERENCES!).
>
> Your *organization* is important:
>
> - an *introduction of three sentences* with a *thesis statement at the end,*
> - *development* paragraphs (2–3) with
> - keyword and "most important" transitions in each paragraph
> - *comparison transition* in the body of each paragraph
> - a *conclusion* of at least *three sentences.*
>
> Your ideas should be thoroughly developed (*5 + sentences per paragraph*) for high "content."

The focus on correct form and organization corresponded with what the students seemed to expect of the class. When asked what good writing entails or what they needed in order to improve their writing, most students focused on features related to organization or mechanics. One student, when asked what he likes most about the class, said, "I like how she gives us the structures of essays. For example, putting a comma before the word 'and' in a series. I was taught not to put the comma in my country."

Peer editing was conducted but without any opportunity to discuss the ideas in papers. Rather, students were given 5 minutes to both read a paper and assign it up to 20 points each in five categories (e.g., content, vocabulary, organization, language use, and mechanics). Students filled these out very quickly, sometimes barely looking back at the paper they were supposed to be grading.

USES OF TECHNOLOGY

During the third week of class, a quiet Polynesian student made the exciting realization that she could use the computer system to write not only to her classmates but also to her faraway friends. She quickly jotted out a note to a friend at another university, using colloquial language (starting with "Hey girl, wassup?") and asked Mary how to fill in the e-mail address and send it. Mary glanced at her letter and sternly told her to check her grammar first. The class ended without the student learning how to address the message, and it went unsent.

A similar situation occurred later when the students first learned how to use the World Wide Web. For many people, one of the most exciting features of the Internet is how the World Wide Web can be used quickly to gather information of a great variety of sources all over the world. Mary's students did not discover this fact on that day nor, to my knowledge, until much later in the semester. Rather, they were given instructions on how to navigate through the college's Web pages to find an online grammatical exercise, which they then completed.

The students worked in small electronic groups throughout the semester, e-mailing paragraphs that their classmates corrected for grammar and spelling and e-mailed back. The students also decided in advance their topic sentences for each paragraph and e-mailed these to their classmates for correction and feedback. The students wrote weekly essays that they e-mailed to the teacher for correction and comment. The students then sent the corrected essays, with a sentence or two of introduction, as letters (of a sort) to their long-distance keypals. Each letter was retyped (or, for the more computer-literate students, cut and pasted) in four different messages with a slightly different introduction to four different keypals and then was given a grade. A bold print warning on the first handout notified students that "the instructor will *not* give credit for e-mailed keypal letters which have not been submitted in draft form for prior response on the due date" (emphasis in original).

These examples illustrate how electronic technology was used as a tool to implement and reinforce the rule-based functions of the class. Students spent about 4 hours a week completing computer-based grammar exercises. They also spent additional hours completing typing tutor exercises, which were mandatory even for those students who knew how to type. Most important, almost all electronic communication, whether between the students and teacher, among the students in the class, or with long-distance penpals, was directed toward correct form rather than expression of meaning.

Although students were generally interested in improving their grammar and form, they still chafed at the tremendous amount of time they spent at the computer at tasks they saw as weakly related to developing their writing skills. As Katina, a Samoan student, said:

The whole thing is a big overload. There's a typing 101 class, so all this typing is a big overload. For some of us who know how to type, it's a big waste of time. But if it's helping us with our grade in the class, we do it. But why should we spend our time on this instead of on something useful?

Many students found the posting of essays to keypals particularly frustrating. As Minda, a Tongan student, commented, "I'm just trying to write the same thing to eight people, to write the same thing in a little bit different ways. It's a waste of time."

TOPICS AND CONTENT

Following a suggestion I had originally made, the writing assignments for the semester were all built around the theme of culture. However, this topic did not lead to the kind of critical sociocultural analysis I had intended. Rather, as Mary wrote on the board one day, in her class culture consisted of climate, food/clothing, music/dance/entertainment, school/education, and family/values. Students' essays thus tended to focus on describing tourist sites in the United States and their countries, comparing food, music, and entertainment, and describing why they chose to come to this college. The essays were inevitably in a standard five-paragraph form, with the first paragraph introducing the three points (i.e., Three main reasons why I want to get an education are....), the next three paragraphs explaining each point, and the last paragraph repeating the points. The essays were often coherent and cohesive, but to an outsider's eye they lacked creativity or originality, as seen by the following essay written by a Korean student named Hae.

So many people come to Miller College each semester to get an education. I am one of them who is learning and searching for something I have been pursuing my whole life. Three main reasons why I want to get an education are to get a better job, to build up self-confidence and to influence people for good.

The first reason of getting an education is to get a better job. There could be a lot of benefits to getting a good job. You can develop your talent and you can earn a lot of money out of it. Money doesn't guarantee happiness, but it surely helps. You can do lots of good things with money. It is great to get a kind of job you like and it is possible only when you have a degree.

In addition to getting a better job, building up self-confidence is another reason why I want to get an education. After I graduated from high school, I was able to work at one of the big companies in my hometown, yet they didn't treat me that great because I didn't have a degree from a college. One of the good things about having a degree from a university is that you will often be referred to as an expert, even though you may not have the slightest clue as to what is actually being discussed. It sounds scary but that is how it is in my home country. For sure, you will be treated better and you will be proud of yourself if you have a degree that qualifies you for a job that you want.

The most important reason why I want to study is to be able to influence people for good. As you get an education, you realize that there are many ways you can help those who are in need. Oftentimes you feel like doing something for someone who is in trouble, yet you have no idea of what to do. Through education you learn how to serve, how to lead and by doing so a lot of people will be influenced for good and it also makes it possible for you to make your life better.

Getting an education is crucial for us to get a better job, to build up self-confidence, and to influence people for good. Moreover, it allows us to grow and improve our lives in many ways. I'm so grateful for being here in Miller College having a wonderful opportunity to learn and grow.

The essay's high level of cohesion and coherence, as well as correct grammar, might be considered an accomplishment for many beginning writers. However, Hae is a highly talented Korean writer who had even published a novel in her own country; one suspects she could do better. She herself was not happy with the situation; on several occasions she complained to me about having to follow a formulaic model that she found to be boring.

An alternative perspective on how a cultural exchange might be constructed is provided by Kern (1996), whose beginning French students in Berkeley, California, carried out an e-mail exchange with students in

France. The two classes, both of which included a number of first- or second-generation immigrants, shared several writings on family and community issues leading to final essays on "What does it mean to be French/American?" This type of cultural exchange was designed to encourage students to examine critically the reality of their lives and their society, in response to the questions and concerns raised from afar. Other exchanges that might achieve similar results focus on critical interpretation of literature (Meskill & Rangelova, 1995; Soh & Soon, 1991) or collaborative multi-site social investigations (Sayers, 1993). Mary's topics, in contrast, failed to provide much room for epistemic engagement or the collaborative construction of new knowledge.

RESISTANCE AND CHANGE

At the beginning of the class, students were generally excited about the opportunity to work with computers, which they saw as important to their academic success and careers. As one student told me:

> Using computers, learning different things, e-mail, everything, I hated it before, but there's a saying, "Conquer or you'll be conquered." So I wanna conquer [rather] than be conquered, so I have to learn, I love it. I think it's so important for me.

As the semester went on, nearly all the students became frustrated at the tremendous number of assignments, many of which seemed peripheral to learning how to write. As Katina told me:

> I think this class is called writing. Essay writing is what we should be doing, something that would help us learn how to write. Computer grammar exercises are a waste of time. The style of writing to keypals, just redoing the essays and sending them to the keypals, it's a waste of time. She doesn't see what's going on. On my essay, I always get 19 out of 20. But I fell behind because I couldn't do all those other assignments.

I conducted interviews with students in three rounds at different times in the semester. It was at the time of my second round of interviews, right in the middle of the semester, that student dissatisfaction seemed to be strongest. Although the students weren't accustomed to complaining to the teacher, nor was the teacher accustomed to soliciting their views, the very fact of my interviewing the students seemed to prove a catalyst for change. On the one hand, the students, merely by having the opportunity to voice their opinions to a sympathetic outsider, seemed to gain confidence in their opinions. On the other hand, the teacher, consciously or unconsciously aware that the students were unhappy, now had to contend with the realization that their unhappiness was somehow coming out for inspection.

Immediately after the second round of interviews (which were conducted privately between me and the students), Mary sent me an e-mail urging me to "help us strengthen the positive and improve, as well as help me continue to build the class rapport I've been working at the last couple of weeks." Two days later, following the next meeting of the class, she wrote that

> The class seemed a bit glum when we started and wouldn't look me in the eye this morning ... A couple of them admitted they were discouraged with the keypal bit, so I told them this week's keypal assignment is the last one with an assigned topic ... after that it's free correspondence as long as they get the information they need for a good comparison–contrast research paper and have at least 20 exchanges total among the 2 to 4 keypals. They seemed satisfied with that.

The change, which meant that students could now write what they wished to keypals instead of submitting letters to her for grades, greatly satisfied the students. They felt that with less busy work, they could concentrate more on their writing. As Hae told me, in comments that seemed to reflect the sentiment of many students, "I like the class now, it's getting better 'cause we write a lot. We write more and we don't do a lot of stuff that we think is not necessary."

A number of other improvements were implemented in the following weeks. The students worked together to shoot and edit their own video to be sent to the partner class. Although the topics of the video—climate, food, music, education, and family/values—were still determined by Mary, students were given a great deal of leeway and independence in planning and producing the video. They were quite excited about the chance to learn some video skills and to creatively film and present aspects of their life.

Students also had a chance to have their own work posted on the Web by providing their electronic texts to Mary, who inserted them into a Web page template. The day their papers were first posted, students looked on in amazement. Realizing that their papers were up for the world to see, they diligently checked for errors and sought out other ways to improve their papers. This was the first time I saw them paying close attention to linguistic elements not just to fulfill an assignment but because they were concerned about how real readers might respond to their paper. Students were also taught how to navigate the Web to find articles related to their own interests.

For their last paper, they integrated material from the interviews with their keypals and from the World Wide Web to compare aspects of their own and their keypals' culture. The topic of the paper was constrained by the somewhat limited way that culture was portrayed in the class, but the students nevertheless took some satisfaction in working with real sources to produce a serious paper.

By the end of the semester, a number of students expressed general satisfaction with the class. Others, although noting some improvement, still had a lot of criticisms. The variety of student experiences is captured by looking at two students, Jon and Paulo.

Jon

Jon, 21 years old, was born on a small village of the Cook Islands. He had been a member of the church all his life and saw coming to this college as a natural but wonderful opportunity. He worked in construction for 3 years after high school in order to save enough money for him and his wife to study at Miller College.

Neither Jon nor his wife, Linda (who was also in the class), had had any previous experience with computers, and both seemed disoriented the first weeks of class. Yet both worked quite hard and received excellent marks. Jon beamed with pride as he talked of his accomplishments:

> We learned a lot of tricks on the computer with Mary, how to do e-mail and things. The other day, I was in the computer lab, and there was some guy who's been here a long time and he didn't know how to do it. And it's my first year here and I was showing him how to do things!

Unlike some of the students, Jon didn't find Mary overly strict. In fact, he found her very liberal compared to his village teachers back home. In general, the limited opportunities that he had on his island made him highly motivated to succeed at Miller College and to appreciate what Mary had to offer. That he succeeded in learning how to write essays that were well organized and even had a certain flair is seen by the following paper he wrote:[2]

---

[2]Note the exact same five-paragraph structure as the other student essay shown earlier.

Each year, people from all over the world travel vast distances in search of a place that offers natural beauty, unique experiences, and an environment for relaxation. When thinking of such a place, the Cook Islands which is a group of 15 tropical islands found in the South Pacific Ocean- comes to mind. The capital and largest of these islands is Rarotonga, the island of my birth. Rarotonga has an unblemished natural charm, pristine ocean and unique culture, which offers welcome to people that arrive.

Due to its unspoiled state, the island of Rarotonga offers a unique opportunity for people from the crowded cities of the world to experience a different type of attraction. The rugged green mountain terrains offer excellent mountain climbing and fabulous cross-island trekking. The aroma of the lush bushes and native plants gives us this sense of natural beauty. On hot summer days people can easily take a nice walk to a waterfall, where their bodies can melt into the cold fresh mountain waters. And if one was still not satisfied he/she could head for the white balmy beaches of Muri.

In addition to Rarotonga's unblemished natural charm, its beauty also exists in its unrestricted lagoon. The calm sea is a snorkler's dream where you can kick back and enjoy the safety of the lagoon. Rarotonga's lagoon is also rich with colorful fish, coral life and various other sea creatures. You cannot miss the soft sandy beaches, and the reflection of the calm blue sky onto the clear waters. Not only will people enjoy the beauty of Rarotonga's lagoon but they will also be able to experience a life of great relaxation.

Part of being in Rarotonga is learning to extend a hand and share the "Kia Orana" spirit with us. It is our special way of welcoming you to our necklace of islands in the sun. The traditional arts and crafts of the Cook Islands are distinct from all others in the Pacific. Nowhere else will you feel so naturally as one with the island way of life. These unique and friendly Polynesians have no doubt established their Independence and are enjoying the vigorous and diverse cultures of each island. The magical tranquility highlights the smiling friendliness of the people.

So all these aspects are typical of Rarotonga's beauty and its uniqueness in this world. Such variety in Rarotonga's scenery produces a perfect harmony for people to enjoy and experience. Therefore, when you leave, we will invite you to return again, to share once more the special magic of the Cook Islands "Kia Manuia." -(May good fortunes be with you.)

The course helped Jon learn the language and culture of power that are often inaccessible to minority and immigrant students (Delpit, 1988). He mastered the genre of the five-paragraph essay and entered the discourse community of those who can produce an acceptable freshman essay. This is not a small accomplishment for many foreign students.

However, there is no indication that in this course Jon was ever encouraged to tackle the larger problems of writing, for example how to explain a difficult concept or argue a controversial point. He was not challenged to develop the skills of abstraction, systematic thinking, experimental inquiry, or collaboration that are crucial in today's economy (Reich, 1991). He was not challenged to "talk and write about language as such, to explain and sequence implicit knowledge and rules of planning, and to speak and write for multiple functions in appropriate forms" (Heath, 1992, p.55). Facing these challenges might have assisted Jon to master other genres and enter into a discourse community that values the content of writing and not just its form.

At the same time, what Jon had accomplished was substantial. He had progressed from being in a state of disorientation and confusion to feeling confident, both about computers and about writing. In his last comments to me, he told me:

> I think now like it's the end of the class, the teacher could just give us anything and I think I can write about it now. I feel confident. Whereas before you know, it was hard just thinking about what am I gonna write about and all that.

Paulo

A view opposite to that of Jon was expressed by Paulo, a 19-year-old student from Brazil. Unlike most of the students, Paulo had been in the church only a short time, joining a few months before he entered Miller's College. Paulo had previous experience with computers, and from the first week of class, he impressed me as a confident, quick-learning student who could finish an assignment almost before the other students had even figured out how to get online. His initial writings also seemed to be among the least stilted and most sophisticated in the class. However, Paulo, who was extremely communicative and really enjoyed trying to express an idea, became frustrated with what he saw as the busy work of the class.

> We have so many little assignments. They're not important. But because you get graded on every little thing, I lose my focus, I can't concentrate on the big things. I like to do more essay writing, just give us a chance to write more.... In the beginning I was motivated. I'm motivated in all my other classes, I like them. It's only this class I don't like. Reading—that's the best class. We sit around and discuss. It's personal, no machine.

Paulo also resented the strict organization Mary imposed on students' essays:

> She says, it's gotta be like this, especially like in the beginning of the paragraphs, when you have to write certain words, like linking words, the organization's gotta be like ... that's hard for me, like you got the thesis statement, you gotta repeat,

why do you have to repeat it in each one of the paragraphs? ... It's boring. You start the essay writing on this, then you, by the middle of the essay you just get bored, and you can't write any more.

It's funny because when you read all the essays or whatever we read it's not like that, so it's different, I'm writing something that I don't read, not very often. Even though it helps a lot, it should be helping a lot to understand organization, but there are some things I don't think are needed.

Paulo was the only student who attempted to deviate from the prese-lected topics on his essays, once choosing to write about the contradic-tions between rich and poor in Brazil rather than describing tourist sites there. As I was reading over his paper, he confessed to me that he was worried that Mary wouldn't accept it because it was off-topic. Later, when I asked what happened to it, he said that it had apparently been misplaced because he never received it back from the teacher.

Paulo often told me that he didn't like to write, but I suspect that it was Writing (the course), not writing (the activity), that he actually disliked. His early e-mail messages indicated that he enjoyed writing to communi-cate and was eager to express his views. His enthusiasm plummeted dur-ing the first half of the semester. By the end of the semester, he was very happy that some of the busy work was eliminated but still felt restricted by the organizational structures Mary insisted on:

The class is getting much better now. It's not busy like it used to be. But I still think that sometimes she's very strict because if you couldn't do this the way she tells us to do, the organization is wrong. I think we should be more free to write. When you have to follow a certain pattern, it's hard. I don't feel to write whatever I want to.

THE SOCIAL CONTEXT OF LEARNING

In trying to make sense of the teaching and learning practices I observed in Mary's class, I found it necessary to examine four overlying contexts: (1) the church and college, (2) the English Language Program, (3) Mary's personal background and beliefs, and (4) the triangular relation-ship that developed among teacher, researcher, and students.

The Church and Miller College

This particular church is known for two features: its fundamentalist doc-trine and its missionary zeal. A recent book, displayed prominently near the entrance to the campus book store, contains chapters such as "One

True Church" and "Teaching Pure Doctrine."[3] The book explains that doctrine cannot be learned through experience or active interpretation but rather must be taught from above. Another recent book, also on prominent display, emphasizes the importance of teaching the principles of the gospel rather than teaching ethics. The church has a long history of zealously working to bring this doctrine and these principles to the people of developing nations.

The church's institutes of higher learning, including Miller College, were established for the purpose of assisting missionary goals, both by training students in church doctrine and preparing them to serve the church. The college catalogue states that "All students at Miller College should be taught the truths of the gospel of Jesus Christ." The Church President stated that "Those who are blessed to attend [the church college] have a great responsibility to make certain that the Church's investment in them provides dividends through service and dedication to others as they labor in the Church and in the world."

Miller College is tied in with the church's missionary role throughout the Pacific region. American students who attend Miller are generally involved in missionary work in Asia and the Pacific. The majority of Miller's students are not Americans but rather foreign students from the Pacific. Nearly all have been involved in church activities in their countries and are coming to learn the principles and to develop the leadership skills to return as capable church representatives.

Students at Miller College lead a regimented life. In addition to the aforementioned dress code, they also make a commitment to abstain from physical familiarity outside the bonds of marriage; to eschew alcohol, drugs, and tobacco; and to attend Church meetings regularly, support Church leaders, and fulfill callings. Students are also required to complete a course on religious education every semester.

Mary's teaching approach, with an emphasis on discipline, order, and principles, is perfectly congruent with the philosophy and goals of the church and college. Yet I personally know other teachers at the college who have a more open teaching approach. For example, I visited the course of a Spanish instructor who also teaches via computer-assisted activities, but in his case the online activities focus on student–student discussion rather than mastering rules.

---

[3]Citations and references for church-related books are omitted so as to protect the anonymity of the institution.

The English Language Program

Unlike the previously mentioned Spanish course, the students in the English Language Program were not Americans but rather international students newly arrived at Miller College. As Atkinson and Ramanathan (1995) pointed out, such ESL programs often emphasize a basic skills approach to writing rather than the more sophisticated approaches found in writing courses for native speakers. This seemed to be the case at Miller College. For example, Mary reported that a colleague reacted very negatively to her idea to grade students on take-home essays, which they would have a chance to revise, because that would be grading them on effort rather than product. Mary took this advice to heart and decided to base most of her grade on the more traditional in-class essays and other assignments such as typing and grammar.

The department indicated its conservative nature not only in its writing courses but also in its reading courses. The department's language lab recently jettisoned a meaning-based approach for practicing reading skills in favor of a computer-based activity involving memorization of isolated, decontextualized vocabulary words.

From a broader social view, the ESL program within Miller College plays a particular socializing role beyond that played by ESL programs in secular colleges. Miller's ESL department is closely tied to the church's overseas role. Mary and other members of the department spend their vacations traveling to developing countries to teach at special church-sponsored institutes. Promising students from those institutes are then recruited to come to Miller College to study. They are required to abandon aspects of their native culture in order to conform to church policy. They need to learn the rules of the game, both inside and outside of class.

It is thus not surprising that they are subjected to strict discipline; this in fact conforms to a pattern found to have existed in the United States throughout the century (Cuban, 1993): Minority and immigrant children are forced to endure frequent tests and quizzes; teacher-directed procedures for seatwork, recitation, and reports; and numerous other rules and regulations that "enable schools to socialize and sort these students to meet the requirements" (p. 250) of society. In contrast, the students studying Spanish at Miller College are overwhelmingly White, American, and native English speakers, and thus they are more likely to fit another pattern noted by Cuban: whereby opportunities for "individual choice, expressiveness, group learning skills, derivations of knowledge from many sources, joint student–teacher decisionmaking, and student participation in both the verbal and physical life of the classroom" are generally reserved for American, upper middle-class students because these "classroom practices and student behaviors.... are tailored for future professionals, managers, and executives" (pp. 250–251).

Finally, the historical relationship between the church affiliated with Miller College and the non-White minorities who are represented in the English Language Program has, in many people's eyes, not always been based on equality and mutual respect. It could be considered risky to the church's interests to foster a critical approach to education among groups of people whose focus of criticism might become the church itself.

The Teacher's Personal Background and Beliefs

In a 10-year study of technology in education in U.S. public schools, Sandholtz, Ringstaff, and Dwyer (1997) confirm that sociocultural context strongly influences how computers are used with students. However, they found that this influence is neither total nor direct but is mediated by the beliefs of individual teachers. It is thus important to consider Mary's personal background and beliefs.

Mary grew up in a rural area of a very conservative state in the United States. Her childhood experiences likely included few contacts with people of other races or religions. She received her B.A. and M.A. in a university run by her church. She completed both degrees in the 1970s, a time when many of the ideas on communicative language teaching or alternative approaches to writing had barely penetrated the profession, much less the conservative university she attended.

Mary had a strong personal preference for highly structured learning and writing environments, as she explained to me one day:

> When I was in college, I took a composition class, I didn't know what the teacher expected or required. I kept getting C's, then eventually I got an A. But I didn't know why. I was really bothered by the lack of structure. That's why I wanted this to be structured. Perhaps that's why I took German, because it was so structured.

Mary once told me that she fit in perfectly at Miller College in her earlier years there. She explained that more recently some of her ideas about teaching had started to change as she attended many conferences and got exposed to more innovative ways of using new technologies. She was concerned that this was causing some tension between her and her colleagues. It seemed clear that Mary's belief system was deeply shaped by a conservative view of education and writing but that she was also open to considering alternative approaches.

The Relationship Among Teacher, Researcher, and Students

The last element of sociocultural context I examine is the relationship that Mary and I developed and the possible influence this relationship had on the class. As indicated earlier, our initial conversations were quite fruitful, and we both agreed to view this experience as collaborative. In those early discussions, I failed to recognize what differences there may be between us, both in outlook and in background, and as these differences became more evident in the first few weeks of the course, I continued to shy away from the difficult task of acknowledging and working through our different views.

As Briggs (1996) noted, "Humanity is gained as the world, in the spaces between people, is acknowledged rather than denied or pushed away" (p. 6). I pushed our differences away rather than confronting them, and Mary collaborated in this process of denial. My failure to help bring about an "articulation of difference" (Minh-ha, 1994, cited in Briggs, 1996) made it difficult for us to heal the split between us.

In a sense it was the students themselves who rescued us from this situation, when, in the interviews, they forthrightly shared their thoughts and opinions of the class, thus creating a context in which Mary and I could no longer easily afford to ignore the difficulties. Mary felt obliged to make some changes, even though the complaints had not been made to her directly. It seems that Mary's actions can be explained in part by the metaphor of the *panopticon* (Foucault, 1997). Foucault selected Jeremy Bentham's circular prison, with the prisoners on the periphery under potentially constant but unverifiable gaze from the guards in a central observation tower, as a metaphor for how power is wielded and knowledge shaped in the real world. According to Foucault, the guards too are always subject to unverifiable gaze, not only from their supervisors but even from outside society, thus guaranteeing the control of the controllers.

Mary found herself caught up in the panoptic gaze of the outside research community. Simply knowing that I was interviewing the students, without being able to verify the content of the interviews, made her aware of the need to conform to outside standards. Yet whereas in Foucault's metaphor the outside and inside controllers are all part of one more or less homogeneous system, Mary was perhaps caught up in two competing panopticons—that of her college and church, with its own set of values, and that of the outside university research community, with a different set of values.

This description does not suggest that the two sets of values are totally contradictory and that only one set is accepted by Mary personally. Rather, it appears that Mary is trying to find her way through a number of different paths and is eclectically appling a variety of approaches and perspectives. In this case, the triangular interaction of students–teacher–researcher seemed to help introduce a critical perspective that resulted in Mary reassessing her teaching in midstream and making some adjustments.

This minicrisis around the time of the second set of interviews, followed by changes in class procedure, helped bring about more openness between Mary and me, as we discussed more frankly our views about how the class should be taught. Once again, Mary started to grow more distant before the third round of interviews and even sent me an e-mail message (that I didn't receive until later) asking me not to come that day because the students were "stressed." After this third round was over, tensions receded and we spoke more freely again, engaging in some interesting discussion about the class.

Thus, over time and with many pushes and pulls, we slowly achieved a degree of intersubjectivity, which, as Eugene Matusov (1996) pointed out, is "a *process* of coordination of individual contributions to the joint activity rather than a *state* of agreement between the participants" (p. 26, emphasis in original). The challenge for me, which I never fully met, was to maintain a critical perspective without attempting to impose it, to acknowledge the borders between us while still venturing into the borderlands (Rosaldo, 1989).

SOCIALIZATION AND SITUATIONALLY CONSTRAINED CHOICE

Susan Jungck (1987) reminds us that "computer literacy is theoretically an empowering concept; its development in practice can have contradictory effects" (p. 492). For Mary's ESL composition students, the introduction of computers into the curriculum brought some knowledge of basic computer skills, but it did little to advance their abilities of systemic analysis or critical inquiry. Instead they learned to come on time, to follow rules of studying and rules of writing, to talk and write about culture from a superficial standpoint, and to use technology as a tool to accomplish busy work.

The students seemed aware that their success was due in large part to figuring out the rules of the game. As Jon told me, "This semester we didn't know what to expect. We sort of have an idea [now] of how the system works, and the teachers."

Students who did poorly in the class were not necessarily the worst writers but rather those who failed this socialization process. One example is Sun, a student from Korea, who told me early that she really liked to discuss ideas and hoped that the class would include more discussion. Sun always tried to find ways to express her personal thoughts in her e-mail messages, even if that was counter to the particular assignment at hand. Sun either could not or chose not to keep pace with the frequent grammar exercises, typing assignments, and repetitive keypal mailings. She showed up to class less and less frequently as the semester continued. Another frequent no-show was Don, the Tongan student who couldn't complete the quizzes within the 5 minutes allotted. And then there is the case of Katina, who did well on the essays but complained about the large amount of busy work assignments; Katina received a D in the course despite writing an excellent final research paper that received a mark of 98 (out of 100).

The failure of Katina, Don, and Sun should not be construed to mean that the course was not a success, at least from the point of view of Mary and the institution. The majority of students made it through the initiation period and learned the appropriate behaviors and attitudes for Miller College. They also learned to write cohesive and coherent essays, with few controversial ideas but with correct transitional phrases. They are well prepared for their remaining courses at Miller College.

This result is explained well by Cuban's (1986, 1993) model of constancy and change in American schools, originally developed for K–12 schools although applicable to the highly structured environment of Miller College. Cuban studied previous educational innovations over 110 years, including the introduction of film, radio, and television, and found that none of these innovations qualitatively altered American education. Cuban suggested that deeply held cultural beliefs about the nature of knowledge, how teaching should occur, and how children should learn steer policymakers and teachers toward certain forms of instruction and that these forms of instruction are guided by the broader role of the schools to "inculcate into children the prevailing social norms, values, and behaviors that will prepare them for economic, social, and political participation in the larger culture" (Cuban, 1993, p. 249). Technologies in schools are almost always implemented in a top-down fashion, which leaves in place traditional teacher-centered instruction, especially when the students are members of lower socioeconomic status ethnic and language minority groups. Cuban's model does not suggest that all teacher behavior is strictly determined from above but rather that teachers have "situationally constrained choice" (p. 260), in other words, a degree of autonomy within the constraints of established school and classroom structures. When changes are adapted, they are most likely to affect issues of peripheral importance rather than decisions that "touch the core of the teacher's authority" (p. 270). Cuban pointed out that changes are also often made in the middle of the semester, once teachers feel they have already exerted a certain amount of control over the class.

In this case, we can see that Mary faced numerous sociocultural constraints, such as the strict disciplinary atmosphere of the church and college, the role of the college as a training school for missionaries, the relationship between the college and the international students, and the conservative expectations of colleagues in the English Language Program. Mary indicated a willingness to make changes, but only in the middle of the semester and only on peripheral issues, such as how many papers students wrote, rather than on more central issues of control, such as who would determine the topics of essays or the content of lessons. Adapting technology to her own sociocultural milieu and outlook, Mary continued teaching in a way that served to socialize international students into the roles established for them by the church and college.

In spite of the differences that we had, I certainly do not view negatively Mary's efforts to better her teaching. Rather, I endorse Cuban's view : "That teachers even initiate incremental changes in the face of considerable constraints speaks of their strong impulses toward improvement" (p. 287). Mary demonstrated her impulses toward improvement by devoting hundreds of extra hours to introduce new technologies to her students, by bravely inviting an outside researcher to observe her class the entire semester, and by admitting mistakes and changing course policies that were upsetting to her students. These efforts were quite impressive for somebody who was still relatively new to online teaching.

Her courage to consider new ideas continued after the class. When I mailed her a report that included in summarized form many of the points from this chapter, she wrote me back, saying

> I like the report very much.... Your words helped me to understand ourselves a bit more as well! ... I am going to keep your report in my professional development folder where I can refer to it frequently and think about my search for self-improvement in teaching.... .The learning experience was good for the class I taught the following spring term, with more reason in balancing the students' homework load and in emphasizing the writing, with the computer used more in support of learning as students felt they wanted to use it.

Later, we even co-authored a short paper that summarized what we had learned from the experience, including the need to involve students in decision-making when integrating Internet-based activities into the curriculum.

I left Mary's class optimistic that she was beginning to find ways of teaching that would ultimately be more rewarding to both her and her students. At the same time, I was concerned about whether she would find sufficient institutional support to continue the process of reform she had started.

I learned some important personal lessons as well. In the future, I hope I can better "recognize and articulate contradictions, complexities, and differences" (Briggs, 1996, p.17) between researcher and classroom teacher, thus practicing the same critical, collaborative communication that is the goal of student-centered online learning.

3

Networking into Academic Discourse

ক্ষ•ড়

To learn to use tools as practitioners use them, a student, like an apprentice, must enter that community and its culture. Thus in a significant way, learning is ... a process of enculturation.
—John Seely Brown, Allan Collins, and Paul Duguid (1989, p. 33)

My study in Mary's class, reported in chapter 2, effectively served as a pilot for the remainder of the classrooms I studied. It clarified for me the questions and situations that I wanted to investigate. In particular, it strengthened my interest in working with teachers who seemed to have a critical perspective on language, writing, and education. I wanted to look at a classroom in which a teacher was consciously trying to use online tools to strengthen student involvement and empowerment, in an institutional environment where such a perspective would be supported.

I found such an environment at the English Language Institute (ELI) at the University of Hawai'i.[1] Like the ELP program at Miller College, the ELI offers supplemental English classes for foreign students who had been admitted to the university but whose test scores indicated that they needed additional help. Beyond this similarity, however, there were important differences.

First, the ELI was located within the major public university in the state, an institution with a conservative top administration but with a liberal faculty and student body. The ELI is headed by Professor Kate Wolfe-Quintero, an enthusiastic advocate of devolving power to students. In her term as director of the ELI, she has actively worked to im-

---

[1]I have used the actual name of the university and English Language Institute per the research requirements of the institute and the request of the director. The names of the teacher and students are pseudonyms.

plement educational innovations and to invite graduate students to join in helping encourage and study these innovations.

All the teachers in the ELI are graduate students at the university, either in the M.A. program in English as a second language or the Ph.D. program in second language acquisition. Luz Santos is one of the most exceptional of these graduate students. A native of Spain, Luz had several years teaching experience in Europe before coming to the United States for graduate study. She distinguished herself as a superb student in the M.A. program in ESL and then immediately entered the Ph.D. program in second language acquisition. She has a number of publications in her own research area, which is related to the acquisition of syntax.

When Luz and I first talked about working together, she was about to begin her third semester of teaching an ELI writing course for graduate students. Alhough she had not used computers in this course before, she was very interested in doing so and invited me to be a full partner in the project. We agreed that I would be a co-teacher of the class; Luz would take overall responsibility for the course curriculum and instruction, but I would work closely with her and with the students in designing and implementing aspects of the course related to new technologies.

Luz was to teach Writing for Foreign Graduate Students (ELI 83), a noncredit writing course for graduate students. Though each ELI course has its own challenges, instructors report that they find ELI 83 to be a particularly challenging course. The students range from unclassified graduate students in their early 20s who are thinking of entering a masters' program to older doctoral students who have years of academic writing and publishing experience in their own language. Some students are enthusiastic about taking the course for the opportunity to improve their writing. Some see the class as an unfortunate requirement that can only interrupt their more serious academic work. Even those who start off with enthusiasm often feel the pressure of competing requirements from credit courses in their own fields.

This particular section of ELI 83 was made up of 15 graduate students from China, Japan, Cambodia, Indonesia, Hong Kong, Thailand, and Brazil. Two were doctoral students, 12 were master's students, and one was an unclassified graduate student hoping to enter a master's program.

Luz, based on her own personal experiences and teaching philosophy, had a well-developed approach toward teaching this course. She sought to focus not on language mechanics or even on writing organization but rather to assist students to integrate into academic life in their disciplines. As she explained:

I don't believe that this class should teach them language or grammar because I think that's beyond our possibilities for one semester. Some of the students have such a low level of language ability in terms of grammar that they wouldn't benefit from just a focus on that for a semester. I think the problem is bigger than that. What they really need is just learn all the skills involved in studying, writing, reading, relating to their professors and other students in their departments. And they need to realize what graduate life is about, how to become more academic in this system.

Luz's approach to the teaching of writing is consistent with a discourse community perspective on college writing promoted by composition theorists such as Bartholomae (1986) and Bizzel (1992). This perspective emerged in opposition to both the formalist approaches of the 1950s and 1960s, which emphasized the production of correct forms, and the psycholinguistic approaches of the 1970s, which viewed writing as an individual cognitive process. In contrast, Bartholomae and Bizzel view learning to write as a sociocultural process of gaining access to particular discourse communities. As Bartholomae (1986) explained,

Every time a student sits down to write for us, he has to invent the university for the occasion ... He has to learn to speak our language, to speak as we do, to try on the peculiar ways of knowing, selecting, evaluating, reporting, concluding, and arguing that define the discourse of our community. (p. 4)

As sociolinguist James Gee (1996) explained, this sociocultural process is true not only of college writing but of literacy development in general. Though Gee focused the following passage on reading, from a sociocultural perspective it applies equally to writing:

One does not learn to read texts of type X in way Y unless one has had experience in settings where texts of type X are read in way Y. These settings are various sorts of social institutions, like churches, banks, schools, government offices, or social groups with certain sorts of interests.... One has to be socialized into a practice to learn to read texts of type X in way Y. Since this is so, we can turn literacy on its head ... and refer crucially to the social institutions or social groups that have these practices, rather than the practices themselves. When we do this, something odd happens: the practices of such social groups are never just literacy practices. They also involve ways of talking, interacting, thinking, valuing, and believing. (p. 41)

Though Luz had not studied composition theorists before teaching this course, her approach very much mirrored these views. She sought to involve her students in the ways of talking, interacting, thinking, valuing, and believing of new academic discourse communities and thus help her students reinvent, if not the whole university, at least the particular departments they were entering.

Consistent with this approach, Luz's courses were organized around students' learning about ways of knowing and writing within their own particular disciplines. Students were not required to write any general papers but rather were given a series of writing assignments based on the completion of a serious academic paper in their own special area. Students were encouraged to work on a paper that had been assigned in another course. Specific assignments for this paper included the submission of a literature review halfway through the semester as well as two or three drafts of the complete paper toward the end of the semester. Some discussions and assignments throughout the semester focused on particular issues related to writing, ranging from plagiarism to academic citations to library research to uses of connecting words. Other discussions and assignments dealt with broader issues related to academic life, student–professor relationships, academic networking, and international students' cultural adjustment.

Luz's attitude toward integrating computers in the course flowed from her general perspective that a major part of the teaching of writing involved enculturating students into the way of academic life in the United States. As she explained:

> I'm sure they are very academic and very successful in *their* systems, but here things work very differently, and one big, big component is computers. I mean it doesn't work if you don't know how to use a word processor to write your thesis or your dissertation. You simply cannot do anything in this system just handwriting or using a typewriter or giving your work to someone to type on the computer, it just doesn't work.... I think obviously the [ELI students'] level of using technology for graduate life is very, very low, and it just makes their work so much more difficult.

Though Luz had a general idea of why she wanted to integrate technology into the class, she lacked specific knowledge of what kind of computer-based activities would be possible and was enthusiastic about working with me to develop a plan. Luz and I thus met several times before the semester started to jointly develop an ambitious plan for integrating technology into the course. For two of the three weekly 50-minute classes, the students would meet in a networked computer lab with Power Macintosh computers, a laser printer, Internet access, and a scanner. The students would be trained in using electronic mail, the World Wide Web, and a program for real-time electronic discussion called Daedalus Interchange (Daedalus Inc., 1989). They would hold regular discussions with each other via computer using both e-mail and

Interchange and would complete a number of technology-based assignments, including subscribing to and participating on an academic e-mail discussion list in their field of study, making one or more pages for the World Wide Web, and reflecting on their experiences in dialogue journals submitted via e-mail to the instructors.

All technology assignments had a purpose. E-mail dialogue journals with the instructors were to facilitate personal reflection and apprenticeship learning as students struggled to grasp the nature of new discourse communities. Students' computer-mediated discussions, both by e-mail and Interchange, were similarly designed to assist students in reflecting on new discourse communities and the nature of academic writing. Participation in academic e-mail discussion lists and the creation of public World Wide Web pages was designed to put students into direct contact with graduate students and professors in their particular fields so as to once again assist their entry into new discourse communities.

The computer was thus designed to play several roles, corresponding to several notions of apprenticeship learning. First, it would be a medium of communication for apprenticeship learning between teacher and student, allowing more teacher guidance and individual student reflection, thus corresponding to a *tutor–tutee* model of apprenticeship learning (see discussion in Wertsch & Bivens, 1992). Second, it would be a medium of communication for student-student communication and social construction of knowledge, thus corresponding to a *collaborative* model of apprenticeship learning, with students providing scaffolding for each other (Bayer, 1990). Third, it would allow students to learn through direct contact with broader discourse communities, thus corresponding to a *peripheral participation* model of apprenticeship learning. This third model, discussed in detail by Lave and Wenger (1991), posits that learners in diverse settings learn best by limited but steadily increasing participation on the periphery of communities they seek to enter.

Finally, technology would not only be the medium of this apprenticeship learning; it would be the content as well. Students would use technology in order to learn and would be learning about technology at the same time.

It was an ambitious plan, perhaps overly ambitious. The extent to which it was achieved or not achieved is perhaps best illustrated by analyzing the types of apprenticeship learning that did appear to take place in the class.

ELECTRONIC MAIL AND TEACHER-STUDENT APPRENTICESHIP

In order to encourage reflective learning, teacher–student dialogue journals were implemented on a regular basis. Every two weeks, Luz or I sent some questions to all the students via the class e-mail list, and they responded individually. Depending on the nature of their responses, we replied to them individually, commented on the issue in an e-mail to the whole class, or discussed some of the points raised during class meetings. Journal assignments dealt with topics such as the nature of the writing process, the structure of an academic paper, students' own writing experience, students' understanding of the issue of plagiarism, students' experiences with subscribing to academic e-mail lists, and students' thoughts and questions about the role of e-mail and the World Wide Web in academic communication and networking.

Students were allowed to submit their journals any way they wanted but were strongly encouraged to do so by e-mail to facilitate a rapid response and to get students accustomed to the electronic medium. In addition, we were aware of earlier research by Wang (1993), who had compared students using e-mail and students using paper notebooks for dialogue journals and had found that the e-mail group wrote more, asked more questions, and got more response than did the paper group.

All students in the class completed some of the journal assignments, with an average of about 60% of the students completing each assignment. According to Luz, this was a far greater percentage than had participated in the past when students submitted journals by paper. As she explained:

> I did a journal in the first semester, written, normal journal, and it was a disaster, no one would do it, they would feel it was a drag, so we had to switch into normal assignments, short assignments, nothing like a journal. Whereas now at least the ones who do the journal do a lot of good thinking.

Luz usually replied to journals within 24 hours and often with lengthy, detailed comments. As a result of these thoughtful interchanges, a number of the students started e-mailing Luz with their own questions and concerns, beyond those that we had raised in journal topics. Electronic mail thus became a vehicle for broader student–teacher contact. Once again, Luz found that this exceeded the type of contact she had had in earlier semesters, with students being too shy to raise issues in class or come to her office hours for extended discussion.

Two students who made the most out of this teacher–student contact were Miyako and Zhong.

Miyako

Miyako is a 25-year-old first-semester master's student in Asian Studies from Japan, with a special interest in studying Indonesia. Like many female Japanese students at the University of Hawai'i, Miyako was very quiet and polite in class. Discussions with her outside of class indicated that she was feeling somewhat overwhelmed by the newness of being a master's student in Hawai'i and wasn't quite certain what graduate school was really all about. She was also coping with cultural differences between Japan and the United States in terms of what was expected from students.

Though quiet in class, Miyako participated avidly in e-mail, sending messages about once a week to Luz as well as many additional messages to classmates. Whereas her early e-mail messages were all in response to teacher-initiated journals or other assignments, during the second half of the semester about half her messages were at her own initiative. She often used her messages to Luz to raise questions, doubts, and concerns about academic life in the United States. Over the course of the semester, this process appeared to contribute a good deal to Miyako's coming to grips with her new role as a graduate student.

A look at some of Miyako's communications illustrates this process. Halfway through the semester, the students read an article published on the World Wide Web by communications professor Philip Agre (1997), called "Networking on the Network." The article discussed the importance of professional networking for graduate students and offered suggestions on how to effectively take advantage of computer-mediated communication to carry out this networking. In a Daedalus Interchange electronic discussion on the article during class, Miyako first started to reflect some of her doubts, when she posed a general concern and then asked one of her classmates to comment on his own experiences:[2]

Miyako:

I just wonder.... I am really hard to catch up with study now. In my case, I don't have time to think about academic relationship or academic culture.

---

[2]E-mail messages are reprinted verbatim, including spelling errors.

Miyako:

To Ping
I have a question. You are in the second year in your MA program. then What kind of professional networking have you ever created in HK?

Ping:

To Miyako:
An academic network is very important to you. First, you have to understand what are you working on actually? Does it worth? These people can give you advice.

Second, these people can recommend you when you wan to continue youe studies. Or you can know other people through these people.
Lastly, academic politics....

In Hong Kong, I maintain good relation with professors in dept. Once I chose my topic, I have to know other specialists in this field. These people are easy to find, since this is a small community. Now, my thesis committee has four members. One is my supervisor, one is a professor in our dept. another professor from University of Hong Kong

Later that same day, Miyako sent an e-mail to Luz, further reflecting on the issue of networking for graduate students.

Date:Mon, 21 Oct 1996 12:38:23 -1000
From:Miyako <miyako@hawaii.edu>
To:Luz <luz@hawaii.edu>
Subject: Today's discussion

I have one more question. Creating professional network sounds very strange for me becasue I don't want to go to Ph.D and I just want to get MA Degree. I would like to create good relationship to my academic adviser and the other professors who in my department through the lecture. I would like to learn alot of things from them. I thought it is enough to study here. I have not ever imagined to create network byong my department or this university. What do you think my opinion? Maybe I don't know how important the academic/professional network mean.
thank you for your time, Luz. :)
Miyako

The same day, Luz gave a lengthy, detailed reply which is indicative of the care she put into responding to student concerns,

Date: Mon, 21 Oct 1996 15:37:47 -1000 (HST)
From: Luz <luz@hawaii.edu>
To: Miyako <miyako@hawaii.edu>
Subject: Re: Today's discussion

Miyako,
I understand your concerns and would like to give you my opinion. Please don't feel obliged to agree with me!

In reponse to your comment that professional networking seems a little bit irrelevant to your situation, because you're not planning to stay in academia and become a PhD but your goal is to just get your MA here and then work:
I understand your position and I think you're partly right, networking seems less immediate of a goal or need for students without a plan to become professors or researchers. However, some degree of professional networking can help you get better grades, learn more about your subject-matter, and have better chances of a REAL good job once you finish your MA. Let me give you examples of "professional networking" at the MA level:

-Pay visits to professors' offices, make appointments to talk about general and specific academic issues, use the office hours and student-conferencing system: Do you pay attention to your relationships to your academic advisor and the professors you take classes from? American students regularly make appointments and discuss their progress in the program or in the class with their professors. This helps professors "remember" their names, faces, and personalities. It also helps them "connect" that person who often comes to talk about academic stuff as a conscientious, motivated, responsible student who cares about his/her progress and learning. For international students who don't know exactly what's valued in the system, going to professors offices to talk about papers, academic issues, etc. is embarrassign, difficult, or even not very clear to talk about what? This means that the p[orfessors never "remember" their names, faces, and personalities, and that they often "connect" the lack of memory about these students with low-motivated students, students who don't seem to care enough about their learning to put some extra time outside class for office hours ... Can you see how networking is working towards a better grade, a more sympathetic reading of your paper, extra help and feedback that improves the final quality of your work ... Lots of advantages that we miss if we don't do "networking" at the MA level!

- Exchange drafts and papers (and ideas) with fellow students in your grad courses: Do you systematically try to engage in conversation and academic exchanges with the best students in your class? If you do so, you'll get feedback from them about the assignments, about how "networking" works with each professor, etc. These exchanges work almost exactly as the excahgning of manuscript before publishing them for scholars and PhDs (the ones that Agre talks about in his article): You improve the quality of yor work thanks to these relationships, and you're expected and willing to reciprocate and help out other students in other occasions; you should do it as something positive for all students involved and keep an equal-to-equal attitude when you talk to those you consider really good students in a class.

-Use e-mail to give other students useful extra information about papers, exams, etc. Soon, they will start doing the same thing for you! Use e-mail lists and e-mail addresses to find out about sources, good topics for papers, professors' little peculiarities in grading papers or liking certain topics, etc. All this information very often is out there in students' minds and mouths ... But asking about things through e-mail makes things easier and clearer.

-Create a "graduate student persona" during your grad years ... For instance, you have now your homepage and you will put a paper on the Web; well, let other people in your field know about this. For the American system, grad students should have an academic dimension and a social dimension: volunteer to do social work in your department, such as monitoring for the Reading Room or the language lab, helping organize receptions, department-wide events, or department-related events. People will remember you and your involvement in the department, and they'll be able to recommend you in the future (you can also put it in your resume, at least in your English resume!). Or if you don't want to be so active in public, you can at least make sure you attend lectures and informal talks (or other optional events) organized in your department. This shows you're a good, motivated student who doesn't view classes as the ONLY single way of "learning", but knows that other departmental activities are equally valuable (otherwise, why do busy professors bother to organize talks and lectures, or social events?).

Two more additional reasons to try to create SOME degree of professional network are:

-you need to get some first-hand experience in professional networking if you need to teach academically and professionally oriented students yourself (for example, back in your country you may need to "teach" how professional networking works in the American education system); and

-you never know, but if some time in the far future you suddenly would want to commit to academia or do a PhD, you'll find yourself in a very bad position if you didn't pay attention to networking during the years of your MA at UH (you'll need letters of recommendation that no MA professor will be able to write because they don't "remember" you ... just seeing that you got an A with them won't help in American universities for letters of recommendation to be written to you for admission in a PhD program or even for regular jobs in the States).

I'm afraid I wrote way too much and you had to put up with my verbosity!! Do you mind if I send a copy of this message to the rest of the students in class? I think we could maybe discuss these points on Wednesday as a whole class (together with Agre's paper). Please let me know if you don't mind and I'll send a copy of this message to the write-I list.

Luz

Miyako replied back the following day:

Date:Tue, 22 Oct 1996 14:19:43 -1000
From:Miyako <miyako@hawaii.edu>
To:Luz <luz@hawaii.edu>
Subject: Re: Today's discussion

thank you very much for your very detailed information. :)

Now I think I got the picture what Agre said in hid paper and why you and Mark picked up this topic to discuss in our class. :)

I have never thought about academic society at university in America. I didn't even have idea about what is a graduate student. I almost lost the way in my study!! I came to America to study and I wanted the different place than Japan, so I should try to participate in not only study but also the relationship with professors and students positively. Even if I would get MA without involving that kind of activities, I think MA degree doesn't mean. We, students, have to learn a lot of things other than earning degree throughout out campus life. :)

Please feel free to use my mail and your answer for my classmate.

I am really happy if my small question can contribute to the class. Is this also important role as a student, right?
Again, thank you for your kindness. I am really happy that I have a teacher like you who always answers my question politely. :)
Miyako

Following this exchange, Miyako's attitude toward relationships within her department started to change. As she explained to me:

After I got an answer from Luz, I went to a Indonesian party, that was organized by Dr. Perez. And I met some student in the same department and I realized that it's very important to make networking, I mean meet the people, the students and professors in my same field, because the students in the same department give me a lot of information about books and articles, so I found it's very useful, helpful for me.

I also think it's very good for me to talk to the student who is the excellent one in the class. So I started talking to the one who everybody says she's great, so it's also helpful to me. Just makes me feel comfortable, because if I go to the class, I don't know anybody, it makes me nervous, if I don't get everything, I don't understand whole lecture. But if I have a person, like if I have a student I know at the class, I haven't asked any question to her yet, but if I got stuck I can ask her something. So it makes me feel comfortable.

Maybe because I'm from Japan. At the Japanese University, we don't need to make network. Just make connection with the teacher (that's how it is). If I go to graduate school in Japan, maybe I work by myself and sometimes talk to my professor, I don't need to make network.

As for her opinions about the class, she told me:

I like the most is, when I write something, and I have a question, I'd like to ask many questions, and then I send journal or I send my questions over e-mail to Luz, she replies to me immediately, it's very helpful. Whenever I took an English class it was like that, but I couldn't use e-mail so I have to make an appointment and I have to find the professor first, sometimes it takes time to ask question, but now I can type and send it and I just wait the reply and it's easier.

When I interviewed Miyako again several months after the semester ended, she told me that she had continued her contacts with Professor Perez and was going on a summer study trip to Indonesia that he had organized. She added that

I think now I can see what is networking, what networking is, I can see, a little bit, because my department is a very small department, so it's very easy to know each other. If I get to know one person, that person will introduce me to two or three other students, so now I can find out many people in my department and also, not only say hi on the campus, we can exchange information about the colloquiums or I can ask about the thesis. A student in the third year gave me some excellent advice about my thesis. Last time I didn't know what grad student is, what I was supposed to do. But now I can imagine what I'm going to do to earn master's degree.

These were not the only benefits that Miyako got out of the class. She also discussed in her interviews how she learned much about the academic writing process from Luz—how to effectively use the library, take notes, brainstorm, and organize her papers. This case study of Miyako illustrates how becoming an academic writer involves broader ways of thinking and acting and the role that electronic communication played in fostering some of that broader reflection in this course.

Miyako's experiences are not surprising when viewed in light of social science research on the effects of computer-mediated communication on organizational dynamics. This research has found that peripheral members of organizations are likely to benefit in several ways from the introduction of computer-mediated communication. First, they are more likely to initiate communication with their superiors because they don't have to go through the risk of a face-to-face encounter (Sproull & Kiesler, 1986). Second, they are more likely to communicate with their peers because they have more opportunities to do so (Eveland & Bikson, 1988). Third, by participating in electronic group discussion, they can benefit from additional access to information and varied perspectives even without direct participation (Finholt & Sproull, 1990).

Sproull and Kiesler (1991), in their review of research on the effects of introducing online communications into organizations, concluded that the most peripheral members of organizations tend to benefit the most because they are the most shut out via traditional means of communication:

> Participation plans [in organizations] typically rely on communications initiated from the center and representation of the periphery to the center. Management initiates most participation plans. Employees receive participation overtures rather than initiation them ... Electronic communication may offer peripheral employees new opportunities to initiate connections within the organization to reduce the information gap and increase motivation. If connectivity is high, there are potentially many people accessible via the network ... [Electronic] interactions increase both connections between the periphery and the center of the organization and connections among peripheral workers. (pp. 79–81)

These conclusions have been confirmed in classroom studies, which show that the introduction of e-mail increases the involvement of students who due to anxiety (Mabrito, 1991) or ability (Hartman et al., 1991) are the least likely to participate in traditional classrooms.

If we see learning how to write and education more generally as a process of apprenticeship, with students gradually achieving more involvement with and participation in new discourse communities, these research results are significant. They indicate that computer-mediated communication may help involve students who in the past have been most shut out.

Miyako is a bright student, but as a first-year M.A. student, without a strong background in her chosen major, she is by definition on the periphery of her chosen field. Her process of apprenticeship is made more difficult by the fact that she is an international student, lacking the native English fluency and background knowledge of American academic life that American graduate students at the University of Hawai'i take for granted. Even among her non-native peers in ELI 83 she is somewhat on the periphery, due to her shyness in face-to-face communication.[3] Yet given the opportunity, she was able to take ample advantage of electronic communication—with both her teacher and her peers—to compensate for her shyness and thus more fully integrate into graduate life.

As Freire (1970/1994) explained, "Liberating education consists in acts of cognition, not transferrals of information" (p. 60). He further explained that such cognition can only be achieved through dialogue: "If it is in speaking their word that people, by naming the world, transform it, dialogue imposes itself as the way by which they achieve significance as human beings. Dialogue is thus an existential necessity" (pp. 69–70).

Luz provided her students an additional medium for achieving dialogue. Miyako seized that chance, contributing to her richer understanding of, and participation in, academic life in the United States.

Zhong

Another case of teacher–student apprenticeship learning facilitated by e-mail is illustrated by Zhong's experiences in the ELI writing course. Zhong, a graduate student in public health from China, represents the opposite end of the spectrum from Miyako. Whereas Miyako was a newcomer to graduate research, Zhong was already a professor at a Chinese university. He had carried out substantial research in China and had published extensively in Chinese academic books and journals. He was in the United States on a 2-year

---

[3]This reticence appears to be typical of Japanese ESL students in the United States. In a previous study, I found that Japanese students, compared to Chinese, Vietnamese, and Filipino students, participated the least in face-to-face discussion and increased their participation the most in computer-mediated discussion (Warschauer, 1996).

fellowship sponsored by both the University of Hawai'i and China's ministry of public health.

As in the case of Miyako, the concrete problems that Zhong confronted also dealt with issues of academic and professional networking. For Zhong, though, the issue was not his relationships with students and faculty in his University of Hawai'i department but rather those with colleagues halfway across the world.

Some Swedish researchers had worked with Zhong in Shanghai to carry out research related to community public health. Zhong had been responsible for most of the field work, and he and the rest of the team had an agreed on arrangement as to who had first authorship rights over which part of the data.

To Zhong's surprise, he received an e-mail message from one of the Swedish colleagues (himself a graduate student) asserting authorship over data that Zhong had gathered. Zhong was trying to figure out how to use e-mail to communicate with this colleague in a way that would protect Zhong's own rights while maintaining a positive professional and personal relationship.

Over the next few days, Zhong sent several e-mail messages to Luz asking her assistance in this real-world writing challenge. The following e-mail represents Zhong's first draft of an e-mail message that he asked Luz to comment on:

Dear Svet:

How about your decision for your mothers treatment. I am sorry I can not give advice because I do not know what cancer she suffered from. As I know, tumor hospital of our university is skilled in many types of cancer while Zhongshan hospital and Changhai hospital are good in primary liver cancer. Zhongshan hospital has special wards for foreign guests. If you can tell me and Hengjin in detail, we can supply more information about hospital and doctors. It is sure that she will be treated by best doctors if you decide to send her to Shanghai because you know hospitals in China usually pay more attention to foreign guests. However, you have to balance because you have to pay all medical service while it is not in Sweden.

I surprised that you also select maternal health care to write paper. When we discussed in Shanghai (during the end of September and the beginning of October. Charles Krot, You, Wang Lau, Li Wen and I joint the discussion), we divided the project to four divisions according to Krot's advice. You are in charge for finance and equity, Wang for drug use, Li for schistosomiasis, and I for maternal and child health and family planning. Since then, we prepared literature and data analysis strategy. When we analyzed the data in Stockholm, nobody proposed to reorganize the task. So three of us worked accordingly in individuals fields. At the end of our visiting, Wang and I presented our most refined result in seminar (Feb. 12, 1996). After then, I tried to complete the paper.

However, I can not find enough time until I came Honolulu. As I mentioned in previous message, under the pressure of English writing class and help of my teacher, I finally completed it.

After I read your paper, I surprisingly found that we used almost the same result that I presented in seminar. In your paper, you add table 8 while I add more literature and discussion in my paper. I understood that you had to publish one more paper and two more unpublished papers for your Ph.D requirement if Hengjin and I can publish each with your name as second author. However, I had written it ready with more than half of my efforts in four topics which distributed to me according to our agreement. My MCH advisor here is finding journal for publishing. I am afraid we can only publish one paper base on the result, and put my name as second or later author in this paper is unreasonable. I think you can use a lot of the result in your equity paper, but not all. If you interest in MCH and FP, I think you can write paper on family planning base on my result. Ms Xu Qian had written a paper in Chinese on family planning, but most of the result is not used. You can find the file that I left to you and get Dr Monicas advice easily on this topic.

If you have some questions on data analysis or data management, I am willing to give my advice. If you need, I can send data set about FP to you by email.

Best regard

Sincerely

Zhong Lu

There are several noteworthy aspects of this draft, but most prominent are that (1) the first paragraph mentions nothing at all about the issue at hand, (2) when Zhong does discuss the issue, he does so in such an indirect way that it's almost impossible to know what he's requesting, and (3) Zhong presents himself not as an experienced professional writing for publication but rather as an English student writing for his teacher.

Luz shared her advice to Zhong in several e-mail messages, including one that was written even before this draft (urging Zhong to stand up for his rights), one that gave some general comments on this draft, and one that offered specific comments on a second draft. As a result of the feedback Zhong received from Luz and other correspondents, he eventually settled on this version, which he e-mailed to his Swedish colleague:

Date: Sun, 10 Nov 1996 21:38:53 -1000 (HST)
From: Zhong Lu <zhong@hawaii.edu>
To: Svet Nord <svet@uni.edu.se>
Cc: Charles Krot <ckrot@uni.edu.se>,
Wang Lau <wlau@uni.edu.cn>
Subject: About MCH paper

Dear Svet:

When I received your email message of Nov 4, I was very surprised to see that you went ahead with your paper on maternal health care. As you must be aware after our discussion in Shanghai last September-October, when we distributed all the topics among us, the topic of maternal health care was incumbent on me for analysis and publication.

Indeed, after analyzing the data in Stockholm, I presented the result on this topic in seminar (Feb 12, 1996). The same results will be also presented in an international symposium in Wuhan, Hubei Province soon (Ms Limin Mao must have told you about this when you visited Shanghai).

I may have not been clear enough when I told you in my message of Nov 6 that I had completed the paper. In fact, my advisor here, Dr Baruffi and Dr Morens, have suggested several possible international journals. We are in the process of agreeing which of the options looks like the most appropriate for this paper.

I have carefully read what you wrote on the paper. I must tell you that your analysis does not seem to add or modify much of the result that I presented at the seminar in February in Stockholm. Table 8 is the only addition for the result in your paper compared to the data I presented then. I frankly am not very clear how this table fits into the overall results in that topic. Myself, I expanded on my presentation in Stockholm and added quite a bit in the literature review and the discussion sections of my paper. Overall, I cannot see how publishing your paper not mine would serve the best interests of our research team.

In conclusion, I am afraid the only satisfactory solution I can see is to publish my paper with me as the first author. This was what we all had agreed on before. I am truly sorry if I was unclear in my communication with you on this matter. I would be happy to agree to your authorship of papers on the topic of equity, using a portion of our results (such as MCH, drug use), or maybe a paper on family planning using my results. We can discuss this further if you are interested. However, I am afraid my authorship on the maternal health care topic is not negotiable.

Best regards,

Zhong Lu

This e-mail message was obviously much more direct and forthright then the first draft. Zhong explained very clearly what the problem was and asserted his professional rights. In response, the Swedish colleague acceded to Zhong's wishes. Though there were some ruffled feathers, Zhong smoothed things out with some softer messages that followed.

Later, Zhong decided to share his experiences with the rest of the class through an e-mail message to the class list. His lengthy message, which included two appendices and a number of interactive questions to the class, is excerpted here:

Date: Sun, 24 Nov 1996 12:50:04 -1000
From: Zhong <zhong@hawaii.edu>
To: write-l@hawaii.edu
Subject: Academic disputation analysis

I just finished a disputation on authorship of a paper. It lasted two weeks, used more than 50 email messages..... .
IF YOU WERE ME, WHAT WOULD YOU DO ACCORDING TO YOUR NATIVE CULTURE? ...

According to Chinese culture, I replied him implicitly. PLEASE GUESS WHAT WILL HAPPEN?....

From the disputation, at least I got two experiences:

1) When we communicate with somebody in English, as well as other languages, we have to understand the culture of whom you are communicating, and think according to this culture. Further, to familiar the culture other than you native culture may be more difficult than language learning itself.

2) Nowadays, INTERNET provide a great environment to communicate more frequent, wide and fast than before. During the disputation, I communicated with 14 persons, over 50 emails. Supposed without email, we would spend at least 2 months to discuss. During this two month period, both of us can complete one paper each.

IF MY EXPERIENCE LIGHT YOUR REFLECTION, PLEASE SHARE WITH OUR CLASS.

Zhong Lu

Zhong's experience raises several issues about the role of electronic learning in this class. One issue is that of *authenticity*. Studies have indicated that much of the writing that takes place in English for Academic Purpose classes is far removed from the real writing needs of undergraduate and particularly graduate students. Some teachers, including Luz, have tried to remedy this situation by allowing students to work on their content-class writing assignments in their English class. In Luz's class, for example, students who were taking a biology or political science class could work on and submit their papers from those classes to fulfill Luz's writing assignments. Even in this situation, however, one class assignment is being substituted for another; there is still no guarantee that the writing assignment matches the needs that students might have outside of class assignment—for example, in writing for publication or communicating with professional colleagues.

In Zhong's case, due to the individualized contact he had with the teacher, facilitated by easy access via electronic communication, he received writing attention at the point of real need, rather than in dealing with some abstract or arbitrary possibility. In a situation like this it is unlikely that the lessons he learned—for example, about the need for directness in Western professional correspondence—would soon be forgotten.

Zhong's experience helps illustrate the nature of electronic communication and in particular how it achieves the benefits of both speech and writing. Zhong was able not to interact with a lot of people in a short time and also to do so in a written medium that allowed Luz and other correspondents to reflect on what Zhong had written and give an interpretive but rapid response. Zhong in turn could reflect on Luz's (and others') responses and take them into account in further interaction. Through this process, a dialogism was achieved in which Zhong successfully incorporated the words and ideas of several correspondents into his eventual e-mail message to Sweden.

This example also shows the importance of learning not only *via* electronic communication, but also *about* electronic communication. The vast amount of time that most academics and business people spend sending and reading e-mail should indicate that this is a very important communications medium in today's world, but it is a medium that is not often addressed in the English class. In this particular case, Zhong was the first to point out that if he had been communicating face-to-face with his Swedish colleague, he could have handled the conflict easily without outside assistance. It was thus not the communication in general that was difficult; it was the particular medium of communication that represented a challenge. Fortunately, Zhong and Luz were able to use e-mail to learn about e-mail, and thus Zhong could not only get through this hurdle but also learn some lessons for future communication.

DAEDALUS INTERCHANGE AND COLLABORATIVE APPRENTICESHIP

A second type of apprenticeship learning that Luz tried to promote can be termed *collaborative apprenticeship* (see, for example, Bayer, 1990). This model de-emphasizes the tutoring role of the teacher and instead emphasizes how students collaborate to socially construct knowledge. For collaborative apprenticeship learning to take place, the following elements are believed to be important: (1) an opportunity for students to freely express their ideas (Bayer, 1990), (2) an active process of reflection on ideas that are expressed (Bayer, 1990; Wells & Chang-Wells, 1992), and (3) an epistemic engagement with texts, whereby students are seeking not only to understand information but to critically interpret it and construct new knowledge (Wells & Chang-Wells, 1992).

In recent years, computer-assisted classroom discussion has become an increasingly popular medium for trying to promote these goals. Computer-assisted discussion takes place in special classrooms with networked computers. Each student sits at a personal computer using special software and typing comments. For example, with the Daedalus Interchange program used at the University of Hawai'i, each participant's screen is divided in two parts. The student or teacher types on the top of the screen and then clicks on a button to send the comments to the rest of the class or group. Within a few seconds, the comments appear on the bottom of everybody's screen, together with the name of the writer. All comments are logged in chronological order, so students can stroll back and forth to refer to various parts of the discussion. The teacher also has the option of electronically saving and printing the discussion and then making it available to students in either electronic form or hard copy.

Computer-assisted classroom discussion is believed to benefit collaborative learning in several ways. First, computer-mediated discussion, compared to face-to-face discussion, has been shown to feature more equal and democratic participation (for reviews, see Sproull & Kiesler, 1991; Warschauer, 1997). Reasons for this benefit include that computer-mediated communication (1) reduces social context clues related to race, gender, handicap, accent, and status, which sometime reinforce unequal participation in other types of interaction (Sproull & Kiesler, 1986); (2) reduces dynamic cues, such as frowning and hesitation, which can intimidate by reminding students that their comments are being evaluated (Finholt, Kiesler, & Sproull, 1986); and (3) allows individuals to contribute at their own time and pace, thus neutralizing the advantage of those who tend to speak out loudest and interrupt the most and allowing students to initiate communication without seeking permission (Sproull & Kiesler, 1991). Numerous studies have shown that computer-assisted classroom discussion features relatively greater student participation (as compared to the teacher dominance of most classroom oral discussion; see, for example, Chun, 1992; Kern, 1995) and also more balanced student participation (with shy students participating more than in face-to-face discussion; see, for example, Sullivan & Pratt, 1996; Warschauer, 1996).

Computer-assisted classroom discussion is also said to facilitate critical thinking by encouraging a combination of interaction and reflection. This benefit has also been demonstrated through empirical studies based on content analyses comparing face-to-face and computer-assisted discussion (see, for example, Newman, Johnson, Cochrane, & Webb, 1996).

Although these features of computer-assisted discussion make it a potentially beneficial tool in a range of content classes, writing teachers have been particularly enthralled with the possibilities, as every verbalization can be seen as an act of collaborative authoring. As DiMatteo (1990) explained:

> My students confront a writing situation that privileges their own speech. They create intensely visible language out of what they consider to be forgettable, facile

words—their own talk and conversation. They develop a sense that when they talk, they are "drafting" themselves, composing their own identities through a speech that is also a writing made utterly tangible ...

My students, divided into groups of talk-writers, face the otherness of language directly. No longer working in just a medium of self-expression, they project a self whose power resides not in separation from others but in an ability to collaborate with them. This empowerment of the individual within an enabling group demands a reorientation of thinking about the conventional definitions of the writer and his or her audience. The group unit, emerging from the erasure of the isolated self, must write to converse, a collective activity. (pp. 76–77)

Although it is uncertain whether Luz's students achieved these lofty goals, it appeared that computer-assisted discussion played a positive role in the class. Students used computer-assisted discussion on about eight occasions throughout the semester, sometimes conversing in small groups and sometimes in the whole class. A comparison of transcripts from face-to-face and computer-assisted discussions illustrates the complementary roles these two discussion media played in Luz's class.

A Sample Face-to-Face Discussion

The following transcript represents part of a whole class face-to-face discussion that took place in the middle of the semester. The topic of the discussion was various types of documentation styles used in academic writing.

Luz:	Do you use/ well, okay, so this is for publishing in journals, right? Should we care about our papers following styles and becoming publishable papers in journals? Why should we care about that if our papers are going to our professors? They're not going to journals in principle, yeah? They may end up being in journals, but sometimes we're not aiming at publishing in journals ... We just want to give our papers to our professors and get our grade! Why should we care about the documentation style and about the structure of journals ...?
Atsuko:	As someone mentioned before, each department has their own mode of style, so we need to start using the, so in writing papers or dissertations etc you should ask your department
Luz:	Any other opinions about why should we care if we only are writing term papers. Or should we care?
Mei:	I think we should care for ... when we're in the final paper we may want to go to publish our final paper ... It should be.... The possibility to publish is is ...
Luz:	is always there
Mei:	yeah [laughs]

Luz: So if we can get lucky and finally publish something out of a term pa-
            per; we need training to be able in the future to publish ... Any other
            reasons?

Hae: Well actually, I once heard that the professor said he will look at the
            question of formality at first, and then content. So I was I was won-
            dered I mean the content is more important than the formality but
            but he he didn't say like that so ... The question is is is very interest-
            ing to to me ... I think the ... the ... the reason that documentation
            style is important is easy to to to follow the article.. actual ...

Luz: That's true, the reader who knows one documentation style and can
            just fly over the lines because everything is familiar- all the conven-
            tions are there so is much much easier to read [silence]. Any other
            reasons? The ones that didn't ask their departments yet ... The ones
            who cannot find an answer. Why should we care, or should we care
            at all? Just for our own term papers? ... I think one very good reason
            is that our professors–although they read a lot of student papers,
            they are not ... uhm ... they are not part of the community of stu-
            dent papers—or students. They are part of the academic commu-
            nity, what they really read their whole life is journals, published
            articles, very high quality papers. Yeah? And so, when they're read-
            ing our papers and they are grading our papers, they can't help it,
            even if they don't want to: They compare our papers with the stan-
            dards that they have. They are used to talking, writing, and reading
            at that high level for everything! [laughs] And when they see our
            papers and they read them and they grade them, they just have this
            whole reference of "up here in the journals." Even if they are, you
            know, they are aware that we're just students—we're just begin-
            ning, we don't need to publish, right? We've been one semester.
            They can't help it! because that's their world, that's their commu-
            nity, of scholars, their community of researchers ... And so, the very
            best way of trying to get a good grade is by making sure that we pay
            attention to all those things! By making sure we are aiming at those
            models in the journals. It's like our best model and we should try to
            become more and more like that, as much as we can. 'Cause for
            them, that's the real world. And that's what they know, and that's
            their values and when they are reading or grading ... they under-
            stand we're students, but still they have this kind of comparison all
            the time. It's good that that your professor explicitly said, "Look, I'm
            looking at formality first and content second." Many professors
            don't say it; they don't know that's what they are doing—but that's
            what they are doing when they give you a grade. And so it's good to
            know that ourselves as students.

The IRF Sequence

This discussion—and virtually every other whole-class face-to-face discussion I observed in Luz's classroom—narrowly followed the traditional IRF communication pattern consisting of an *initiating* move by the teacher, a *responding* move by a student, and a *follow-up* move by the teacher.[4] Numerous studies have shown that this pattern is the dominant structure of classroom discourse in the United States and other countries (Cazden, 1988; Lemke, 1990; Mehan, 1985; Poole, 1990).

What then is the general function of such discourse? Researchers claim that it is an established pattern for the teacher transmitting information to the classroom. As Lemke (1990) explained, "The triad structure [IRF] can be understood as a teacher-monolog in which some key T Inform has been transformed into a T Question/S answer pair, with T Evaluation required to confirm their equivalence to the 'underlying' T Inform" (p. 46). In commenting on Lemke's analysis, Cazden (1988) added that "the entire lesson can be seen as an interactional transformation of a lecture [the teacher] could have given herself but preferred to transform into [IRF] sequences, with slots for student responses in order to keep their attention" (p. 50).

An analysis of the face-to-face discussion, reported previously shows the same function. Luz knew why we should care about documentation style, but she initiated a series of IRF sequences in order to involve students in providing this information. This was a pattern I observed throughout the semester.

Discourse based on IRF sequences can likely play a positive role in education. After all, teachers have a lot of knowledge to share with students, and sharing that knowledge through IRF is certainly more engaging than through lecture. The problem is not so much that IRF exists but rather that it is ubiquitous. Even teachers such as Luz who favor more student-centered discussion have an extremely difficult time bringing it about, at least during whole class discussions. As Cazden (1988) commented:

> It is easy to imagine talk in which ideas are explored rather than answers to teachers' test questions provided and evaluated; in which teachers talk less than the usual two-thirds of the time and students talk correspondingly more; in which students themselves decide when to speak rather than waiting to be called on by the teacher; and in which students address each other directly. Easy to imagine, but not easy to do.

---

[4]Also referred to as IRE: Initiation, Response, and Evaluation.

Observers have a hard time finding such discussions, and teachers sometimes have a hard time creating them even when they want to. (p. 54)

Daedalus Discussion on Plagiarism

Cazden's words may have been true when she wrote them in 1988, but 10 years later observers have an easy time finding such discussions—on the computer. Numerous studies show that student-centered discussion tends to be the norm in synchronous computer-assisted classroom discussion (see Warschauer, 1997, for a review).

This was certainly the case in Luz's class. The following are excerpts of a Daedalus Interchange discussion on the topic of plagiarism.

Bagus: The main principle a scientist or researcher should keep in mind is "honesty". That is why it is not polite or ethic to say or write something that is not your own thought or finding without acknowledging the resource or the person from whom you get or extract his or her ideas even though from the writings, without being in direct contact with him or her. So, plagiarism here mainly deals with (according to my understanding) using other people thoughts and or ideas in your writings without giving acknowlegement to the sources. So, plagiarism can also be said as a "theft or robbery" in writings.

Atsuko: To avoid plagiarism, we always have to be careful. But sometimes the border line is not clear to recognize. For example, if I read an article and I agree with it, then I digest the idea and reorganize it in my brain. In such case, border of my own idea and idea from sources is not very clear to me. After several days, weeks, months later, if I use it in my writing without citation of source, it may be plagiarism. Is it same as copy or steal other people's idea?

Kazue: To Atsuko I do not think it is same as plagiarism in such case. When you use it after you completely understand and reorganized, the idea will be mixed with your knowledge about the issue so that probably you will write it with your own thinking and words.

Atsuko: If a writer used other people's idea from a published source without citation, it is clear that is plagiarism. But, in case he/she uses an idea from unpublished source, for example other people's draft, scholarly paper, or opinion in the discussion, how can we recognize it?

Xiao Hui: I agree with Atsuko's opinion. In case of the unpublished sources, how can we tell? Besides, if we want to cite some idea from an unpublished source, how to cite it? For instance, if I want to use some ideas from my professor's unpublished writing or from the e-mail discussion group, how can I cite them? I am really confused about it.

Sang: To Atsuko

The Bible says "There is nothing new under the sun." That means everybodys ideas or thoughts are come or influenced partly from other's ideas or thoughts or written materials. Therfore if you haven't clear intention to plagiarize other people's thoughts or ideas, and it is not so important in your writing, I think it would make big problem. That depend on your conscience. But I think as long as you know the source, it would be better to mention it.

Bagus: I would like to comments on Atsuko.s Question. Eventhough the source is not being published you can also acknowlege the person by putting a footnote about it on your paper, or just in the literature review just put "personal communication" or "pers.com". So after all it goes back to the writer him or herself. We can not justify him or her but the very important thing is that we donot follow their steps. Let us be honest ... Amen.

Kazue: To tell the truth, I have no good idea to avoid to be accused of being plagiarized. How we can know whether we do plagiarism or not if it is only by lack of knowledge or attention? But it may be one of the strategies to ask someone who is an expert of the field to check our writing.

Zhong: In our country, plagiarism (Chinese name "Piao Qie") is a action in academic profession which used somebody else's finding, data, idea without writing the name and source in references. This action is considered a cheating, and is looked down on by peers. If somebody act as PLAGIARISM, his/her retutation in professional activities will be so bad as to difficult to find collaborator in future. Maybe he/she have to change profession. Sometimes the action that a supervisor or advisor occupied the first authorship in his/her student or supervisee's reseach paper also can call "plagiarsm".

Luz: Okay, stealing ideas is plagiarism (that is, taking ideas from a source without acknowledging it) and copying word by word without acknowledging that we are quoting (by using quotation marks and page number) is plagiarism. But is plagiarism intentional always? Does the person "want" to steal and consciously "steals"?? Many international students tell me that the language is a big problem for them and that they cannot avoid copying more than normal because their English is not good enough to express themselves without the "help" of other people's words ... What do you all think? Is that case plagiarism? Can we talk about

	plagiarism if the person didn't intend to "steal" ideas or words, if the person wasn't consciously "dishonest"? What do you think?
Miyako:	As Luz said, I sometimes have to make sentence which is like the one from the book I read for paper to write my idea clearly. Then I think "Is it plagiarism?" How you all compose your sentences without making resemble sentences in your refference books?
Atsuko:	As Luz wrote, some plagiarism cases are not done by intentionally. In my case, since I could not have established my writing style, I have to refer to other people's (native speakers) writing. My writing is easily influenced by the source which I am referring to. Of course I'm paying attention not to copy an idea from the source, but I'm afraid that I already commit a kind of plagiarism in my papers.
Hae:	In order to avoid the plargiarism, I think, it is necessary to mention the author, the article that you make use of their ideas in your paper. When I was in the university in Korea, I saw some cases of plargiarism. In one time, when I was working in the press center for the students, one of my collegue was accused of plargiarism. That time, she wrote an article for press but, the editor pointed out that her idea was from another daily newspaper. However, she insisted that her article was original, because she did not read the daily newspaper. In that respect, I agree with her in that our ideas sometimes can be same especially in some controversial political issue. Actually, in academic writing I saw some cases of someone's ideas are same with another. Therefore, it is easy to think that the case is plagiarism. But, to the one who wrote the article, it may be impossible to think his/her idea to be plagiarised. Seeing with these two cases, it is not easy to judge plagiarism.

This example indicates several features that were dramatically different than the face-to-face discussion presented earlier. Other participants, rather than the teacher, can play the central role (in this case a leading role was played by a student named Atsuko). Students' comments were generally more substantial and thoughtful. Students followed up on each others' points and at times responded directly to each other. The teacher continued to participate, but in order to push the discussion along or raise key points, rather than as the single sole arbiter.

It is particularly interesting and important that such a discussion took place on the topic of plagiarism. Plagiarism is often simplified to the issue of wholesale copying, without attribution, of others' papers, but the issue involves much more subtle decisions about whether and to what extent one can use phrases or sentences from other writers (or even from one's own previous work) with or without citation. It is an especially important issue for non-native writers, who have to make narrow decisions as to whether imitation is a successful language learning strategy or whether it's stealing. Finally, as Pennycook (1996) pointed out, perspectives on plagiarism vary greatly across cultures, and there is nothing inherently more logical or morally superior about the North American or European perspective than any other.

This dialogue thus represents an excellent example of where a teacher-fronted whole class face-to-face IRF discussion would be inadequate. Even small-group face-to-face discussions might be less than ideal because students would only be able to share ideas with the small number of people in their groups. In this case though, students were able to learn the ideas of everyone in the class, while also having full opportunity to jump in and offer their views without having to interrupt anyone. They were able to address important issues such as the relation between using someone's ideas and using their words, the differences between citing published and unpublished information, strategies for avoiding plagiarism, and even the possibility (raised by Zhong, of course) of graduate students themselves being victims of plagiarism.

When Luz and I were later looking over the transcripts of both face-to-face and Daedalus discussions, Luz commented that she asks questions in face-to-face interaction not only to keep students' attention but "also because I feel [it's] essential to know first what students believe and how they perceive a given issue before I try to 'convince' them of the official perspective or of my perspective." She also expressed her conclusion that "this is precisely what Daedalus achieves much better than a teacher-centered class: Students get to voice their own perceptions."

Other Daedalus Discussions

Not all the Daedalus discussions were as rich as this plagiarism discussion in terms of exchange of content, but every Daedalus discussion featured more decentralized discussion than any of the whole class face-to-face discussions. Students sought each others' opinions, built on what other students had said, and expressed solidarity with each other in ways that didn't happen in oral whole-class interaction. Here is an excerpt of another Daedalus discussion early in the semester on the topic of students' experiences so far in the university. Although the topic might not be considered as academically serious as plagiarism, the discussion seemed to serve a valuable purpose of allowing students to offer support to one another.

Ho Shan: Aloha: This is my second semest in UH. In general, I enjoy the student life. But I feel a little bit hard in studing. because I've left school for eight years already. In the other hand, the lanuage is a big obstacle for me. Sometime, I really want to quit the school. But I can't. I like studing. Especially I really want to improve my Enlish. This is a main purpose that I come to here.

Miyako: To Ho Shan: Maybe everybody feels hard to learn English, so please don't feel so depressed. Someday, you will be all right. We need patience.

Ho Shan: TO Miyako: I am very glad to have your encourage. Thank you. Mahalo.

Marina: Hi, I'am realy interested in every thing I've been learning .It is a challend to me go back to school , and try to improve my self.Iwas out off school for almost 10 years'and just 2year ago I decided to go back.I still writing very slow;but Miyako has been helping me.MAHALO!!!! [thank you]

Kazue: To Marina; I understand your feeling because I had also graduated university about 10 years ago,and decided to go back to school 3 years ago. It is little bit difficult to accostum myself to a student life, but it is nice and interesting, don't you think so?

It's noteworthy that all the participants in this discussion were women. I found that female students used Daedalus to offer words of support, thanks, and encouragement more frequently than men did, and they were especially appreciative of the opportunity to share solidarity in computer-assisted discussion. As a young Thai woman named Puanani told me,

I think [Interchange] is amazing ... I feel better because I feel like there's some other people that have problems like me. And we don't have to see each other, just read from there, and I think sometimes we can write something that we don't want to talk.

Another female student, Hao Jie from China, told me that

Daedalus is wonderful education in class, people can like networking, you can talk to each other and everybody can see. It's helpful. You can more active about your thoughts, you can thinking about yours, and other people don't interrupt what you're thinking. Other people compared to yours you just look at. If you're talking, talking, they can interrupt you. Daedalus is very useful for learning.

Other students told me that they benefited from the exchange of ideas on Daedalus. Bagus, for example, was an older student from Indonesia. Like Zhong, Bagus was a professor in his own country. Bagus had substantial research experience and was a skilled writer. His main needs revolved around learning acceptable ways of presenting information in an American context. Bagus participated very actively in Interchange discussions, articulating his views in detail and responding carefully to other participants. After the class ended, he told me that the single greatest benefit he got from the class was a better understanding of the differences between American and Indonesian approaches to plagiarism—a topic explored in depth in Daedalus and on e-mail.

Finally, some students commented on the writing practice that they got through Daedalus. Zhong explained that

> It's practice in writing … If we talk face-to-face, maybe the grammar and the words, make some mistakes. If use Interchange, we can improve our grammar and words, because we have to think a lot. Everyone can read and understand what we are writing and pays more attention.

Ho Shan, a Chinese woman, commented that

> You can take from somebody else, what they thought and their writing style, you can learn from each other. English is all our second language, we just translate, we do it the wrong way, not the right way, so we can see somebody else, the way they do it—I mean the structure.

Not all students felt positively about Daedalus. In personal interviews, three of the 15 students expressed frustrations, ranging from shyness about writing in a public forum to difficulty in reading so many incoming messages. The overall sentiment of both the students and the teacher, however, was that Daedalus offered a beneficial way to complement but not replace face-to-face discussions.

Whole-class face-to-face discussion proved an effective medium for Luz to share information with the whole class. Small group face-to-face discussion was useful when students needed to explore an issue in depth, with lots of rapid back-and-forth inquiries. Both whole-class and face-to-face discussion were better than computer-assisted discussion when a consensus needed to be reached. Computer-assisted discussion, and electronic communication in general (see, for example, Weisband, 1992), are not good tools for arriving at consensus or decisions because several people are communicating at once and it is thus hard to control the floor. Daedalus was useful for student-centered discussion on topics that required neither decision nor consensus but rather a reflective exchange of ideas.

THE INTERNET AND PERIPHERAL PARTICIPATION

In their book, *Situated Learning: Legitimate Peripheral Participation*, Lave and Wenger (1991) explain the theory of peripheral participation as follows:

> Newcomers' legitimate peripherality provides them with more than an "observational" lookout post: It crucially involves *participation* as a way of learning—of both absorbing and being absorbed in—the "culture of practice." An extended period of legitimate peripherality provides learners with opportunities to make the culture of practice theirs. From a broadly peripheral perspective, apprentices gradually assemble a general idea of what constitutes the practice of the community. This uneven sketch of the enterprise (available if there is legitimate access) might include who is involved; what they do; what everyday life is like; how masters talk, walk, work, and generally conduct their lives; how people who are not part of the community of practice interact with it; what other learners are doing; and what learners need to learn to become full practitioners. It includes an increasing understanding of how, when, and about what old-timers collaborate, collude, and collide, and what they enjoy, dislike, respect, and admire. In particular, it offers exemplars (which are grounds and motivation for learning activity), including masters, finished products, and more advanced apprentices in the process of becoming full practitioners (p. 1995).

Luz was constantly trying to find ways to support her students' entry into the communities of practice of their field. A number of class assignments involved having students investigate practices in their fields through talking with their professors, consulting fellow graduate students, or investigating journals at the library.

For Luz, computing was an important aspect of this process, first because it provided an additional medium for accessing the practices of the field and second because it represented part of the content involved in becoming a skilled academician. A number of class assignments were designed with these goals in mind. All students were given basic instruction in using e-mail, to fulfill assignments for this class and also because it was seen as a vital academic skill. All students were also required to join one academic listserver (i.e., e-mail discussion list) in order to get a better sense of the concerns and issues discussed by people in their field. All students were given instructions in how to search the World Wide Web as an important skill of academic research, and students were taught how to create their own Web pages, including both a personal home page and one for their academic articles, as a way of establishing their presence in their academic communities.

Results from these activities were mixed. Almost all the students were in their first semester at a U.S. university, and many had little previous experience with computers. About half the students did not know how to type. Few knew anything about the Macintosh operating system. This low level of computer knowledge meant that students needed a fair amount of instruction and practice in order to use the computer for electronic communication. There was thus a tension between providing this instruction and practice without turning the class into a computer skills class instead of a writing class.

A few class sessions were devoted entirely to computing skills (including how to use e-mail, how to search the Web, and how to make basic Web pages). Beyond this, students were encouraged to try to learn by themselves outside of class. Most students expressed satisfaction with the amount of time spent learning about using computers, though two students felt that there was too much time on this topic and one student, in contrast, felt it should have been given even more time.

What they learned in the course was far more than computer skills as traditionally defined. Much discussion and class activity was devoted to the use of the computer as an academic tool and how this affected the genres and use of computer-mediated communication. This topic came up in particular around the dispute between Zhong and his colleagues but also occurred in different guises throughout the semester. One frequent topic of discussion, for example, was the appropriateness of using e-mail for communication with professors, with students coming to the realization that this was a matter they had to explore over time with the individual professors.

Home Pages

Another topic of discussion was the role of Web home pages. Luz tried to emphasize the role that Web pages could have in projecting a professional presence by including a curriculum vitae, a description of research interests, or the students' published or unpublished papers. Yet the students, most of whom were beginning master's students, did not yet have much of a curriculum vitae, were unclear of their research interests, and had not yet written papers that they would be proud to share. When they searched the Web to look for home pages of other faculty or graduate students in their own departments, often they found very little.

Most students created home pages by the end of the semester, a couple of which were very professional in terms of both content and form. Many were done cursorily, and some did not have the academic tone that Luz wished for. For example, Ping's home page included a picture of himself, a few of his favorite links, and the following content:

Ping Chu Homepage

under construction

This forthcoming homepage is under construction. Come again.
Well, I am still confused on what I can put on this homepage, and I am busy to
make some changes as well, may you have any suggestions, please let me
know. Any help from you would be much appreciated.

E-mail address:ping@hawaii.edu

Ping Chu is a Hong Kong graduate student studying political science.

Other students also indicated they were confused about the purpose. As
Miyako told me, "It's interesting but kind of embarrassing, I don't know what
kind of people look at my home page, so I don't know what kind of things I
have to write on my home page."

Academic Listservers

Subscribing to and participating in listservers was also a challenging task for
students. Students were taught ways of searching the Internet for appropriate
listservers, and some managed to find useful lists either through searches or
consulting with other students or faculty. Ping, a Chinese student majoring in
political science, found and subscribed to a listserver that sent out a weekly
newsletter about events in China and provided much more current political
news than he could find in the library. Miyako subscribed to a list about
Southeast Asian affairs and said that she benefited from newspaper articles
from Southeast Asian countries, which were regularly translated and posted.
Xiao Hui, a female graduate student in linguistics, became a real listserver enthusiast, subscribing to five lists related to her major.

Few students however were bold enough to send messages to lists. One
exception was Atsuko.

Atsuko is a shy, soft-spoken Japanese student in her late 20s. She was a
first-semester graduate student in the master's program in English as a Second Language. For several reasons Atsuko was in a particularly challenging
situation. The University of Hawai'i ESL Department is top-rated with a
competitive atmosphere. Students are expected to complete sophisticated
research papers from the first year of their M.A. program. They are also expected to demonstrate native-like proficiency of English because they are
becoming teachers of that subject. Atsuko was a non-native speaker who
had completed an undergraduate major in a different field and then had
worked in the business sector for several years. She faced a difficult task in

succeeding in the ESL department, seeking to become an ESL professional while being an ESL student herself.

Atsuko was a very thoughtful and diligent student who took her academic work very seriously. She spent a great deal of time on assignments, both in her major and in her writing class. She also was able to benefit from the fact that both Luz and I were in the same academic field as she was, and we could thus give her extra guidance and advice beyond what we could offer other students.

Alhough Atsuko had little previous exposure to the Internet, she took very well to the electronic medium. She participated actively in Daedalus discussions (as evidenced by the exchange on plagiarism excerpted earlier). She completed all her e-mail journal assignments and wrote to Luz or me on many other occasions to ask questions. She told me that she spent several hours a week using e-mail and even got an additional private account so that she could more easily send e-mail from home as well as from the university.[5]

Atsuko sent messages to colleagues in the field twice in order to get support for class assignments. On the first occasion she was writing a critique of a textbook for teaching listening comprehension. Through e-mail she was able to find and contact ESL teachers at the University of Hawai'i who had used the text in their classes. Atsuko solicited their comments and incorporated them in a paper that Luz and I found to be very sophisticated for a first-semester graduate student.

On another occasion, Atsuko sent the following message to JALTCALL, an academic listserver in Japan made up of English language teachers in that country.

Date: Thu, 5 Dec 1996 16:53:35 -1000
From: Atsuko <atsuko@hawaii.edu>
Subject: Journals in ESL field

Hello everybody, I have following questions about Journals in English as a Second Language field.

I am a graduate students in ESL department in the US, I'm now working on my final paper of this semester and it's about content comparison of following journals;

* Tesol Quarterly
* ELT Jounal

---

[5]After Atsuko had exchanged several e-mail messages with Luz, she then started visiting Luz's office regularly. Luz felt that the e-mail exchange had served to break the ice and give Atsuko more confidence to approach her face-to-face.

* Studies in Second Language Acquisition
* TESOL Jounal.

I'm doing it because I'd like to know what kind or type of journal really benefit teachers.
I would be grateful if you could give me your answer and opinion upon followng questions.

1. Do you think classroom teachers need to keep up with current research findings?
2. Do you think reading journals is good way for teacher development?
3. One or more of these jounals availble in Japan?
4. If yes, which one do you prefer and why?
5. What kind of information do you(as a teacher) want to gain from journals?
6. Is there any research-oriented ESL journal in Japan like TQ or SSLA? (as far as I know, there are two major jounals "GENDAI EIGOKYOUIKU" & "EIGOKYOUIKU",I think both of them are teacher-oriented ones.)

Besides answering these questions, any opinion would be really helpful for me to develop my idea, because I have no experience as an English teacher in Japan.

Thank you in advance.

Atsuko Yoshinaga
University of Hawai'i
Department of ESL
atsuko@hawaii.edu

Although Atsuko received some helpful responses, she unfortunately also received a rude response that criticized her use of English. Atsuko later sent Luz and me an e-mail explaining and commenting on what had happened.

Date:Sat, 1 Mar 1997 01:21:51 -1000
From:Atsuko <atsuko@msn.com>
To:Luz <luz@hawaii.edu>
Cc:markw@hawaii.edu

... I am not sure about the formality of e-mail writing style. An e-mail correspondence is neither an oral conversation nor a letter. Usually, I write casually (to my friends, to you etc.). But when I try to send something to list server, I'm not sure about the etiquette or unwritten rule of formality. Do you think teachers can or have to teach about such criteria when they encourage their students electronic networking? I became to think about this matter when I first (and only once) sent some questions to the JALTCALL list server. I usualy keep myself as ROM (Read Only Member) even in HATESL list, but at that time I encouraged myself to try something new. I had to nerve myself to attempt to do so. Actually, I could get some useful comments, answers and advice. But one of the respondents gave me a feedback about my English. This person pointed out that I made many grammatical and spelling mistakes. It was true, so I was so ashamed and embarassed. I am intimidated to say anything on the e-mail discussion list now.

> If we really need to be careful about such formality, correctness and
> so on when we comunicate with people on lists, it is not easy expecially for
> non-native speakers to do. Uneasiness about such things undermine students
> motivation.....

Atsuko's message raises some important points, both about the hazards of the world of e-mail and also about the nature of Luz's and my approach to this situation. Although we had not required students to post to lists, we had encouraged them to do so, perhaps without sufficient warning as to the potential hazards. Like the real world, the electronic world can be a nasty one; in some ways it is worse because the relative anonymity makes open expressions of rudeness and hostility far too common. The theory of peripheral participation suggests taking measured steps in which "the costs of errors are small" (Lave & Wenger, 1991, p. 110). I do not believe that Atsuko made any error in sending her e-mail request for information; her message seemed completely appropriate to me, and any deviations from standard English are the kind that frequently appear in e-mail messages to discussion lists, even messages written by native speakers. Yet by venturing out into a public list, she was entering a danger zone that entailed some risk. Teachers who want their students to venture out publicly into the Internet, whether via e-mail or the World Wide Web, should prepare them for possible consequences.

COMPUTERS AND LITERACY

The interrelation between computers and literacy is a complex one and was experienced by different students in different ways throughout the class. Students from the least developed countries were often the ones who felt they had the most stake in learning about computers, as both they and their countries were trying to catch up.

Bagus, the older Ph.D. student who is a professor in his native Indonesia, stressed the emerging role of computers in his own institution located in an isolated region of his country:

> We are a small university, far from Jakarta, we get very little funding from the department to attend outside seminars. Sometimes we can attend seminars in Jakarta, but only once could I attend outside the country, in the Philippines. We have a library but it needs to be improved. The computer right now is very important, you can get information from outside and I can also submit my findings or what I have done, because maybe I cannot attend seminars, because I cannot buy tickets, but by computer I can distribute the results of my research, so everybody else can know what I've done or find out.

Bagus devoted a great deal of time and energy to trying to learn about computers. He diligently copied down all computer-related instructions given in class, including those thrown out casually, and often asked that instructions be repeated. He sometimes came to my office for extra assistance or questions regarding using computers, both related to uses of the Internet and also related to formatting problems with his papers. He also used Interchange discussions to ask other students for computer-related tips, such as how to improve his typing. In spite of limited funding, he bought his own laptop computer during the semester, and by the end of the semester he was in regular e-mail contact with his colleagues in Jakarta.

Prasit, an M.A. student from Cambodia, had similar feelings about the importance of computers. He told me that

> It's very important, because in Cambodia, if you to ask for a job at an NGO [non-governmental organization] or somewhere else, the first thing they ask is computer skills and English-speaking. They're very important for my career.... I like this class very much, because it use computer and make me very interested. Some time I sit in the class for one hour, and it feels like five minutes....

Prasit told me that he preferred discussing things via Interchange than in face-to-face discussion because he had extra opportunity to practice typing and using the computer. He once suggested that we devote an hour of class discussion to sharing ideas about how students learn computer skills.

Zhong, who already knew quite a bit about computers going into the class, still learned skills he found quite useful. After the semester ended, he started to set up his own business making Web pages in order to help put himself through school. One of his two scholarships was ending, and he needed an additional source of income if he was going to stay in the United States and continue to study.

Sang, an M.A. student in political science from Korea, had a very different attitude toward the use of computers in the class and toward the class overall. Unlike some of the other students, who were concentrating on ESL classes in their first semester, Sang was already taking several classes in his major. He was feeling great pressure from having to complete many writing assignments and saw much of the activity in the class as irrelevant to his immediate situation. He was frequently absent, missed several assignments, and often paid little attention to class activities. Here were his comments about using Interchange:

> To be quite frankly, that was useless, because, Ping, maybe Ping is in the political science department, but except he, nobody is in the political science department, so actually we don't have information, that was just chatting, huh, I don't think it's useful to

write my papers or to grouping my idea, maybe I can get better ideas or better information about the students, but it's not useful for my writing, just chatting. Somebody don't know about brainstorming or about writing, they're just chatting on Daedalus.

This is a writing course, so we'd better concentrate more writing…. We have very limited time. I don't know about the other department, but as for my department, I have a lot of writing, so I have to do a lot of papers, I need a lot of writing skills in a short time….

Later in the semester he felt that there had been some improvement, but he still obviously had some concerns. Here are excerpts from an e-mail message he sent me.

Date: Mon, 18 Nov 1996 08:55:40 -1000
From: Sang <sang@hawaii.edu>
To: Mark Warschauer <markw@hawaii.edu>
Subject: Reply to your Nov. 15 question

…. I think this class have improved much more toward concentration on writing. I said that this class is not a computer class, but an English writing class for Graduate level, and most of the students are foreigners. Too much stuff in the curriculum couldn't be accomplished completely any one of that. Even though I think combining writing with computer is a very good idea because most papers are supposed to be written in computers, but the problem is how much emphasis is laid on the computer skills. We can learn computer skills at any time and from anyone who knows how to operate it skillfully. But not the writing skills. That's why I said to you that this class should concentrate more on the writing skills. Even though I'm not quite satisfied, I feel much better nowadays.

Luz had never taught with computers before, and some aspects had not gone that smoothly. She felt, and I agreed, that she could do a better job of integrating computers more seamlessly in the future. Nevertheless, even in this first try it was clear that most students felt that the knowledge and experiences they gained were worth the occasional rough edges.

DISCOURSE AND DIALOGISM

As discussed earlier, Luz viewed learning academic writing as a process of entering a new discourse community. She thus tried to arrange class activities in order to give her students as much exposure as possible to the norms of the communities they sought to enter as well as opportunities to apprentice into those new modes of discourse. But the language of the academy is not a monolithic discourse that can be packaged and transmitted to students (Zamel, 1995). Rather, as Harris (1989) pointed out,

> The borders of most discourses are hazily marked and often travelled, and ... the communities they define are thus often indistinct and overlapping.... One does not step cleanly and wholly from one community to another, but is caught instead in an always changing mix of dominant, residual, and emerging discourses. (p. 17)

Harris went on to suggest that "rather than framing our work in terms of helping students move from one community of discourse into another, ... it might prove more useful (and accurate) to view our task as adding to or complicating their uses of language" (p. 17; see also Coles, 1988; Williams, 1977).

This "adding to" or "complicating" language uses, if it is to take place, clearly involves a process of critical reflection rather than one-way transmission of ideas. Students need opportunities to compare their own ways of thinking, acting, and communicating with the ways of different communities and to decide on their own which borders to attempt to cross and how. It becomes a matter not only of reinventing the university but also of reinventing their own relationship to the university, and perhaps even of reinventing themselves.

For the students in ELI 83, technology was an important part of this process, in several ways. On the one hand, learning about technology gave them better access to the tools needed for success in academic discourse. Students entered the class with a keen sense that they and their countries were on the periphery of global technological advances. Students' desire to catch up with new technologies helps explain why, according to Luz, students in this class showed much greater motivation than did her students in previous sections of the same class taught without a computer lab.

Perhaps most important, the students were able to put the tool to immediate effect in writing about their own experiences, questions, thoughts, and concerns. They could put out their own experiences in a written form that other students and the teacher could reflect on and respond to. In at least some cases, this proved to be a powerful tool for assisting students in invention and reinvention, discovery and exploration, reflection and negotiation—enhancing students' opportunities to think critically about the academy and their role in it. Computer-mediated communication was not the only means by which the process of critical reflection occurred, but it did seem to be an effective medium for facilitating this process.

In interpreting what took place in the class, it is useful to consider not only the discourse community approach to writing but also alternative approaches. In the 1980s, the discourse community approach existed in contention with a process-oriented approach favored by theorists such as Peter Elbow. Elbow, Bartholomae, and others debated whether writing was principally an individual cognitive process (see, for example, Elbow, 1995) or a social process involving gaining access to a new discourse community (see, for example, Bartholomae, 1995).

Nystrand, Greene, and Wiemelt suggested that this dichotomy is overcome by another approach, that of *dialogism*. Dialogism is based on the ideas of Bakhtin (e.g., 1986) who sharply critiqued the view that language is either an individual activity or an abstract system, positing instead that "language is a continuous generative process implemented in the social–verbal interaction of speakers" (Volosinov, 1973). According to Nystrand et al. (1993),

> Bakhtin viewed discourse as a forum where the forces of individual cognition, on the one hand, and social ideology and convention, on the other, "dialectically interpenetrate" each other .... In other words, the individual and the social provide neither competing nor even alternative perspectives on meaning in discourse; rather, context and cognition operate always and only in an interpenetrating, coconstitutive relationship. (p. 295)

How exactly does this take place? In Bakhtin's (1986) view, all utterances (spoken or written) are filled with dialogic overtones, based on "echoes and reverberations of other utterances to which it is related by the communality" (p. 91) of communication. The unique language experience of each individual is thus shaped through constant interaction, and more focused interaction leads to higher forms of learning. "Words, intonations, and inner-word gestures that have undergone the experience of outward expression" acquire "a high social polish and lustre by the effect of reactions and responses, resistance or support, on the part of a social audience" (Volosinov, 1973); this intense social interaction is also where "creative energies build up through whose agency partial or radical restructuring of ideological systems comes about." (p. 92)

Many have speculated that it is in the electronic era that Bakhtin's ideas are seeing their fullest and clearest expression, as computer-networked writing facilitates the kind of dialogic interpenetration that Bakhtin described (Landow, 1992). As Tuman (1992) explained,

> Bakhtin, as it were, turns the world of print literacy on its head, and in so doing becomes a rallying point for all language educators ... who want to move beyond the

CHAPTER 3   81

pedagogic and, at a deeper level, the moral limits of print literacy. The specific appeal of the networked classroom is that it literally embodies the structure of post-print literacy. Such a classroom, for example, automatically seems to refute one of the principal tenets of print literacy, that of the writer as isolated individual, replacing it with a parallel tenet of online literacy, that of writing and knowledge generally as social construction. (p. 91)

This dialogical perspective proves useful for interpeting the types of electronic interaction which took place in Luz's class. In Miyako's case, she began by reading an article that talked about the importance of graduate students' professional networking, but that principally focused on how students can use electronic media to share their ideas and drafts with professional colleagues around the country. Then, through electronic interaction and reflection with her colleagues and teacher, Miyako began to reinterpret this article in terms of her own immediate needs as a new M.A. student, creating her own understanding of what networking means for her in her own social context. This intense social interaction helped her achieve a new understanding of her role as a graduate student, combining the perspectives of the original author of the article, her classmates, her teacher, and herself. In the case of Zhong, the multivocality is perhaps even more immediately obvious, because he incorporated the electronically expressed voices of different people not only into his ideology but also into his own immediate written output. Both Zhong and Miyako made use of the electronic medium to make visible for reflection their own thoughts and ideas, share these ideas rapidly with a number of people, hold and reflect on the responses of others, and incorporate these responses into a restructuring of their own thoughts, language, and behavior.

Mary and Luz

Luz's classroom, like Mary's at Miller College, was shaped by a broader sociocultural context. The fact that the class took place in a progressive English language institute within a liberal department shaped the expectations of both the teacher and students. The language unit that Luz taught her class in was also influenced by a progressive pedagogy; Luz herself had attended several computer workshops that emphasized the use of the Internet as a way of devolving power to students and giving them authentic writing practice. Luz, like Mary, had also been influenced by her own background as a student. Luz told me on several instances that she herself knew a good deal about writing before she came to University of Hawai'i and that what was difficult for her was becoming familiar with a new system. Viewing her students through her own background, she sought to give them the types of experiences that she found to be most beneficial when she was a graduate student.

Like Mary, Luz was teaching writing in a computer-networked class-room for the first time. As she herself was still learning some of the tech-nology, a number of her lessons were awkward, confusing, or ill-timed. This resulted in not infrequent wasted time and frustration, not only for Sang but also for other students. Luz hopes to learn from her lessons and do a better job next time.

But just as Mary's "mistakes" did not obscure her fundamental underlying approach, neither did Luz's. Both taught in ways consistent with their views of composition and education. Just as Mary used technology as part of her overriding goal of focusing on structure, Luz was able to use technology as part of her overriding goal of apprenticing her students into new discourses. Luz ended the semester with great enthusiasm for the computer-networked writing class and made ambitious plans to continue and expand her use of computers in her own and other ELI writing classes.

4

Computer-Assisted
Language Revitalization

ཊ•ཊ

I ka ʻōlelo no ka ʻola, i ka ʻōlelo ke makemake
In language there is life, in language there is death
—Hawaiian proverb

The third class I worked with, Kapili Manaole's Hawaiian 201 class at the University of Hawaiʻi,[1] was different than the other classes in several important ways. First, it was a class in Hawaiian, not in English. Second, it was as much a language class as a writing class. Third, the students in the class were not international students but were almost all born in Hawaiʻi. Finally, my own relationship to the class was very different than other situations, as explained later in this chapter. However, before introducing more details about the class, it is necessary to provide some background information on the Hawaiian language and its role in society and at the University.

Ka ʻŌlelo Hawaiʻi

Ka ʻōlelo Hawaiʻi, the Hawaiian language, is a member of the Polynesian language family, similar to Tahitian, Samoan, and Māori (Scühtz, 1995). It was the sole language spoken throughout the Hawaiian islands, with minor dialectal variation, until the arrival of Europeans to Hawaiʻi (Wilson, in press). Hawaiian was a strictly oral language until the discovery of the islands by Europeans in

---

[1] I use the real name of the university but pseudonyms for the teacher and students..

1778, followed by the arrival in 1820 of American missionaries, who developed an alphabet in order to better proselytize (Schütz, 1994).

Hawaiian literacy flourished in the 19th century when Hawai'i was a kingdom with a parliamentary government. Dozens of newspapers were published, a number of religious and literary works were translated into Hawaiian, and Hawaiians transcribed a wealth of traditional oral literature. Hawaiian was the language of government, religion, retail business, the media, education, and inter-ethnic communication throughout the era of the monarchy (Wilson, in press). At the same time, the Hawaiian people and their culture were being devastated by Western colonization. Diseases introduced by colonizers reduced the Hawaiian population from some 300,000 in 1778 to less than 45,000 a century later (Reinecke, 1969).

In the latter part of the 19th century, with American landowners strengthening their hold on the Hawaiian economy and large numbers of agricultural workers brought in from Asia, English gradually began to supplant Hawaiian as a medium of instruction in the schools (Reinecke, 1969). A small but powerful American elite sought not only to spread the use of English but also to actively repress Hawaiian, the use of which was seen as an impediment to "the Americanization of the islands" (Foreign Relations of the United States, 1894, p. 825).

The coup de grâce was delivered by the 1893 U.S.-backed overthrow of the sovereign Hawaiian monarchy and the forced annexation of Hawai'i to U.S. territorial status 5 years later. The Hawaiian language was banned from both public and private schools, and children who continued to speak Hawaiian in school were punished. Teachers were even sent into the community to coerce the adoption of English in the home (Wilson, in press). As a consequence of these policies, a century later the Hawaiian language

> is now faced with extinction. It is estimated that there are fewer than 1,000 native speakers remaining. Except for its use by approximately 200 Hawaiians from the island of Ni'ihau ... Hawaiian is not spoken as a language of daily communication. Most native speakers of Hawaiian outside of the Ni'ihau community are over the age of seventy. (Warner, 1996, p. 5)

Today, most native Hawaiian people on the islands, as well as most other people born in Hawai'i, speak as a native tongue Hawai'i Creole English (HCE; Sato, 1985). HCE evolved out of a pidgin spoken in the late 19th century by agricultural workers of many nationalities.[2] It then became the

---

[2]There is disagreement over the original roots of HCE, with linguists divided as to whether it originated from a "makeshift dialect of English" spoken in whaling ports (Reinecke,1936, p. 7; also see Reinecke,1969), or in a Pidgin Hawaiian spoken on plantations (Bickerton & Wilson, 1987; Roberts, 1991, 1995).

native language of most children born in Hawaii, thus transforming into a Creole (pidgins creoles are spoken only as second languages, and creoles are spoken as native languages). Nevertheless, the language is still called Pidgin by its speakers. Though HCE, or Pidgin, shares some vocabulary, idioms, intonational features, and syntactical features with Hawaiian (Reinecke, 1936, 1969), it is dominated by English vocabulary and is generally regarded as a nonstandard dialect of English.[3]

HAWAIIAN LANGUAGE REVITALIZATION

A Hawaiian renaissance movement began in the 1960s and 1970s, parallel to other national and international movements for native people's rights. The 1970s witnessed a renaissance "of everything Hawaiian from music and dance to land and political rights, to traditional voyaging" (Wilson, in press).

Efforts for Hawaiian language revitalization had both a cultural and political character. On the one hand, from a cultural perspective, "language itself is seen as a procreative force of great power in Hawaiian culture. Words, especially in the poetic form of *mele* [chanted poetry] ... have the power of life and death. The chant itself creates reality" (Wilson, in press). Cultural groups related to hula and chanting have played an important role in preserving the language, and many of the participants in these groups have struggled for broader language rights. Other activists saw Hawaiian language rights as part of an effort to gain broader political and economic rights—including some form of political sovereignty—for the native Hawaiian people, who were at the bottom of virtually every social, economic, and educational indicator.[4]

In the face of grassroots pressure, legal restrictions on the use of Hawaiian in the schools were removed, and in 1978 Hawaiian was once again made an

---

[3]For a discussion of the political status of HCE in Hawaii, see Sato (1991).

[4]Native Hawaiians are a group including both "pure" Hawaiians, estimated at some 3,000, or roughly 1/4 of 1% of the state's population (Barringer, 1995), and part Hawaiians, estimated in 1990 at 18.9% of the population (Hawaii State Department of Health, 1990). Socioeconomic problems facing the Native Hawaiian community include disproportionally high rates of poverty, unemployment, infant mortality, and arrest, and low rates of educational achievement (Barringer, 1995; Takenaka, 1995; Takeuchi, Agbayani, & Kuniyoshi, 1990).

official state language together with English. In 1984, Hawaiian language scholars and community leaders established a number of Hawaiian medium *Pūnana Leo* (language nest) preschools. In 1987, the state board of education approved the formation of the Papahana Kaiapuni ʻŌlelo Hawaiʻi (Hawaiian Language Immersion Program), and two immersion kindergarten/first grade classes were formed to receive graduates of the Pūnana Leo pre-schools. Additional years of Hawaiian immersion education have been added each year, and the lead immersion class is now in the 10th grade. New schools in both the preschool and immersion programs have been added, with the total student population now 200 children in 9 Hawaiian-medium preschools and 1,200 children in 14 elementary and secondary immersion schools.[5]

The success to date of the Hawaiian immersion program represents an important victory in preventing the extinction of the Hawaiian language. Children in the immersion program are reaching near-native speaker fluency (Warner, 1996) and thus provide a basis for the continued survival of *ka ʻōlelo Hawaiʻi*. Whether Hawaiian will eventually be more fully revived as a language of daily communication outside the schools is probably dependent on broader factors, such as efforts by Native Hawaiians to achieve some sort of political sovereignty.[6]

HAWAIIAN AT THE UNIVERSITY

The University of Hawaiʻi has played a critical role in the revitalization of the Hawaiian language. Scholars at the university began to teach the language in 1921 and have continued until now. Although only small numbers of students took Hawaiian from the 1920s to 1960s, the university's teaching, research, and publication of grammars and dictionaries helped keep the language alive through its darkest years.

Enrollment in Hawaiian language courses at the University of Hawaiʻi rose from only 27 in 1961–1962 to 623 in 1973–1974 to 1,277 in 1992–1993

---

[5]Information provided by the Hale Kuamoʻo office, University of Hawaiʻi at Hilo.

[6]There is a large and diverse sovereignty movement in Hawaiʻi, with demands ranging from full independence for the state to creation of a sovereign Hawaiian nation within the United States (similar to the legal status of some Native American nations in the United States and Canada) to some forms of political autonomy within the state. See Dudley (1993) and Trask (1993).

(Schütz, 1994). The number of students has continued to grow since then, with Hawaiian language enrollment recently surpassing enrollment in Spanish and catching up to Japanese, still the most widely taught language at the University of Hawai'i (due to its instrumental value in the tourist industry as well as its heritage value in a university where 26% of the university students are of Japanese ancestry[7]). The University of Hawai'i's second-largest 4-year campus, at Hilo, won approval in 1996 for a master's program in Hawaiian Language Studies, representing the first graduate degree program in an indigenous language in the United States.

HAWAIIAN 201

Kapili Manaole's Hawaiian 201 course was a third-semester Hawaiian language class. It was a general language class, focusing on reading, writing, speaking, listening, grammar, and culture.

Although there were 17 Hawaiian 201 sections offered that semester, Kapili's was one of only two that had been designated as writing intensive. The writing-intensive program was started at the University of Hawai'i in 1987 as part of an effort to promote the development of writing across the curriculum. University of Hawai'i students must take a total of five writing-intensive courses in order to graduate. These writing intensive courses can be in virtually any subject, from mathematics to anthropology to language. Courses are designated writing intensive at the petition of the professor, who must agree that.

1. Writing will be used to promote learning of the course material.
2. Students and professors will interact on the writing during the writing process.
3. Writing will play a major role in determining the grade for the course.
4. Students will be required to do a substantial amount of writing—a minimum of 4,000 words, or about 16 typewritten pages.
5. Class enrollment will be limited to 20 students.

In addition to fulfilling a writing intensive requirement, the course also fulfills the university's 2-year foreign or second language requirement.

---

[7]Figures for 1993–1994 (Office of the Vice President for Student Affairs, 1994).

The Students

Fourteen students were enrolled in Hawaiian 201, mostly college sopho-
mores. Most students were still in the process of deciding their majors; their
interests ranged across a number of subjects, such as journalism, education,
marketing, biology, and computer science.

All the students in the class were born in Hawai'i, with about half from
Honolulu and about half from outlying areas of Oahu or the neighbor islands (as people on O'ahu refer to the other islands of Hawai'i). Thirteen of
the 14 students in the class were of part Hawaiian ancestry and the other
student was of Japanese ancestry. Students explained to me that their interest in learning about and promoting their Hawaiian cultural heritage was an
important part of their decision to take Hawaiian. As Kaipo, a 20-year-old
female student of Hawaiian, Filipino, and Portuguese ancestry, told me, "I
figured since I was Hawaiian I might as well learn. My grandmother never
spoke and that kind of disappointed me, she never knew a lot of stuff so I figured I might as well learn it, teach my kids."

Although it's common to think of American university students as
Internet-savvy, that was definitely not the case with this class. Six of the 14
students in the class had never even tried the World Wide Web before the
semester started, and 2 more had used it only once. Only 4 students used
e-mail on a regular basis before the class started.

The Teacher

Kapili Manaole, a woman in her early 40s, has been involved in Hawaiian revitalization for some 20 years. As she told me,

> When I was a teenager, I started dancing hula, and in our halau [hula house group] we
> had kupuna [elders] who taught us Hawaiian. And then I went away for 2 years to
> Santa Cruz, and went to school there, and then I just figured I had to come home and
> learn, 'cause I didn't know much. Yeah, high school really didn't teach you anything
> about being Hawaiian. And it was just a point on the university campus here that eth-
> nic studies was just starting up, and so there was just a handful of us taking language,
> and I think it really was because of being in hula that people knew they had to know
> their language and got real inspired.

Kapili helped start the Pūnana Leo preschool program and enrolled all
three of her children in it. Her children are all now in a Hawaiian immersion
school; her daughter is in the lead class (10th grade) and thus in 2 years will
be part of the first group of Hawaiians in over a century to complete Hawaiian medium K–12.

Kapili has been teaching Hawaiian for more than 10 years at the high school and university level. It seems that almost every moment of her life is filled with activity on behalf of Hawaiian language and culture. During the year I worked with her, she led the immersion students' canoeing club, arranged and accompanied a student delegation to New Zealand to meet with Māori counterparts, and participated in state-wide committees related to curriculum and language.

One of Kapili's strongest contributions has been in the area of technology. She has been making videos of *kupuna* (elders) for several years, helping perpetuate the voices of the last generation of native speakers. At the local Hawaiian immersion K–12 school, where she consults two days a week in addition to her university teaching job, she has organized a group of students to write and publish a Hawaiian-language newspaper, and she has been the first Hawaiian language instructor to integrate new online technologies into her teaching at the University of Hawai'i.

I first met Kapili when she attended a workshop I was giving for language teachers on using Daedalus Interchange. After the workshop, she used Daedalus in her Hawaiian 201 class in the spring, 1997, and was very satisfied with the results. I then began to speak with her about working with her in the fall, 1997, as part of my research. She readily agreed and was enthusiastic about attempting to integrate additional uses of computers into her course with my assistance.

Participant–Observer–Student

My personal role was different in Hawaiian than in the other classes discussed in this book. First, whereas I speak English as my native tongue, I was a learner of Hawaiian. I had attended two semesters of Hawaiian language courses at the university, as had the other students in the Hawaiian 201 class. Kapili and I agreed that I would play several roles in her class, as a student participating with other students in language learning activities, an assistant teacher helping out with computer-based activities, and a researcher examining computer-mediated texts, taping classes, and interviewing students.

From the beginning of the semester, I realized that this was going to be a challenging task. I am usually a good language learner, but I was at a disadvantage to the rest of the students in several regards. As indicated earlier, there are some similarities of vocabulary, syntax, and intonation between Hawaiian and Hawai'i Creole English, similarities that Kapili was quick to point out. Because all students in the class except me either spoke HCE or had heard it most of their lives, they could potentially take advantage of these similarities in ways I could not. In addition, students had heard a fair amount of Hawaiian in popular songs, chants, sayings, and expressions while growing up. Their Native Hawaiian background also provided them with more understanding of the cultural context of the language and, according to their reports, increased their motivation. In many cases they had Hawaiian-speaking relatives, roommates, or close friends to practice with, which I did not. Finally, my research and work commitments prevented me from putting as much time into the class as the students did. Even while I was in class, I was trying to concentrate on observing the class as much or more than on learning the language. This affected not only my ability to learn the language but of course also at times my ability to observe the class.

Nevertheless, in spite of these difficulties, I believe my role as a learner in the class contributed positively to the study in two important ways. It gave me insight into the issues I was investigating from a learner's perspective, and it facilitated my contact with the other students, as I was able to interact fully with them on a daily basis.

Planning the Class

Kapili and I met a few times before the semester started to discuss elements of the class. We also met with a Hawaiian teacher from a local community college, Susan, who was interested in working on some joint electronic projects with Kapili.

Kapili and I agreed on three ways that computers would be integrated into her Hawaiian 201 class. First, students would meet in the computer lab once a week for computer-assisted classroom discussion, using Daedalus Interchange. This was a continuation of an activity that Kapili had already done the semester before, and she felt quite comfortable with it. Second, about a month into the semester, we would begin a weekly e-mail exchange between Kapili's class and Susan's Hawaiian 201 class from Pearl Community College. Third, at the end of the semester Kapili's students would publish research reports on the World Wide Web.

An Eclectic Approach

It's difficult to characterize Kapili's general approach and method to teaching Hawaiian. Like many language teachers, Kapili's approach is eclectic, drawing on many different perspectives and sources.

From the first day of class, I noticed important distinctions between this class and the previous Hawaiian classes I had taken. To begin with, almost all the instruction and discussion was in Hawaiian. Although this pleased me quite a bit—as it matched my own learning style—it was also quite a challenge, because my first-year Hawaiian class, and presumably the first-year classes of some other students, was taught mostly in English. Yet students caught on quickly and seemed to appreciate the chance to use Hawaiian in class.

The first week was marked by a great deal of communicative and collaborative activities. In information-gap activities, we walked around the class to find out (using only Hawaiian) which student in the class drove a moped to school or was born on the island of Kaua'i. In small group discussions, we analyzed reading passages to find and correct grammatical errors.

By the second week, the class was beginning to settle into a fairly traditional language class. We studied reading passages, reviewed vocabulary, and did associated grammar exercises. Much work was done in small groups, usually related to review of exercises and analysis of syntactic or lexical elements.

The content of the course was based on native Hawaiian culture, land, and life. Stories and articles we read included *Ka Hau* (about a lowland tree found in Hawai'i), *Ka ʻOama* (about a type of goatfish prominent in native Hawaiian fishing), *Ka Kōlea* (about a Pacific migratory bird), *Nā Mōhai ʻUlu* "The Sacrifice of the Breadfruit," a proverb about Hawaiian gods), and *Ua Hiki Anei Ka ʻŌlelo Hawaiʻi Ke Ola?* ("Can the Hawaiian Language Survive?").

Kapili sometimes used the content of the stories to introduce more political concerns. She used a proverb in one story—*ʻAi nō ke kōlea a momona, hoʻi i Kahiki* ("the plover eats until fat, then returns to the land from which it came")—to raise questions about who has gotten wealthy from the plunder of Hawaiʻi's natural resources. She used a proverb in another story—*Pūʻali ka hau nui I ka hua iki* ("the small branch grooves the large branch")—to discuss how a small group of Hawaiians took on the powerful U.S. military to eventually win back native control of the Hawaiian island of Kahoʻolawe.

The importance of Hawaiian culture was most strongly felt in two special activities, reciting of *haʻiʻōlelo* (chants) and meeting with *kūpuna* (elders). We memorized two traditional Hawaiian chants, each about a dozen lines long, throughout the semester and recited them together frequently, as is very common in Hawaiian culture. We also met in small groups with native-speaking elders several times throughout the semester to practice our

Hawaiian. My group met with Tutu Kalanui ("Grandma Kalanui"), a very kind woman of about 80 years of age who had learned Hawaiian as a child from her own grandmother. Tutu Kalanui told us stories about her life, starting from when she was beaten by her teachers for speaking Hawaiian. She also taught us some Hawaiian crafts, like lei making. Meeting with Tutu Kalanui gave us a chance not only to practice authentic Hawaiian but to learn more about Hawaiian life and culture.

Daedalus Interchange

Starting from the second week of the semester, the class went to the computer lab once a week for computer-assisted classroom discussion using Daedalus Interchange. There was palpable excitement, and a lot of confusion, from the very first day in the lab. Several students were unfamiliar with personal computers or the Macintosh and thus needed a lot of help in tasks like finding applications or opening folders.

The main problem, however, lay with font difficulties. The Hawaiian language has two special diacritical marks not found in the English-language alphabet, the 'okina ['], which signifies a glottal stop, and the kahakō, or macron, which is placed over vowels to lengthen them (ā ē ī ō ū). Although there are a number of special Hawaiian-language computer fonts that handle these diacritical marks, the current version of Daedalus Interchange is not able to handle nonstandard character sets. We found a way to handle this problem using an additional program called Fontpatchin' (Hara, 1992), but this involved several extra steps by the individual user. What complicated the matter even further was that the students were only to use the Fontpatchin' program with Daedalus Interchange. When sending e-mail or using the World Wide Web, they had to follow a different set of procedures for using Hawaiian fonts. Confusion about changing fonts was a bothersome problem all semester.

Once the students got through computer glitches, they eagerly plunged into computer-assisted discussion. Every week the teacher posted questions or topics for them to discuss. In the beginning of the semester, these were simple topics such as discussing favorite films, musical groups, and free time activities. As the semester developed, Kapili chose more complex topics, such as students' opinions on upcoming elections or social issues such as prayer in the schools.

The lab was a buzz of activity during Daedalus sessions, with students checking back and forth between different Interchange conferences on different topics, reading incoming messages, scrolling back to read previous messages, writing messages addressed to individuals, writing messages to the whole group, consulting dictionaries, laughing, and chatting with one another. The teacher sent sporadic messages in the Interchange sessions and spent much of her time either reading the messages or helping students with problems.

Follow Daedalus sessions, Kapili usually provided the students, either electronically or in hard copy, partial or complete transcripts of the Daedalus sessions for their perusal. Sometimes she gave each student a copy of the comments that students had written, with errors marked. This was for the students' own use; no correction was required.

From observing the students in the lab, noting my own behavior as I participated, reading over the transcripts, and interviewing students, I noted a number of aspects of the use of Daedalus. Although these aspects overlapped with what I observed in Luz's class, there were differences as well—mostly because this was a third-semester language class, with students still coping with writing simple sentences, while Luz's was a graduate writing class, with students more concerned with learning how to write papers in their majors.

One benefit, as in Luz's class, was the high degree of student-student interaction. After the first week, normal classroom sessions were dominated by Kapili, with brief comments or questions, almost always to the teacher, made occasionally by students. In contrast, the Daedalus sessions were a free-for-all of student interaction. In one early Daedalus session, for example, students took an average of 12.5 turns each, with every student taking at least 5 turns and all but two taking at least 9 turns. The teacher took only 7 turns, and all the students' comments were directed to other students.

The increased interaction was also very democratic, extending to even the shyest students. Kalei, a reticent student who almost never spoke up voluntarily in class, took 14 turns in this particular Daedalus session. Another quiet student, Onaona, took 16 turns. When I later interviewed Onaona, she told me,

> I really like Daedalus a lot, 'cause I think you lose some of your inhibitions that you have when talking to somebody face-to-face, you know, 'cause you're not necessarily strong in verbal speaking, so you kind of hold back a little bit, but when you're at a computer talking to everybody else you can just go for it and not really worry that much.

The experience was very motivating for the students. I never saw the bored faces that I sometimes saw in the regular classroom. In the computer lab, students continued to write until the very last minute and groaned with disappointment when Kapili told them that the period had ended and they had to stop.

The excitement seemed to stem from both the fun of using the computer and the joy of communicating with people in a low-stress environment. Students didn't have to seize the floor and speak in front of the whole class. They didn't have to worry about pronunciation difficulties, and they were less fearful of mistakes because they could check their messages before sending.

Finally, students achieved the language learning benefit of written interaction. Because Hawaiian 201 was a writing intensive class, Kapili had attempted to have authentic, interactive writing assignments even in semesters before she used computers. She had accomplished this task previously by having students write dialogue journals to the teacher on note cards once a week. To attempt to make the task interactive, Kapili had occasionally responded with a comment or two of her own written on the note cards. Needless to say, such interaction was pretty uninspiring compared to using the language for real-time writing to a large group of classmates. (I myself had written such dialogue journal cards in a previous Hawaiian class and gotten very little out of it.)

In contrast, real-time written interaction gave students a chance to see not only one or two sentences written by the teacher but dozens of comments made by other students and by the teacher. The ability to take from these comments, as well as from other sources, provided an excellent environment for language learning. As Bakhtin (1986) said, discussing the learning and development of language:

> The unique speech experience of each individual is shaped and developed in continuous and constant interaction with others' individual utterances. This experience can be characterized to some degree as the process of *assimilation*—more or less creative—of others' words (and not the words of a language). Our speech, that is, all our utterances (including creative works) is filled with others' words, varying degrees of otherness or varying degrees of "our-own-ness," varying degrees of awareness and detachment. These words of others carry with them their own expression, their own evaluative tone, which we assimilate, rework, and re-accentuate. (p. 89)

In the last 20 years, a good deal of research has demonstrated that second languages are learned through interaction (see summaries of research by Long, 1996; Pica, 1994). However, for teenage and adult learners, interaction is not sufficient for language learning. People who learn language only through interaction tend to fossilize at a level far below that of native speakers, with some form of pidginized syntax (see, for example, Schmidt, 1983). Rather, some kind of attention to the form of language is necessary to allow students to stretch their language abilities continually.

Finding the best ways to combine form and meaning is one of the main challenges of the language educator. One approach has been first to teach a variety of forms and then to allow students time to practice these forms. This method has been criticized as in violation of natural learning sequences (Long, 1991). An approach that is gaining increasing interest is maintaining an overall emphasis on communication and meaning but attending to form issues that arise within this process. This technique is quite challenging because interaction is by nature fast paced and attempts to halt interaction to attend to form can short-circuit the communicative process.

Computer-mediated interaction provides, in theory, a vehicle for helping overcome this contradiction. Students have more opportunity than they do in oral discussion to notice structures in incoming messages, a condition believed to be critical for learning (Schmidt, 1993). Working privately at their own seats, students can attend to formal aspects without interrupting communication—by rereading previous messages and, if appropriate, consulting texts, dictionaries, or even their neighbors. They can take advantage of increased planning time to write their messages, a feature also shown beneficial in stretching language (for a review, see Crookes, 1989). In rewriting their messages, they can borrow liberally and easily from earlier messages, thus achieving the assimilation suggested by Bakhtin (1986). Finally, the teacher can make use of the students' written messages for further analysis together with students.

Through observations, interviews, and analysis of texts, as well as attention to my own behavior, I attempted to assess the extent to which this process occurred. As a learner myself (albeit probably more conscious of second language learning theory than the other participants), I actively consulted others' words in writing my own messages. Indeed, the ability to do so was one thing that made the process so exciting for me. I often felt frustrated in class when oral conversation went by me; either I didn't understand something, or, even if I did understand, I didn't feel I could incorporate it in my own production. In Daedalus, I could always take time to understand everything and incorporate new words or phrases into my own production. For example, when the teacher wrote that we should discuss *kau hana ma kou manawa ka'awele* ("your activities in your free time"), the phrase *manawa ka'awele* ("free time") was brand new to me. Nevertheless, it was easy for me to use the teacher's phrase and then write to a student, *E Kalei, he aha kau hana ma kou manawa ka'awele?* ("Kalei, what are your activities in your free time?"). Later in the same discussion, another student wrote, *"Nānā i ke ki'i'oni'oni kahiko ka'u hana punahele* ("watching movies is my favorite activity")." *Ki'i'oni'oni* ("movie") was a word that I had heard but had never quite caught. *Punahele* ("favorite") was a concept that I had often wanted to use in oral discussion but never had, because I didn't know the word. Yet with both of these words now provided to me in a written example, I easily incorporated them into my own original sentence, *"E Onaona, he aha kau ki'i'oni'oni punahele?* ("Onaona, what's your favorite movie?").

Although it is impossible to learn from transcripts precisely the situations in which learners were using vocabulary they already knew and situations in which they were assimilating new words or phrases, there were indications that many students were going through the same process that I was. I observed students frequently consulting previous messages as they wrote their own messages. They also checked with dictionaries, each other, and occasionally the teacher.

When a teacher or student used a new phrase that had not come up in class before, many students immediately used it in their own sentences. For example, on one occasion the teacher asked a question about nā moho i lanakila i ke koho bālota 'ana i ka pule aku neia ("the candidates that won the voting last week")—a syntactically complex sentence with several new vocabulary words. A number of the students immediately incorporated phrases from the sentence into their own writing. On another occasion, when one student asked another, *"Hele 'oe i ke kalapu?"* ("Do you go to clubs?"), "many others immediately used the word *kalapu*, and the phrase *i ke kalapu* ("to clubs") even though the word "kalapu" had never been taught in class. Although the word *kalapu* is not difficult, because it was adopted from the English word *club*, the sentence *Hele 'oe i ke kalapu* might be difficult for an English speaker because it uses the singular expression *ke kalapu* ("the club") rather than a plural expression *nā kalapu* ("the clubs"), to express a meaning that requires a plural in English. In spite of this potential difficulty, the students immediately adopted the phrase for their own use.

Students' ability to make use of such phrases is consistent with research on the role of formulaic language in second language acquisition (Weinert, 1995), research that provides support for the views of Bakhtin (1986). This research has found that learners acquire chunks of unanalyzed language that they then put to productive use, and this process assists them in mastering similar patterns (Bolanderr, 1987; Wong-Fillmore, 1976). This has led Weinert (1995) to conclude that

> "lexical phrases" which exist somewhere between grammar and the lexicon may be given a more central role in language teaching and may provide a suitable compromise between approaches which rely too heavily on either the notion of linguistic competence or communicative competence.[8] (p. 199)

In interviews, most students commented about the benefits of written interaction, and several spoke in particular about how they picked up words and phrases from each other. One female student, 'Iolani, told me:

> You learn vocabulary, 'cause there's people who know some vocabulary that you don't know, so when you see it on the screen, you can look it up or something, or you can see how they're using the patterns and stuff when you read it, it's like you're reading the patterns over and over and over. It helps too, even if you don't write, I guess reading it. But the writing helps too, 'cause you're thinking and you're writing. When you talk, it's like you have to get what you know in your head, it's more pronunciation. But when you're writing you're solely concentrating on the patterns and everything else.

Similar comments were made by Kamahele, a male student, who said:

> Well, it seems like there's a bunch of people who can either speak really well or can write well. So it's kind of like there's two sides, 'cause I know a lot of people that can speak, speak, speak and just talk story for hours, but then when you tell them to write something they think, ah, they're missing kahakō's or 'okina's and all the other things, but then, there's another bunch of people that can't talk that well, but, when you give them a piece of paper, they can just write beautifully, I mean, all the grammatics is there, all the difficult sentence structures are there, and uh, what I think I have is more of a speaker, and I kind of lack on the writing, and that's why, I think, when you go into the computer lab and this class, and through these two mediums that I get a chance to flex my writing abilities, and the computer makes it a lot easier, 'cause when you're sending messages, and then you write a message and you can see and you send it out, and somebody else writes back to you and then you can see it on the screen, and then, you know, it's a really, really good way to communicate with each other, and kind of learn grammar, spelling, and all those other things. You can kind of read what others say and kind of takes things from them, and add your thoughts on to it. It's really good.

E-mail Interaction

After several weeks of using Daedalus Interchange, the Hawaiian 201 students were looking forward to their next adventure in electronic communi-

---

[8]Weinert made this statement in agreement with a similar suggestion by Nattinger and DeCarrico (1992).

cation—e-mail correspondence with a Hawaiian class at Pearl Community College. This would be their chance to use their Hawaiian not only with their classmates but with other students on another part of the island. As a student named Kai told me, "It's new people—we already know everybody in this class!"

The exchange with students at Pearl had been planned before the semester started, in meetings between Kapili, Susan, and me. Susan was the teacher at Pearl and was a real enthusiast about new technologies. She had attended a summer institute at University of Hawai'i to learn about the Internet for language teaching and was anxious to put what she had learned into practice.

During our first meetings, Susan stressed that things were just getting started at Pearl and that she wanted to take things slowly. She explained a lot of obstacles that she would have to go through in setting up the project. I later saw those obstacles first-hand during several visits to Pearl. Almost none of her students had e-mail accounts or any previous experience with e-mail. Applying for e-mail accounts for students was a slow and cumbersome process that took more than a month. The college had no computer labs especially dedicated for language students; Susan's class had to use the regular college computer lab, which as yet had no software installed to allow foreign language e-mailing. That lab was also not available on a regular basis. Susan could reserve it only five times for the whole semester, and students had to go to a separate lab for individual e-mail work (which was also not yet set up for foreign language e-mailing). Susan worked hard to overcome these problems, but in the end they proved insurmountable. An e-mail exchange was eventually arranged, but it was so plagued with problems that it was a disappointment to all.

This is more or less what took place. First, students from the two classes were placed into groups of four or five, made up of two students from Kapili's class and two to three students from Susan's class. Students were to send weekly messages to the other members of their group, with copies to the teachers.

Each week the students were given topics that they were to discuss with their groupmates over e-mail. Topics were set by Susan and Kapili and evolved from simple topics in the beginning (i.e., personal introductions, describing respective schools) to more complex issues later on, such as how students felt about plans to build a new university campus in the western part of the island. On a couple of occasions they were also supposed to talk about the topics of their own research papers.

The main problem was that students in Susan's class did not have the consistent access to the lab needed to master the procedures for sending and receiving e-mail. Most students in her class participated sporadically, if at all. As a result, many messages from Kapili's students went unanswered.

Problems were not only on the Pearl end. Many of Kapili's students were also not used to using e-mail and had no ready access to it. Unlike the Daedalus exchanges, the e-mail work was to be done outside of class. The computer lab they were most familiar with was frequently full, and they had a hard time finding times to complete the assignment. Few had the necessary software at home to send foreign language e-mail. In addition, many of the assigned topics were not well integrated into the class activities. This same situation existed to a certain extent in Daedalus, when students sometimes were given topics to discuss that had not appeared elsewhere in the class, but the informal interactive nature of the Daedalus exchanges encouraged students to plow ahead anyway. For the e-mail messages, which were being forwarded to the teacher and which seemed a bit more formal, students experienced some anxiety writing about topics that were unfamiliar to them (i.e., the building of a new university campus).

As a result of all these problems, e-mail messages, when they were written, became more of a series of asocial monologues rather than an authentic forum for communication. Students tended to view their weekly topics as assignments that they would fulfill simply by writing a message to the rest of the group. For example, one student, Donald, explained to me a formula that he used for all his messages:

> Every time I wrote my e-mail pals over there, I write two paragraphs, the first paragraph I ask how they're doing and general information, like I talk about what I'm gonna do on the weekend, 'cause I always write it on Friday, and I ask what are they doing on the weekend and I tell them what I'm doing on the weekend, and the second paragraph is usually about the topic that *kumu* [teacher] gives us.

Here's an example of one of Donald's messages. Note that although it's a very friendly and sociable message, it makes no reference at all to anything that anybody's ever said to him.

```
Date: Mon, 7 Oct 1996 13:23:45 -1000
To: keona@hawaii.edu, iolani@hawaii.edu, kamealoha@hawaii.edu,
sandy@hawaii.edu, kumu-l@hawaii.edu
From: dflores@hawaii.edu (Donald Gomez)
Subject: Re: Aloha
```

Aloha nui loa kākou! Pehea kākou? Maikaʻi nō au a hauʻoli loa, no
ka mea ʻo ka "Pōʻalima Aloha" kēia lā. "ʻAʻole hana ā hiki i ka Pōʻakahi".

No laila, he aha ʻoukou e hana ai i kēia hopena pule? E holoholo ana au me koʻu mau hoa aloha. Nānā mākou i ka pāʻani pō peku. ʻAʻole au i makemake i ka pāʻani pō peku akā, he pāʻani Homecoming ko mākou. Ua puka au i ke kula kiʻekiʻe ʻo Darlington. E hōʻaʻano ana mākou i ke kula kiʻekiʻe ʻo Waimano. Manaʻo au, ʻoi aku ka maikaʻi i ka pāʻani pō paʻi ma mua o ka pāʻani pō peku.

Pehea ʻoukou ʻimi noiʻi? He aha ʻoukou i ke kumuhana? E ʻōlelo ana au e pili ana i ka nēnē. Kākau anei ʻoukou i ka ʻekolu ʻaoʻao? Kākau mākou i ka ʻekolu ʻaoʻao. I kēia manawa, ʻaʻole maopopo iaʻu he aha e kākau e pili ana i ka nēnē. Ma hope iho paha, maopopo au. E kākau ana au iā ʻoukou ma hope iho.

A hui hou,
Donald Gomez

[Translation:

Greetings everybody. How are you? I'm well and very happy, because to-day is "Aloha Friday". "There's no more work until Monday." So, what are your plans this weekend? I'm going out with my friends. We're watching a football game. I don't like football, but it's our Homecoming. I graduated from Darlington. We're playing Waimano. I think that volleyball is better than football.

How's your research? What are your topics? I'm going to speak about geese. Are you writing three pages? We're writing three pages. Right now, I don't know what to write about geese. Perhaps later I'll know. I'll write to you later.

Bye,
Donald Gomez]

Some students, including Donald, stopped writing at all when they didn't get any responses from Pearl for several weeks. As one student, Kalei, told me, "I haven't been sending any e-mail, because they don't send it back to us. Nobody, not since September. I only got one message, two sentences from one girl at Pearl College. Only one."

It's interesting to note that e-mail class exchanges, which are often viewed as one of the best uses of the Internet for teaching language and writing, proved disappointing for both Mary's class at Miller College and Kapili's class at the University of Hawaiʻi. It appears that successful e-mail projects involve a tremendous amount of coordination, with teachers from two or more different schools co-managing both curricular goals and practical matters. Cross-cultural psychologist Bruce Roberts has pointed out that

There is a significant difference in educational outcome depending on whether a teacher chooses to incorporate email classroom connections as (1) an ADD-ON process, like one would include a guest speaker, or (2) an INTEGRATED process, in the way one would include a new textbook. The email classroom connections seems sufficiently complex and time consuming that if there are goals beyond merely having each student send a letter to a person at a distant school, the

ADD-ON approach can lead to frustration and less-than-expected academic results—the necessary time and resources come from other things that also need to be
done. On the other hand, when the e-mail classroom connections processes are truly
integrated into the ongoing structure of homework and student classroom interaction, then the results can be educationally transforming. (Bruce Roberts, posting on
IECC-discussion@stolaf.edu, March 22, 1994, cited in Warschauer, 1995a, p. 95)

Kapili and Susan both recognized that a successful e-mail exchange
would necessitate much better coordination and planning. They began to
make plans for an improved e-mail exchange for the following semester, but
Susan was not rehired in her position as a Hawaiian teacher at Pearl, and the
collaboration ended.

In spite of the many problems with e-mail, there were times when I could
catch a glimpse of its potential. Kamahele was a student with very strong
speaking skills but less developed writing skills. He also had a very strong
sense of pride in the Hawaiian language and culture. A couple of times when
the computer lab was busy, Kamahele came to my office to write his e-mail. I
noticed that he stayed a very long time, putting a great deal of effort into pol-
ishing his messages. He told me once that

The e-mail is really good. Because I'm sending it to somebody, I tend to take a little bit
more time, just because I want to try out complex sentence patterns. I don't want to
just like—I don't know, we're sharing between two schools and like, that's just my 'ano
(way), it's not competitive or anything, but I wanna just send out interesting things
and put it in an interesting way, so I wouldn't just say things like "How are you doing?"
I would make this into just a little more interesting, like "How are you doing on this
great day today?" I mean like, just like flower up the sentence so it looks a little bit
more, not impressive, but just a little bit more interesting to read. That's why I take a
little bit longer. I also try to correct my things before I send it out. That's how I do it.
But I'm not too familiar with e-mail, so that's why too I have a hard time, I'm still learning how to use e-mail.

The World Wide Web

The other main computer-based project in the class involved the World
Wide Web. Kapili assigned her students to do one in-depth research paper
due at the end of the semester. Students were taught how to use the Web in
order to find material for their research, and they were then taught how to
publish their papers on the Web. By the end of the semester, all the pages
were up on the Web and were linked together to a class page.

Work on the project began early in the semester, when students were told
to start thinking of their topic, which could be anything related to Hawai'i,
such as the Hawaiian people, historic events in Hawai'i, Hawaiian geogra-

phy or nature, or activities in Hawai'i. Students were to choose their topics and present a basic outline of the paper by the sixth week of class. Topics were discussed orally in class and also in Daedalus and e-mail discussions. A first draft of the paper was due in the 9th week of class, and a final draft due in the 12th week. This schedule allowed two weeks for students to put their paper on the Web.

Kapili worked very closely with the students throughout this whole process. Although technically only two drafts were required, many students submitted several drafts in their efforts to develop top-notch papers. Kapili provided both general feedback in terms of the content and organization of the papers and detailed feedback on language errors.

After the initial outline was turned in, students spent a couple of class sessions learning how to use the Web to search for information for their papers. This was quite an adventure, as about half the class had virtually no prior experience on the World Wide Web. Kapili provided basic instruction, and I assisted in helping the students.

Students had a number of interesting experiences when they first ventured out onto the Web. 'Iolani had found a page of Hawaiian photography and went to sign the guest book. She found a comment in the guest book from someone on the U.S. mainland who asked, "Hey, where are the girls in grass skirts?" She decided to try to inform the person about Hawai'i by sending him the following e-mail (which in my eyes was surprisingly polite):

Date: Wed, 23 Oct 1996 14:11:47 -1000
From: 'Iolani Smith <iolan@hawaii.edu>
To: jonathon@waycon.net

Aloha!
Noho au ma Kane'ohe Hawai'i ma ka mokupuni 'o O'ahu.. (I live in Kane'ohe Hawai'i on the island of Oahu). There aren't any ladys walking around here in grass skirts. It really isn't the total paradise that people make it out to be. Of course there are beautiful mountains, beaches, and waterfalls, however due to western contact, much of the original native beauty is gone. Take care. A hui hou! (Until we meet again)
Write back if you want to! =) I just wanted to share a little bit about Hawai'i with you.

Students generally did very well in navigating the net and finding information. Kalei found information for her paper on the taro plant, and Donald found information for his paper on the Hawaiian goose. However, students also noted the lack of pages in the Hawaiian language or with detailed information on Hawaiian culture. Kamahele, for example, found some texts of

Hawaiian chants on the Web, but the pages did not include any audio nor did they include any substantive background information about the role the chants played in Hawaiian life. Kamahele told me that he was motivated to do a better job to help fill this gap.

The real excitement began when students started to put their own papers up on the Web. Kapili had earlier asked me how long I thought this would take, and I answered that it could be done in a single class session, because new software programs allow students to cut and paste word-processed text into an HTML file. To my surprise, for most students this process ended up taking not one day but 2 weeks of daily work in the computer lab.

I had been right in estimating that the creation of the basic text-only Web page was relatively straightforward. What happened was that students insisted on making attractive multimedia Web pages with background colors and graphics; different colors of text; carefully chosen and well-placed photos, graphics, and icons; and hypertext links to additional information. Several students made sites with two or more pages in order to provide additional background information on their topics or to provide personal information about themselves, their family, and friends.

In producing their pages, students had to cope with a broad array of issues, including technical, design, and copyright issues. Students learned to operate a number of software programs in order to edit texts, design web pages, scan and edit photos, view and copy textual or graphical material from the web, and record and edit sound files. They also had to make a number of complex decisions about how to best organize material for their pages, including what kinds of graphics or photos to include, what size the graphics or photos should be, where graphics or photos should be placed on the page, and whether they should have captions or borders. They chose the color or pattern background and the size, font, and color for text; they decided how text interfaced with graphics, whether material was kept on one page or divided into several pages, what kinds of links to include to outside information, and whether to include sound files. In making these design issues, students had to consider not only how the page would appear but how difficult or easy it would be to access. For example, in using graphics, they had to consider not only the appearance of the graphics but also the time they would take to download. This design also involved technical skills, such as how to edit photos in a way that maintained the most content while using the least bandwidth. In making decisions about what graphical or textual material to use, students had to make decisions about a range of copyright issues, including what material on the Web could be freely used; whether or not they could reprint graphics they found in books, magazines, newspapers, or on the Web; and why and how to ask for permission to use other people's material.

In spite of the fact that the students learned a great deal during these 2 weeks, I was still at first somewhat confused by the experience. Most of what the students were working on did not fall within the realm of writing as it is usually conceived (i.e., the creation and editing of texts), and a great deal of their interaction during the weeks took place in English rather than Hawaiian. This did not necessarily have to be the case—these types of interaction around learning new computer and design skills could of course take place in Hawaiian as well but occurred in English in this class for several reasons. All the software programs are in English, necessitating special effort to translate terms into Hawaiian, and students were rushing to finish their projects and thus often used the language of greatest ease and convenience. Also, I was the one who was principally instructing and helping students in Web page design, and my Hawaiian is too weak to easily give that kind of instruction in Hawaiian. As a result, students were using English to talk about issues such as how to create background patterns on Web pages. I began to wonder what this had to do with learning how to write in Hawaiian.

My concerns were offset by what I saw and heard taking place in class. Students were learning important new skills, and they were actively engaged in the learning process. They were spending long hours—any time the computer lab was open, they were there—to work on their projects. This excitement built to a crescendo on the final day, as the students took turns presenting their projects to the rest of the class. There was a feeling of pride and achievement that permeated the whole class.

It was only when talking to the students that I fully realized how much impact the course and project had on their education and lives. A number of the students expressed a profound sense of personal awakening to the power of technology and to its relevance to the present and future of the Hawaiian language. In the remainder of this chapter, I discuss some key themes that emerged in their interviews and in the class. These themes include the changing nature of writing, culturally appropriate education, social identity and investment, technological literacy, and language revitalization.

THE CHANGING NATURE OF WRITING

Students spent a great deal of time working on elements other than text, such as editing and of images and overall page design. To assess whether this time was justified necessitates a broader look at issues regarding the changing nature of writing.

In 1990, Marcia Peoples Halio, then assistant director of the writing program at the University of Delaware, wrote a controversial article entitled *Student Writing: Can the Machine Maim the Message* (Halio, 1990). Halio claimed that the Macintosh computer, with its graphical user interface, was causing students to play frivolously with font and design features and ignore serious writing. She used anecdotal reports, samples of first drafts written on the Macintosh, and computerized style checks of essays written on Macintosh and IBM computers to support her claim that the IBM facilitated serious writing, whereas the Macintosh did not.

Halio's paper sparked a sharp response from computers and writing specialists, with heated discussion talking place on e-mail discussion lists and no fewer than four critical responses and one replication study published in academic journals.[9] Respondents critiqued Halio's inexact research methods and sweeping conclusions and expressed the fear that administrators would use Halio's argument as a reason to stop buying Macintosh computers.

Today, a mere 7 years later, it is true that administrators may be buying fewer Macintosh computers, but for entirely different reasons than those feared in 1990. Rather, Microsoft Corporation has successfully imitated the Macintosh Operating System's graphical interface in its immensely popular Windows program, stealing much of Apple's thunder. Virtually every new personal computer in the world is now sold with a graphical interface and, in a delicious irony, Halio herself is now authoring papers with titles such as Multimedia Narration: Constructing Possible Worlds (Halio, 1996).[10]

In spite of Halio's personal conversion, technology critics such as Neil Postman (1992; 1995), Sven Birkerts (1994), Clifford Stoll (1995), Stephen Talbott (1995), and Todd Oppenheimer (1997) decry the image-oriented emphasis of educational computing, which they feel is debasing attention to the word. Oppenheimer (1997), for example, claimed that lazy students "frequently get seduced by electronic opportunities to make a school paper look snazzy" rather than trying to improve the text (p. 52).

---

[9]Three comments appeared within a few months in the journal *Computers and Composition* (Kaplan & Moulthrop, 1990; Slatin, 1990a; Youra, 1990), with Slatin's signed by 20 of the best-known scholars in the field. A commentary by Anderson (1994) appeared several years later. The replication study by Dierckins (1994), conducted under more rigorous circumstances, failed to find any significant differences between student essays written on Macintosh and IBM computers.

[10]Other of Halio's recent papers include *Webbed writing: Helping students find a voice online in a changing world* (1997) and *Writing the future: How computers are changing writing* (1995).

Writing theorists such as Jay David Bolter (1991, 1006) and Nancy Kaplan (1995) view the matter differently. Bolter (1996), looking at the history of writing and art, explained that human beings have a "desire for the natural sign" (p. 264): "Pictures or moving pictures seem to have a natural correspondence to what they depict. They can satisfy more effectively than prose the desire to cut through to a 'natural' representation that is not a representation at all" (pp. 265–266). In Bolter's view, this desire for the natural was partially suppressed due to the limitations of print but has broken out widely throughout the 20th century, not only in the popularity of film and television but also in recent developments in newspapers and magazines. Use of graphical material in writing thus not only corresponds to a natural human desire for multimodal communication; it also represents an effective way to reach audiences in the current era.

Kaplan (1995) claimed that an emphasis on graphics represents a restoration of something that has been lost:

> In the past, literacy has chiefly meant alphabetic literacy. That meaning has dominated because the chief technologies of literacy, especially the early printing press, have privileged the written language over all other forms of semiosis ... The printing press divorced verbal from iconographic information and representation. This divorce no doubt helped intellectual elites to consolidate their power and authority over public and authorized discourses. (p. 15)

My observations and interviews yielded evidence that students were keenly aware of the new medium they were writing in and that they felt that the media was very appropriate to their Hawaiian cultural traditions. Almost all students showed keen interest in learning the design features of the Web medium. They were not content just to put their text on the Web but wanted to find a presentation that was rhetorically appropriate. This interest included aspects such as finding appropriate graphics, editing the pictures carefully, choosing effective background colors or graphics, and linking to other background information.

An example is seen in the work of Malina, a Hawaiian studies major in her mid 40s. Malina had little previous experience with computers and was unhappy about making Web pages. Later, she warmed up to the activity and spent a great amount of time in the computer lab. She had worked hard on the text all semester, but in the last two weeks she principally worked on selecting the best colors and graphics, editing photos, and placing all the elements in a coherent and attractive design. She ended up producing a beautifully designed page on Hawaiian wetlands, incorporating a combination of poetry, text, drawings, and photos. Malina expressed her thoughts about the new medium, from the point of view as both a writer and a reader:

It was very fascinating to me because suddenly this paper became another kind of medium. And you couldn't just do the same thing, it didn't look good if you just did the same thing.... If you've got a book in front of you, you can put it down anytime, it's kind of right there. But if you have a Web thing, it's different. You're not holding it, you have to kind of look at the screen, and the screen experience to me is, it's hard for me to sit and read that stuff, I can't stand just sitting there reading like that, you gotta keep 'em occupied, with some sort of other interesting thing, and those things can really pull a person into the flavor.

Kamahele's page was unbelievable! I mean the fact that he could get, first of all, you know the chants are just SO good, and anybody, whether they speak Hawaiian or not, if they understand that they can click a Hawaiian chant, I'm sure they're gonna wanna hear it. Cause it's beautiful chanting. But I love how he made his page. The colors were just so powerful in the Web. And the the *ki'i* [pictures] that he had, just outrageous, and you FEEL something and you WANT to read about it. And even if you don't speak the language, you want to press down and go further because something is happening on that page, you know it's some kind of *mana* [spirit] is coming out of that page. And so, the people in the class wanting to put their stuff on there, that's part of their expression, it's part of their *mana*, so it makes the page even much more interesting and inviting. It says in other words, it says not in words, but it says in a different way what they're supposedly trying to convey in a piece. You know, you would think, or at least who wrote it, you know, and you know, so it becomes more interesting. So I think that the graphics are a very integral part, it's very creative.

You know, Hawaiians they weren't a written culture, and I think there's a reason for that, you know they were very alive with everything, so if they're gonna be writing I think this is a great medium because they can be alive here. They can kind of be artistic and do something creative, so, I think it's very good, and very, a lot of *ha'aheo*, a lot of pride can come through there.

Malina's last point raises the issue of the relation of multimedia computing to Hawaiian culture. Several students spoke to this point in their interviews. Among the most eloquent was Kamahele, a 20-year-old biology major. Kamahele has been immersed in native Hawaiian life and culture since childhood. Both his mother and father are Hawaiian, and some of his aunts and uncles spoke the language. Kamahele is a talented hula dancer and a gifted Hawaiian chanter; when he performed chants in class the entire class was mesmerized by the beauty of his deep, powerful voice. He works part time teaching hula and chanting to high school students, and he has traveled to Europe and Asia to participate in Hawaiian cultural presentations. As Malina mentioned Kamahele created a very compelling Web page that incorporated not only texts and images but also included recordings of his own Hawaiian chanting. Kamahele told me:

If you look at hula, the importance of hula isn't the dance performance, the most important thing was the word. But Hawaiians are more than one-dimensional, they like to do things so you hear it and then, and then they'll embellish on it, something like that. So like the pictures really help, because if you've never seen a *kalo* [taro] plant before, you can read about it all you want but if you don't have the picture and stuff like that, then they would help you to understand what *kalo* is or what or maybe what an old Hawaiian chanter looked like and how he dressed, and stuff. So you have maybe a deeper understanding.

Kamahele felt that it was a matter not only of Hawaiian means of expression but also Hawaiian styles of learning. As he explained:

If you look at Hawaiian culture, they weren't one to sit down in a classroom and read something. Ours was more of a, was a spoken language, and so what that means is that you interchange, you speak to each other, you work with ideas, you look at pictures, you look at, and feel different things. And so that the more dimensions that we can get it to, the easier it was for Hawaiians to learn. That's why I think, I don't know, it's just a guess, this is my own opinion, there's no documentation, no fact or anything, but I think maybe that's why Hawaiians are having a little bit of a hard time in the classroom, it's because that's not the *'ano* [way] for thought for maybe 2,000 years, they've been learning through teaching and learning from somebody else, and through visually doing things and working with things instead of just reading out of a book. And so when we add in pictures and colors and voice and everything like that, it's not just a page, words on a page, but actually like jumps at you, and it comes, it, you can feel it more, more in your brain, everywhere, just in your body, I don't know.

A focus on oral and visual learning is one that I've found pervasive in Hawaiian education. Historically, Hawaiian multimodal forms of communication—such as the hula, which combines dance and chant—were opposed as "obscene" by North American missionaries. Today, Hawaiians place great emphasis on maintaining and reviving their oral and visual traditions, both in society and in the classroom.

Earlier, when I took a first-year Hawaiian language class from a different teacher (taught without computers), the students were required to write not traditional final papers but rather picture-stories, encompassing drawings or photos together with descriptive text. Hawaiian language students in both university and K—12 immersion programs often begin their classes with oral chants. On occasions when I've visited immersion schools, I've found a very strong focus on learning through multimedia interaction, whether it be poetry, drawing, or composing songs. As a principal of a Hawaiian immersion school told me:

[Multimedia work] is culturally appropriate. It's not quite so foreign as printed word. The oral nature for the students is much stronger, because you know that's the whole basis of Hawaiian language and culture, I mean it was much more oral. The blending with the western way of doing things and values and things, because we really represent a blend, you know, hopefully a blend of both worlds, where students can learn and recognize when is it appropriate to practice which one.

The computer teacher at the same school strongly emphasized multimedia work. She told me:

The children are so expressive and the more opportunities that we give them to express in their area, they're really great artists. The kids love to sing, they love to perform, and they love to draw, and those kinds of things really, with the medium, are, you know it's really inclusive. They seem to do better when they're there, because you can't compare somebody with somebody else because everybody's doing something different. They can express it in any way that they want to, and that's fine. The students who have behavioral problems have no behavioral problems with me because of the medium that we're working with. They're being challenged and there's no limitations about how they can express themselves, and it's so hands on.

I would certainly not claim that Hawaiian children have an exclusive propensity for learning through singing, drawing, and performing. Learning through a combination of media is indeed considered a general principle of good education because it allows educators to reach out to learners no matter what their preferred learning medium or style is. As has been noted by many other educators, students of all different backgrounds are fascinated by the multimedia capacities of modern computers. Nevertheless, the importance of learning through various media—at not only the K–12 but also the university level—is given special attention by Hawaiian educators as one possible way to help overcome to the text-based modes that have thus far failed the Hawaiian community.[11] In this sense, using multimedia computer applications certainly seems congruent with the goals of Native Hawaiian education.

In summary then, it did not seem to me that students' effort to incorporate additional media into their pages was a matter of frivolous play. Rather, it seemed to indicate that they were aware of the nature of the Web medium and wanted to communicate in as effective a fashion as possible in order to have a positive impact on their readers. They were also communicating in ways they felt to be congruent with their own cultural background. Their pages were not only well designed but also included well-written and edited texts. If we are in fact "coming toward a semiotic view of writing, a view that

---

[11]See Barringer (1995), Takenaka (1995) and Takeuchi, Agbayahi, and Kuniyoshi (1990) for reports on low educational achievement by Hawaiians.

incorporates writing among other forms of communication" (Faigley & Miller, 1982, p. 569), then this seemed like a job exceptionally well done.

CULTURALLY APPROPRIATE EDUCATION

As Kamahele mentioned, Hawaiians have had troubles with the American educational system imposed on them in the 20th century. Among K–12 students, Native Hawaiians achieve the lowest test scores of all major ethnic groups in Hawaii in both reading and mathematics (Takenaka, 1995). Those who make it to college take longer than other groups to graduate and have higher dropout rates (Takeuchi, Agbayani, & Kuniyashi, 1990). As a result, only 8.7% of Native Hawaiians in the state have bachelor's degrees, compared to 21.4% of Whites, 24.2% of ethnic Japanese, and 12% of ethnic Filipinos (Barringer, 1995). Yet Hawaiian education in the 19th century, before the overthrow of the Hawaiian monarchy, achieved one of the highest literacy rates in the world (Judd, 1880). What accounts for the dismal performance of Hawaiians now?

Research confirms Kamahele's comment that at least part of the reason is culturally inappropriate education, with decontextualized modes of school learning at odds with traditional Hawaiian approaches (Au, 180a; Au, 1980b; Boggs, 1985; D'Amato, 1988; Jordan, 1985; Levin, 1992; Martin, 1996). One of the most consistent research findings has been in regard to the importance of social relations in Hawaiian learning. On the one hand, this involves close communication with the people around them, a tradition often referred to in Hawai'i as "talking story" (Au, 1980a). On the other hand, this involves striving toward helping the broader family and community. David Sing, director of Nā Puā Noe'au (i.e., Center for Gifted and Talented Native Hawaiian Children), summarized the results of research that he and others have conducted on these points:

> Hawaiians will work on a task with more vigor and longer if the task involves social interaction. Studies have shown that Hawaiians are motivated to achieve in order to have access to and sustain contact with people. The achievement of personal goals and success provide only secondary motivation.... Hawaiians have been found to achieve less when they are expected to strive toward individualistic and competitive oriented goals.... Another affiliation-oriented behavior of Hawaiians is that they perform better in class when the activity has direct benefit to their family or to a group of which they are part. (Sing, 1986, pp. 26–27)

It is interesting that long before the World Wide Web was developed, Hawaiians used the metaphor of the net to describe their concept of social relations. Here's how one Native Hawaiian program explained the concept of net in Hawaiian culture:

> Hawaiians think of social relationships as binding ties which protectively surround a person. These ties are conduits or connecting paths for emotional exchanges between interrelated individuals. The greater number of positive affective exchange relationships a person has, the more secure and protected the individual. (Mental Health Task Force, 1985)

This sense of a net is evident in Hawaiian classes and in the attitudes of the students that take them. Kapili was able to promote this further through uses of the Internet, both to promote contact among the students and to strengthen their ties to the broader community. One female student, 'Iolani, expressed the sense of working together in the class:

> In Hawaiian classes everybody works together. They're really good. It's my favorite. 'Cause like the other classes you have all different kind of people in your class. But, I don't know, I guess like when we, in Hawaiian class, just put everything together and everybody just helps each other and it's more comfortable, I think, than the rest of the classes, 'cause there are some are so stiff. I guess for Hawaiian language since it's still growing too, the teachers really help you 'cause they want you to learn it, like they don't want, they're not gonna like fail you just to fail you, it's not like math, where everybody can know math, and everybody must take Hawaiian and they're trying to teach everybody, so I think they make more of an effort to make sure they learn everything. It's better, 'cause you get more help, from the teachers and your classmates. 'Cause everybody's trying to work together, like try and bring the language back alive, so everybody's helping each other, if you don't know nothing, they'll just help you. The other classes, I don't know. In Hawaiian, everybody's trying really hard to get their work done and help each other …
>   It's really good to put our papers on the Web. Maybe now if other Hawaiian classes need research, maybe they can look on the Web for research that they need and they can learn how to read it in Hawaiian and get the information in Hawaiian. 'Cause we got all ours from English books and we translated it, and so maybe now instead of looking at English books they can look at our Web pages and they can add on their own, so they can like read in Hawaiian, and then write in Hawaiian, and put their own Hawaiian stuff on the Web page, along with whatever they got from English textbooks, and that can be like texts for other Hawaiian classes.

'Iolani's comments, show the importance of social relations in both senses described earlier: the relations that she has with other students in the class and also the bond that she builds to the broader Hawaiian community through her work on the Web.

Social relations are just one factor related to culturally appropriate Hawaiian education. Darlene Martin (1996), also a coordinator of the Center for Gifted and Talented Native Hawaiian Children, conducted a 2-year study of optimal learning conditions among Hawaiians. According to

Martin, previous research as well as her own study shows that Hawaiians learn best when education emphasizes encouragement and opportunities to develop the whole person through dynamic and experiential learning experiences, a strong connection to one's roots, nurturing and expression of interests and talents, relationships that foster a true sense of belonging and inclusion, and the striving for perfection.

From my observations of class, it was clear that each of these elements was prominent. The work that students did on their Web projects was by any definition dynamic and experiential. A strong connection to Hawaiian roots was emphasized throughout the course. The Web project nurtured student's interests (by allowing them to work on projects of their own choosing) as well as their talents (whether in writing or design). The relations both in the class and to the broader community fostered belonging and inclusion, as 'Iolani's comments show. The striving for perfection was encouraged through opportunities for multiple revision in close cooperation with the teacher.

A comment by Kamahele helps illustrate how several of these features came together in this class. For Kamahele, striving for perfection was closely related to his sense of belonging with the other students and especially his strong roots to the Hawaiian culture:

> Most of us are Hawaiian, and I think we all chose to be in Hawaiian language class because we love Hawaiian language and because that's what we want, we CHOSE to be in Hawaiian language, more than we would choose Japanese or any other culture. We chose the class, so once we did, we have like a desire to learn, and a desire to do things, and I think after that it becomes pride, like whatever we do and whatever we're gonna say, this is Hawaiian, we don't want the world to look at it and go, oh, well, that's interesting, or oh, that's nice—we want them to go WOW, that's Hawaiian! So I think that's why we took a little bit more pride and it took us a little bit more time to do our projects, only because we have pride in our heritage and maybe where we come from, and so we wanted to put our best foot forward. That's what I think and that's how I was feeling.

SOCIAL IDENTITY AND INVESTMENT

Much research on second language learning has focused on the role of individual affect and cognition. Peirce (1993, 1995) critiqued this perspective and suggested that it be complemented by an approach emphasizing social identity and investment. From this perspective, social identity is multiple, a site of struggle, and constantly changing, and the way that social identity changes over time and in different circumstances affects how people invest in learning and using languages.[12] In addition, as Peirce and others have pointed out (e.g., Penuel & Wertsch, 1995), a key aspect of social identity is cultural identity.

This perspective seems especially helpful for understanding what took place in this class. As young adults of mixed ethnic backgrounds, the students' sense of cultural and social identity was multiple and changing. As their comments show many students were in the process of becoming more strongly invested in their sense of being Hawaiian and their concomitant commitment to the Hawaiian language. Kapili was able to use technology to tap into this process further by giving students an opportunity to express and develop their own Hawaiian identity through their online projects. This technique seemed to have a positive impact on many of the students, with one particularly dramatic example being the case of Onaona.

Onaona was a 24-year-old student of Portuguese, German, and Hawaiian ancestry. Though very light-skinned and just 1/8 Hawaiian, her Hawaiian roots were a strong part of her identity. As she explained:

> When I was in elementary school my mother made me take Japanese. It was fun at first, but after taking 2 years in an after-school Elementary program, 3 years in high school and 1 semester in college I began to hate it because it wasn't something I could relate to in terms of heritage and nationality. I only did it for my mum. To this day all I can remember are a few key verbs (*matte*–"wait," *hayaku*–"hurry," etc.) as well as a few hiragana and katakana characters.
>
> But my great-grandfather was Hawaiian. My mum had told me that he used to translate the bible from English to Hawaiian but I'm still trying to trace that. I definitely know that when he'd retired, he worked at the Bishop Museum, on his own time, helping with texts and artifacts, perpetuating the language and making sure that we learned it. I think that was the driving force for me to learn the language, because he was both fluent in Hawaiian and English, and I think like, why aren't we like that? You tend to lose bits of your culture and your history and yourself, when you kind of close yourself off to that side of you and that's what it felt like I had been doing.

Onaona worked at a television studio doing broadcasting and computer graphics. When I first interviewed her, she was planning to take an internship in a New York television studio and contine in a career in broadcast media. However, she wasn't quite sure of her study or career plans and had changed her major several times.

Although Onaona had a Macintosh at home and was more computer savvy than most of the other students, she had little previous experience with the Internet. She had never used e-mail, had rarely used the World

---

[12]Peirce's concept of social identity is based on the work of Weedon (1987). Her concept of investment draws on work of Bordieu (1977) and Ogbu (1978). For further details, see Peirce (1995).

Wide Web, and was somewhat skeptical about the sudden popularity of the Internet, but Onaona really enjoyed the computer work in class, in part because it gave her a chance to express herself (as mentioned earlier in the chapter, she was very shy in oral interaction but expressed herself easily using Daedalus). She also felt the written interaction helped her speaking abilities: "I'm more of like a visual learner, so if I can get it visually down, like in writing, then the correct structure, it will be a lot easier to speak."

It was while working on her research paper, that she really started to shine. Onaona wrote a lengthy and sophisticated paper on the life of one of Hawai'i's last princesses. She then spent countless hours in the computer lab developing the presentation. There was literally not an hour that the lab was open that I could not find her there. She had a fine eye for aesthetic detail, thinking carefully about issues such as how and where to place picture captions or whether to put in borders, and learned much more about some of the software than I knew.

She explained to me the great attention that she paid to both the text and design of her page:

> I was kind of nervous about the text, I tried to make it extra good, revision after revision, going, *kumu* [teacher], is this O.K., does it look all right? I guess because, for me, my name is on it, and so I really want it to look good, and I'm like, a real balance freak, especially if I've got photos, I've got to either have it centered, with things underneath, or on the side with stuff next to it, with text wrapped around it, so I think, plus too, because of my job and the things that I work with, the computer graphics that I work with at the station, I really like to make sure everything's balanced, with my name on it, it's even more so, cause I keep thinking, oh gosh, all these people are gonna see it, and they're gonna go, oh you did that.

Onaona overcame her skepticism about the Internet and started to spend a good deal of time online in various projects. She also started to think more actively how to combine her interests in media and in Hawaiian.

> I think the possibilities are limitless right now, because if you get the people together you could probably have radio, you know even if you wanted radio dramas or even a television station that broadcast only in Hawaiian, or, you know and different learning tools with children, you know like getting some of the legends on tape or on film for them to watch and you can also learn and possibly getting something up with HITS [Hawaiian Interactive Television System] and more of an interaction between kids, you know, on other islands, and they can talk to each other.

She was trying to figure out what her own role would be in this:

> Since taking Hawaiian I've changed my major like 8 million times. I used to be an English major, well, first I was a television production major, then I was an English major,

then a journalist major, then I went back to English, and now I'm thinking of getting an education major, with a minor in Hawaiian studies, and a minor in journalism. I'm not sure yet [about being a teacher], but when we see the video and we see the kids, they're so cute.

Like almost all the other students in the class, Onaona continued with Kapili the next semester in Hawaiian 202. The students made Web pages again, and Onaona produced a page on the history and nature of Hawai'i Creole English (Pidgin). This page, written in Hawaiian, discussed the social and linguistic roots of the language, compared Hawaiian and HCE syntax, gave numerous examples of HCE using sound files, and presented newspaper quotes with sophisticated graphics (including, for example, a blurred graphic of newspaper text with a raised quote typed above it using Adobe Photoshop). The page was presented on a slightly blurred brick background, giving an urban feel to the page, reflecting the working-class roots of today's HCE speakers. Onaona had become quite a talented writer and designer in this medium.

By the time this second semester had ended, she had definitely decided on continuing Hawaiian and becoming a teacher:

Date:Wed, 14 May 1997 00:46:46 -1000
From:"Janet O. Obenho" <chuna@gte.net>
To:Mark Warschauer <markw@hawaii.edu>

As for the summer, I'm taking a few classes ... Hawaiian 301 & 302 :) I've thought of continuing before, but just for fun ... Lately I've been thinking that I would like to continue speaking Hawaiian for years to come ... I don't want to wake up one day and not able to remember how to do that. I finally decided that in teaching Hawaiian (hopefully) I would be able to do this and also aide in my fluency and mastery of Hawaiian.

If you would have told me two years ago I would consider being a teacher, I would have told you were crazy..It's so weird how taking one class can alter your plans so greatly for the future.

Actually it was last semester when I began tinkering with the idea (becoming a teacher) but it wasn't until this semester when I actually said HEY I really wanna do this. I'm still trying to figure out a way to merge my television production background, journalism experience and Hawaiian. To get a career that utilizes all three ... I think would be my dream job *sigh* :) Heck, I'd still like to someday intern for David Letterman ... as long as I know that I can still communicate in Hawaiian via the web.

I really can't put a finger on what exactly in the class changed my mind ... the most obvious reason I can come up with is the exposure to the high-tech trinity; e-mail, the net and creating web pages. I think it's totally amazing that I can put my ideas on the web and someone half-way around the world can read about it!!! Even though I work with a lot high-tech equipment both at school and at work, I am a very conservative creature when it comes to using new technology for recreational use ... I usually have to be dragged kicking

and screaming into using the newfangled machines, but after the initial shock wears off ... WATCH OUT! I have become such an e-mail junkie it's not even funny, I can't believe I'm using phrases like "I'll e-mail you to-night", "can you fax it to me by Monday" and "this is what I found while surfin' the net".
A hui hou, e malama pono [See you later, take care]
Onaona

E ola mau ka 'olelo Hawai'i! [Long live the Hawaiian Language!]

Onaona's social identity evolved in two important ways during the class. First, she changed from seeing herself as someone who was skeptical about the Internet to someone who had strong expertise and interest in it. Second, she began to view herself as someone who was not merely interest-ing in learning about her heritage but rather as someone who should ac-tively promote Hawaiian language and culture throughout her life. The combination of these two views helped her make an important career choice that she felt would allow her to combine her interests in media, Ha-waiian language, and education.

Although few other students in the class changed their majors or ca-reer choices, many students seemed involved in a process of developing their identities as Hawaiians. Kapili tapped into this well by providing students an opportunity to explore and express their sense of Hawaiianness in the online world.

TECHNOLOGICAL LITERACY

In the earlier discussion of Mary's class at Miller College, I analyzed what students were learning apart from the stated curriculum of the class. A similar approach seems useful here. Though the class was ostensibly about the Hawaiian language, clearly what students were learning ex-tended beyond that. Most students seemed to be learning about how to use technology to interpret and construct meaning and what significance that had for their lives as students and as Hawaiians.

In one sense, students could be seen as developing computer literacy, though this term has been rejected by educators who have seen it used in too narrow a fashion. Because computer literacy is sometimes portrayed as little more than how to turn on or operate a machine—and because it fails to account for the way that computers are connected with other new media—educators have sought new terms that emphasize how students learn to work with a variety of technologies and media to interpret and construct meaning. Suggested alternatives—each with its own shade of meaning—have included electronic literacy (Craver, 1997), digital literacy (Gilster, 1997), technological literacies (Lankshear & Knobel, 1995), multiliteracies (New London Group, 1996), and metamedia literacy (Lemke, in press).

Putting the particular terms aside, what is it that made this a particularly powerful literacy experience for the students involved? Several elements seemed to be involved. First, as in Luz's ESL class, there seemed to be a very effective combination of focus on meaning and form. Students were allowed a great deal of latitude in determining their own topics and approaches. They were encouraged by the teacher to deal with topics of importance to their lives as Hawaiians, and they were given many opportunities to discuss together what those topics and issues might be. They were invited to use a variety of media creatively to convey their message and were given the time to develop the skills necessary to do so—even if that seemed to distract from the course's ostensible main purpose of teaching the Hawaiian language.

These learning experiences seemed to differ from the experiences that students had had in previous classes. The majority of students in the class were from economically depressed working-class neighborhoods. Most had gone to high schools where they had little exposure to new technologies, and none had the opportunity to use interactive or multimedia technologies for the creative construction of meaning in either their high school or college classes.

Within this general emphasis on meaning, there was also attention to form. To a certain extent, the medium itself facilitated and encouraged this. The Daedalus and e-mail communications gave students a chance to study the form of incoming messages and to attend to the form of their own messages. The fact that their papers were published on the Web also encouraged students to pay attention to the form. Beyond this, the teacher took special effort to assist the students with form, by giving them printouts of Daedalus discussions with some errors marked or working with them individually to correct and improve their research papers.

A number of educators have pointed out that an overemphasis on expressive communication, combined with an underemphasis on the forms and genres of language, can be detrimental to minority and lower socioeconomic status students, who may lack knowledge of the rules of the culture of power (Delpit, 1988; Martin, Christie, & Rothery, 1994). Indeed, many students in this class expressed a need for better attention to form, in both English and Hawaiian. I'm thinking, for example, of the comments of Donald, a Hawaiian–Filipino student and native speaker of Pidgin. Donald explained to me that he had failed his English class because the teacher had assumed he had knowledge of the genres and forms of written standard English that he didn't have. In contrast, he found Kapili's Hawaiian class to be easier: "Because we're beginners in Hawaiian, they help us along the way, but then like for English they expect you to know these things that I don't know, so Hawaiian is easier for me."

Mary Sanderson's Pacific Island students also felt a need for a focus on form, but somehow the way that she accomplished this task left most of them alienated. In contrast, Kapili achieved a formal focus within a highly motivating context of creative multimedia production in Hawaiian. Whereas Mary's students used in-class communication to complete exercises, Kapili's students wrote freely and then later analyzed the structure, and whereas Mary's students produced Web pages on narrowly defined topics by writing texts that the teacher then inserted in a template, Kapili's students created Web pages on topics of their own choosing through an intense learning experience of multimedia design.

The experiences of Kapua help illustrate many of the previous points. Kapua was a 21-year-old sophomore, planning to major in education. She explained to me that she is part Hawaiian and part Filipino, and that she took Hawaiian "because I wanted to learn my culture ... before I learn any other language I would rather learn Hawaiian." Like other students, Kapua took writing-intensive Hawaiian in part because she thought it would help her master the structure of the language:

> I wanted writing intensive. Because, at the same time I wanted to, you know, learn more about the patterns and you know, the writing and stuff, you might as well learn two things instead of one, writing intensive AND language. I wanted to challenge myself.

Kapua grew up in one of the poorer areas of the state. She had been admitted to the university through the College Opportunity Program for students from low-income areas. She had never previously used the Internet and did not have a computer at home. When I asked her if she had used a computer in high school, she took the opportunity to give me a broader view of what her high school experience was like:

> In high school I don't remember even going on a computer. In elementary school yes, but never in high school. High school was so easy, but it was like I wasn't learning anything, cause the teachers was like O.K., do questions 1 through 10, and then turn it in at the end of the class, and that's the whole class period, you just answer questions from the book, and once a week we would do labs, but we didn't learn anything in the labs. Even English, we would just read paragraphs, like, the teacher would call like, O.K. Kerrie read the first paragraph, Makala read the sec-

ond paragraph. And that's all we did. And we never had conversation, like O.K., what'd you guys think about this. We just read. And then after we read that book, like Macbeth, we would watch the video. That's it.

They're supposed to be teaching us, but we didn't even know what English is, what kind of things that we were supposed to know. Even our book reports, I mean I didn't even know what the term plagiarism was, and I used to plagiarize from even the footnotes, and I used to get a good grade. I mean I didn't know what plagiarism was.

Even though Kapua had never used computers before, she caught on fairly quickly. She really enjoyed using Daedalus and hated leaving class when computer sessions were over. Once, leaving class, she told me, "The time goes fast. We don't wanna leave when it's over. It's not like in the class, when we're looking at the clock, afraid she's gonna call on us. Here, we write what we want." Another time she explained that "Daedalus is better [than writing journal cards] 'cause you get response. If you just get postcards and you just give it to Kumu [teacher], then it's just correction, give it back. But Daedalus is like, constantly talking."

Kapua enjoyed surfing the net and found information about Hawaiian wrestling to put on her Web page on the topic. She was especially amazed at the ability of the computer for multimedia creation and became very excited over the use of the digital camera and Adobe Photoshop for graphical work. By the end of the semester, she began to see computers as very important for her own life and future and for that of her family as well. She discussed her thoughts at length with me at the end of the semester:

It was hard at first, I was a little confused, I mean I was totally lost. She'll explain it, but I didn't understand what we were supposed to do, but then slowly, slowly I got to learn more stuff, especially with the Photoshop. I know that now.

This class is very challenging, very interesting. It's really good. I think this is one of the best classes that I took, that really made me learn so much in a semester. Especially in computers. This is the first class where I used a lot of computers in the class, and I'm thinking of buying me one. I think it will be a good investment. A lot of things that it can do, like making a Web page, that was exciting, I didn't know you could take pictures with a digital camera, and e-mail, that was good too. I think it was really interesting. It just made me like the language more, using the computer you can see what other students have learned in the Hawaiian language, especially with the Web page. Also, when you send e-mail to Pearl like that, I think that's helpful too because you get to talk to people at other schools, instead of just talking to your students here. I think that's helpful.

I was either gonna use the rest of my money from my scholarship to fix my car or to buy a computer. And I think I would rather buy a computer, 'cause my sister and brother are in elementary and intermediate. And I think if I teach them things in the computer, 'cause right now they're just relaxing, they don't really care about school. They're not really studious in their classes, like my sister, she really doesn't care about school. I think computers can motivate them. So I think that would be a good investment.

Next fall I'm gonna try to enter college of education. I'll try to use computers, I think it will be more exciting for kids, too, yeah, instead of those same old boring lectures and writing on the chalkboard kind of stuff. I'll teach science, I think it's interesting. Especially you find all kind of stuff to get the kid's attention, like projects and maps. Computers'll help too 'cause they'll see what other schools have done in that same project that we did.

I believe that Kapua's excitement about using computers did not stem merely from exposure to a new medium. Rather, she was given an opportunity to interpret and construct meaning in that new medium on topics that she found of interest. She started to connect technology to aspects of her personal life, ranging from helping her brothers and sisters to thinking about ways to incorporate computers into her own work as a future teacher.

Kapua's experiences of overcoming difficulties to learn to use computers are seen in some of the other students as well. For example, Malina, the student in her 40s described earlier, had a great deal of difficulty in the beginning:

In the beginning I was cynical because I didn't know how to do the technology. It was very hard, the whole Web thing kind of pissed me off in a way, because this isn't a Web class and I don't know anything about the Web, I didn't know anything about how to make a page and that was very stressful for me. So that kind of was hard for me. That was really hard. And mainly because I thought I wasn't gonna get my project on. That's what I was really upset like, "Oh my God, I'm gonna get graded for this and I can't even get my paper on the screen!"

Eventually, Malina overcame her fears:

But after I was able to get in there and put it up, I thought, what a great idea, because often we write these great papers and no one is there to read 'em, and they're really terrific information. So I thought that was really good and we have another skill and in fact, it's kinda been a crash course for me because my husband's been trying to get me into the computer and my girlfriend who lives in New York, and, she's just been hired for like $175,000 a year to head up this company's computer, the Internet thing, where they, I guess what they do is they get space or they design the page to get the people in to buy the records. And they've all been trying to get me into it cause they've been thinking that I'd be really good at it, and I'd like "Ughhh." But after we did this I actually did get really interested, you know when we started to do the artwork is when I was like, oh this is very cool! You know, the scanning, and going in and putting the borders around and everything, and fixing the page up.

After the semester ended, Malina was very disappointed that she wouldn't be able to continue studying with Kapili due to a time conflict in the following semester. Though she began the semester angry about having to use computers, she was now upset that she might not be able to use them. She still had hopes though that other teachers might follow Kapili's example:

> I'm hoping other teachers will do this too, because it's just a wonderful project. It's a really good way to get people very much, you know, because my criticism of the university as a whole is that they put you in an ivory tower, and you are learning all this stuff that is not gonna do you one bit of good when you get out. You have this degree and you think, O.K. all I have to do is write a paper, and you know you get out there, you can't get a job, nobody's really interested in that. You know they don't think like that on the outside. And I know that because I've been living there on the outside, you know working in businesses, working in my own field. But this way Kapili is kind of showing students that there is something that they could do with their knowledge of Hawaiian. They could write, you know, if they could do this, they could write for a newspaper. If they could do this, they could, you know, I mean they could teach, they could do ANYTHING. And this field is kind of an open field with computers, nobody really knows where it's going. But, um, I just think it opens their vistas. And it's very practical, too. I mean you can see that it might have something to do with your life outside of these walls. So I think that she's doing a really good thing.
>
> Yeah, yeah, I think, you know, you can't, don't separate it, don't make it not a part of the life. It has to be organic. So I think that the Web actually makes it, helps it to be organic—although to me computers aren't necessarily an organic experience—but it helps it to BE organic, because it, you can, you can connect from here to the outside world, and then you have.

Malina's comments illustrate well that it was not the computer per se that engaged her interests—friends had been attempting to get her involved in computers for years—but it was the opportunity to use computers to make a real connection "from here to the outside world" that was relevant for her. This real connection, communicating meaning on relevant issues to an authentic audience, seemed to be central to the literacy experience of many students in this class.

LANGUAGE REVITALIZATION

The last topic bearing discussion is the relation between new technologies and language revitalization. The revitalization of languages is a very complex phenomenon, a full discussion of which is beyond the scope of this volume. However, a few comments are in order.

Joshua Fishman (1991), in his renowned book on reversing language shift, contended that the phenomenon involves two general stages. In the first stage, a community seeks to attain *diglossia*, that is, a situation in which the community language is spoken as a second language in home and social environments. In the second stage a community seeks to transcend diglossia by making its language the dominant one used in all spheres of life, including work, the mass media, and governmental operations.

Hawaiian is within the first stage of reversing language shift, and will likely be so for a long time. The ability to attain the second stage seems to depend on broader social and economic changes, such as those called for by the Hawaiian sovereignty movement (Dudley, 1993; Trask, 1993).

However, even within the first stage, Hawaiian faces special challenges. According to Fishman (1991), the key within the first stage is to achieve "the intergenerational and demographically concentrated home-family-neighborhood: the basis of mother tongue transmission" (p. 395). As Edward Spicer (as cited by Fishman, 1991) explained,

> The persistence of configurations of identity symbols depends on the kind of communication possible in community organizations.... It is in the mileu of the effective local community, uniting household groups, that the basis for choosing to identify with an enduring people becomes established. (p. 358)

With speakers of Hawaiian so few and dispersed, Hawaiian educational leaders have turned to immersion education to try to develop concentrations of Hawaiian speakers and to bring these pockets of speakers together into larger virtual communities through the use of the Internet. To accomplish this, the Hale Kuamo'o Hawaiian language curriculum office in Hilo devoted considerable resources toward developing a graphical-interface Hawaiian language bulletin board system called Leokī (The Powerful Voice), believed to be the first Internet communication system in the world fully based on an indigenous language (Warschauer & Donaghy, 1997). Leokī has been installed in most of the immersion schools and is gradually being installed in other public colleges, community organizations, and, eventually, private homes throughout the state.[13] As Keiki Kawai'ae'a, Director of Curriculum Materials at Hale Kuamo'o explained,

> The concern is linking the language communities, because there's a small community at Keaukaha, and there's a small community of kindergarteners and first graders at Waiamea, and they're all over, there are over 15 schools at the street, but there are pockets of Hawaiian speaking children, that are all second language, the majority of them are second language speakers, and they need to have more peers to speak with.

---

[13]Leokī was not yet installed at the University of Hawai'i at the time this study took place.

Leokī has the feel of a community. In addition to e-mail, Leokī includes public notices, conferences, a store for Hawaiian language books and materials, a newspaper, and—the most popular feature—a live chat room. Kāhealani Naeʻole-Wong, a computer coordinator at an immersion school, has watched students at her school excitedly use Hawaiian with other children and adults around the state, some using Hawaiian outside their own school environment for the first time. She told me that "Leokī's playing a big role now. It's like a virtual community of speakers, it's substituting for the lack of the real community of native speakers, or just speakers."

Another goal of Hawaiian educators in supporting technology has been to promote the notion of Hawaiian as a language of the present and future, not just the past. Nancy Hornberger (1997b), based on her studies of language shift throughout the Americas, contended that in order for a minority language to compete seriously with more dominant languages, it's necessary to create a feeling that it does not belong only to the past but also to the future: "Language revitalization is not about bringing a language back, it's about bringing it forward" (Hornberger, 1997b, n.p.).[14]

Curriculum specialist Kawaiʻaeʻa explains that this idea, promoting Hawaiian as a living language of the future, was behind their effort to develop Leokī and other software with all commands and menus in Hawaiian:

Without changing the language and having the programs in Hawaiian, they wouldn't be able to have computer education *through* Hawaiian, which is really a major hook for kids in our program. They get the traditional content like science and math, and now they are able to utilize this ʻono [really delicious] media called computers! Computer education is just so exciting for our children. In order for Hawaiian to feel like a real living language, like English, it needs to be seen, heard and utilized everywhere, and that includes the use of computers.

This perspective, promoting the use of Hawaiian as a living language of the future, was central to Kapili's thinking as well. As she explained to me,

I think because we're really breaking new ground, using Hawaiian in technology, there's no other place that they would have had this exposure to it, and so wherever they have their first year of Hawaiian, whether it's high school or college, we can bring them to new levels with the technology that we've been able to do with the class. And I think it helps them to look at language that, anyway, for like the life of the Hawaiian language is not just something you do from a textbook or in a class, but it's something

---

[14]See also Hornberger (1997a). The phrase was used earlier by Rosemary Henze, who organized a session (in which Hornberger participated) at the American Anthropological Association national conference in 1995 entitled "Bringing the language forward: Language and cultural revitalization efforts."

for the future as well, you can do Hawaiian language online, and you can do the same things that you're doing with your English language, and I think that's really important that they can feel ownership for the language wherever they are. And as we're moving ahead in technology, and we need people working in computers, developing, so some of them can get sparked, that we communicate in all these different ways, whatever ways that technology has provided for us, and we can do that with our Hawaiian as well as in English. So it gives a status to the language.

I think that's one of the most valuable things, that we don't just look at Hawaiian as the language of our ancestors, it has to be a language for our future, and however we make that bridge, so if we want to say that language is going to be vibrant in the 21st century, so it needs to be in all aspects of our lives, and this machine is definitely part of that.

Students in Kapili's class seemed receptive to this message. On the one hand, the use of technology helped give them a sense of the future of the language. As Kawika, a 20-year-old male student, told me, "It incorporates stuff now with language we're learning, so it's keeping up with the times, it's not just one of the books and papers, it's incorporating current stuff, technology."

Whether or not it serves to revitalize the language, the notion of creating a presence for Hawaiian on the Web was a powerful motivator for students in this class. This was seen in the earlier comments of 'Iolani, who felt that by putting her papers on the Web she was helping to create an important resource for other Hawaiian language students. A similar sentiment was also expressed by Kamahele:

It's like a double advantage for us, we're learning how to use new tools, like new technology and new tools, at the same time we're doing it in Hawaiian language, and so we get to learn two things at once. We learn new technology, and implementing it with Hawaiian language, which I think is really, really good. It looks almost as if it's a thing of the future for Hawaiian, because if you think about it, maybe there's [only] a few Hawaiian language papers. But instead of maybe having a Hawaiian language newspaper, you have something that might be just a little bit better, like the World Wide Web, it's like building things for all the kids who are now in immersion and even for us, someplace to go and get information, and so that's kind of neat what we're doing, we're doing research and then finding out all that we can about a topic and then actually putting it on the World Wide Web, and then having that be useful to somebody else in the future.

Kamahele's comments illustrate to me the interconnection between many of the points discussed in this chapter. For Kamahele and the other students, a new way of writing, culturally appropriate education, social identity and investment, technology literacies, and language revitalization were not isolated themes of the course. All were aspects of an integrated educational experience that helped shape their lives. Whether computers and the Internet will in the long run play a role in the renaissance of Hawaiian remains to be seen, but judging by the results of Kapili's class, the match between technology and language revitalization seems to be a good one.

5

Cyber Service Learning

ᎧᏃ•ᏍᎧ

Literacy within the walls of academe is as foul a fish as Ken Macrorie's "Engfish" a type of writing found only in the rarefied atmospheres of English classrooms, one that smells when it is taken out of the environment.
—Lillian Bridwell-Bowles (1977, p. 25)

Joan Conners, as Assistant Professor of English at Bay Community College in O'ahu, shares Lillian Bridwell-Bowle's concern, and she has thus designed a course specifically to provide a solution. Joan's English 215 course combines two main features—intensive networked written discussion and production of brochures, Web pages, and newsletters for community organizations. Both are designed to provide the kind of authentic communicative writing seldom found in the English classroom.

Located on O'ahu, Bay serves as both a vocational school and a feeder college to the University. Its 6,000 students include recent high school graduates and returning students of various ages. The school has a diverse ethnic mix of locally born students (including ethnic Japanese, Chinese, Hawaiian, Filipino, and almost every other ethnicity found in Hawai'i, a few transplants from the U.S. mainland, and a sizable number of immigrant students from throughout Asia and the Pacific.

If Bay College is noteworthy for anything—other than its scenic Hawaiian campus—it is its devotion to technology. The campus was the host of several national conferences during the last year devoted to technology and education. The provost of the college is finishing his doctorate in Information and Computer Sciences with study on computer-mediated communication. Just as Miller College's newspaper is filled with religious themes, Bay College's paper often features high-tech articles: *New Media Arts Program to Train for Digital Media Jobs, Expert Sees Large Growth for Technology in Hawai'i, Students Get Connected to Web, Take a Virtual Tour of Bay College on the 'Net.*

126

Perhaps no one has done as much to bring technology to Bay College as Joan Conners. Now an assistant professor of English, Joan first got involved in computers and composition in 1978 when she wrote her M.A. thesis on a typewriter terminal in her office connected by modem to a mainframe. She had her own students word processing their papers via mainframe by 1980.

Joan moved to Hawai'i in 1986 and continued her efforts to integrate computers into writing instruction. After looking into and rejecting other computer-assisted instruction programs ("they didn't really involve writing, but just having a student push a key or something"), Joan helped to get a grant to purchase the Daedalus Integrated Writing Environment (Daedalus Inc., 1989) and to set up two dedicated networked class labs for writing instruction. Joan and a colleague designed the class labs so that they would be most suitable for instruction. Joan has taught exclusively in those labs the last 5 years.

In addition to computers and composition, Joan has two other educational passions: writing across the curriculum and service learning. Writing across the curriculum is both a philosophy of education and a program at Bay College (and the larger University of Hawai'i system). It is based on the premise that both writing and critical thinking are improved when students have extensive writing assignments in all their classes and not just in their composition or English classes. Students at Bay College have to take two designated writing-intensive classes to complete their 2-year degree as part of a total of five writing-intensive classes needed to graduate from the University of Hawai'i. Joan had been the Writing Across the Curriculum director in a previous job and was involved in the program at Bay College as well.

Service learning is also both a philosophy of education and a program at Bay Community College. Service learning has been described as "a form of experiential education in which students engage in activities that address human and community needs together with structured opportunities intentionally designed to promote student learning and development" (Jacoby, 1996, p. 5). Rooted in early 20th century progressivists' views of experiential learning (see, for example, Dewey, 1938), service learning has blossomed into a national movement in the last 20 years, with organizations such as Campus Compact and the National Society for Experiential Education promoting and coordinating service learning projects throughout the United States.

Joan helped to start the service learning program at Bay College with a grant from Campus Compact. The grant provided some release time for her as well as funds to purchase desktop publishing software. Using this software, students in Joan's English classes have been publishing a newsletter for a community organization in a low-income neighborhood. Over time, she has had her students work on other service learning projects, including tutoring ESL pupils at a local middle school and providing hands-on Internet training to ESL pupils from a local elementary school. Eventually, Bay College was designated a mentoring school by a national organization, and Joan and others now travel to other colleges throughout Hawai'i to help them set up their own service learning programs. Due in part to Joan's efforts, Hawai'i has become the first state in the nation to have Campus Compact service-learning centers at every one of its public universities and colleges.

ENGLISH 215

Joan's English 215 course allowed her to combine all her academic passions: computers and composition, writing across the curriculum, and service learning. Although the course was officially titled "Advanced Expository Writing," Joan told me that she preferred to think of it as "creative nonfiction." It is an elective course designed to give students advanced nonfiction writing experiences beyond what they get in the basic required English 100 class. Like the Hawaiian 201 class reported in chapter 4, English 215 was an officially designated writing-intensive class. It was also an officially designated service learning class, though unlike writing-intensive classes, service learning classes are not required of Bay College or University of Hawai'i students. Like all Joan's classes, English 215 is taught in a networked computer laboratory.

I first spoke with Joan about researching her class a few months before her English 215 course started. Joan and I had long been acquaintances and colleagues, and I had visited her classes in previous semesters. I was particularly interested in working with her English 215 class when she told me that students would be creating authentic World Wide Web pages for community organizations as part of their service learning requirement.

My relationship with Joan was somewhat different from those I had with Mary, Luz, or Kapili. As a highly experienced teacher of computer-based writing, Joan didn't need or expect any help from me in planning her course. Although Joan and I discussed the course a few times over lunch, and I offered occasional comments or suggestions, my participatory role was not as a co-teacher but rather as a helper. I attended classes regularly and assisted students with computers or writing problems as they arose.

There were 20 students in the class at the beginning of the semester, reflecting the same cultural diversity of the college as a whole, including 5 locally born students of Japanese and Filipino ancestry, 3 White students from other U.S. states, and 12 immigrant or long-term resident students from China (7), Japan (3), Korea (1), and Germany (1). By the end of the semester, two local students had dropped out, leaving a total of 18.[1]

The large number of immigrant students in the class probably stems from the fact that Joan, in addition to teaching English classes, also teaches Bay College's ESL writing classes. With an M.A. in ESL to complement her M.A. in English, Joan has a great deal of training and experience in meeting the special needs of second language learners. Many students in the class had either previously taken Joan's ESL courses or heard about her from friends who had.

Joan's class met twice a week for 75 minutes. I missed the first week of class due to a trip to Australia. When I arrived on the third class session, it was clear that students were already acclimated to the computer lab. In a pattern that would continue throughout the semester, Joan said nothing at the beginning of class. Students already knew that they were to get online and open up the Daedalus program to see their instructions. This is what they found:

English 215W
January 23, 1997

Hello again, welcome back to ENGLISH 215W.
TO DO TODAY:
1. Complete the questionnaire distributed by Mark Warschauer.
2. Use Utilities—Copy a Document to copy the discussions from last time onto your disks. Select all the files with IC beginnings.
3. Take time now to read quickly through the discussions that you were not a part of.
4. Use Activities—Interchange and Interchange—Join a Conference to participate with your assigned group in a final discussion of the essay, "Endou."
5. Under Activity—New Write Window, follow the Mrs. Conner's directions to complete your own writing. Save your file in your own journal folder.
6. As time permits, use Activities—Interchange and Interchange—Join a Conference to participate in disucssions about Chapter 4 in Fact and Artifact.

---

[1]One student dropped the course in the first two weeks. A second left in the middle of the semester for work-related reasons.

I passed out a short questionnaire for the students to fill out. After that, students worked independently on the tasks. Many already had the hang of what to do. The few who needed help asked their neighbors or Joan. I also circulated and helped students as they needed it.

Students appeared to be quite comfortable in class, right from early in the semester. Computers in the class were situated in clusters of four (rather than in rows, as in Miller College, or around the periphery of the room, as at the University of Hawai'i); this clustering of computers allowed students easy access to ask questions of neighboring students. In addition, posters of flowers and parks adorned the walls, and Joan put on soft baroque music on a cassette player when students were working at their computers. A variety of stuffed animals—fuzzy bears, cuddly dogs, woolly sheep, and cute kittens—sat on top of the computer monitors. Joan explained that she and another teacher had brought the animals to make the room feel less threatening than a traditional computer lab. (They later added a few plastic dinosaurs to provide some "boy toys" for the males.) Students occasionally donated animals as well.

IMMERSION PHILOSOPHY

The class continued in much the same vein for the first half of the semester. Students would come in, log on, read some instructions on the screen, and set about their work for the day, which almost always involved some form of computer-mediated writing and interaction. This stemmed from Joan's philosophy of teaching and learning composition. As she explained to me,

> I see myself as a facilitator to set up situations through which the students will write as much as they can write, and they use writing for communicative reasons. I base that on the feeling that this is like an immersion in the language situation. I think the literature is pretty strong to show that the student who is immersed in the language learns the language faster than the student who goes to a classroom two or three times a week, so that's my goal—to provide what could be called an immersion experience in the written language in the classroom.

After many years' experience, Joan was adept at facilitating this kind of immersion experience. She introduced technology in a seamless manner, allowing students the time and opportunity to figure out new skills on their own. (This was facilitated by the fact that many of the students in the class had used Daedalus before in previous Bay College classes.) Joan was thoroughly familiar not only with Daedalus Interchange but also with the other modules of the Daedalus Integrated Writing Environment, and she used these features to have students post their drafts for the class to read, copy documents from Joan or transcripts of Interchange sessions, and conduct written peer review.

Joan was particularly skillful in engaging students in Daedalus discussions. She accomplished this by setting an appropriate size for a group discussion (usually 5–9 students per group), writing thoughtful question prompts (which appeared at the top of the screen at the beginning of the session), and intervening during the sessions with further comments or questions to stimulate more thinking and writing. She also encouraged her students to keep their comments short to facilitate more interaction.

Interchange sessions in Joan's classes almost always featured an interesting exchange of content. The following is an example of an Interchange early in the semester. Seven students were discussing the short story "Endou" by Josephine Foo (1995), in which Foo recounts some of her memories of growing up in Malaysia. Joan had assigned this reading in preparation for her students' work on writing an autobiographical essay, which was the first of four main assignments in the class. She asked this group to discuss the first section of the essay, which is subtitled "Boxes." Participating in the discussion were five American students (Gerald, Hal, Anne, Charlene, and Karl) and two Japanese students (Yoshi and Aki).

(1) Joan: Discuss with others in this group what you think is the reason Foo calls this section "Boxes." Remember that this is a discussion, so keep your comments relatively short.

(2) Gerald: hello?

(3) Hal: hello Gerald

(4) Anne: I think she feels like she lives in a box, apart from the world around her.

(5) Charlene: Hi. I think that it either had to do with her neighbor thinking that she grew up in a box, or that she tried to find her mother's maiden name in boxes.

(6) Karl: Hello everyone

(7) Gerald: I think that she feels that one stereotype about Malaysians are that they are poor.

(8) Hal: Anne where did you get that idea?

(9) Yoshi: I agree with you, Anne, but another thing is that she has left her memories in her "old boxes."

(10) Gerald: but she also appears to be searching for herself

(11) Gerald: she doesn't know where she belongs

(12) Anne: hal, She just seems so alone and confused.

(13) Yoshi: That's a good point, Gerald. I was going to say that, too.

(14) Karl: I agree with Yoshi, that she has thrown away alot of her past away with those boxes.

(15) Hal: I have to agree that she is searching for herself.

(16) Gerald: anybody understand the line "like bars passing the panther in its cage"?

(17) Gerald: does that mean that she feels that life is passing her by?

(18) Anne: why would a neighbor girl think she grew up in a box in Times square?

(19) Karl: It seems that she is stuck in a everyday monotmous lifestyle.

(20) Charlene: Maybe she feels like she's a caged animal.

(21) Aki: She wants to search herself by looking for a box, but she seems that she already got tired.

(22) Anne: good point Aki

(23) Gerald: but if she feels caged, why would the bars be passing the panther?

(24) Joan: She doesn't know where she belongs, and yet others think she lives in a box.

(25) Yoshi: She means that she cannot get away from her lifestyle, no matter how she wants it.

(26) Joan: Do the bars pass the animal or the animal pass the bars?

(27) Joan: I'm seeing some good discussion in this group. Keep it up.

(28) Hal: bars pass the animal

(29) Charlene: I think it means that what you said, that life is passing her by. It might be like a light passing by which makes the shadow of the bars move instead of her or the panther.

(30) Gerald: good point Cheryl

(31) Yoshi: no, animal pass the bars, people has to try to break through the cage at some point.

(32) Gerald: but Yoshi, in the passage, the line reads "like bars passing the panther ... "

(33) Hal: I think that the writer is really in a depressed state of mind, She feels that her life has reached a standpoint for the time being ...

(34) Anne: she feels like she's outside looking in

(35) Gerald: so has she given up the future?

(36) Yoshi: she means that someday bars passes her, but from what I've read in the passage, she is still in the cage.

(37) Anne: she needs to know her history , to know where to go

(38) Charlene: I can relate to what Hal and Anne said because I often feel that way and when I'm sad or depressed, I know I don't make sense. That's why it's a little hard to understand it.

(39) Karl: I feel that she is stuck inside looking out thru the bars and seeing pass her by. Which also reminds her of her life being at a stand still.

(40) Joan: Lots of good points. Perhaps it is now time to move on to another
           section of the essay and see where she goes with these ideas.
(41) Aki: She is struggling in the kitchen like panther roaming in the cage.
(42) Gerald: so what section next?
(43) Charlene: I was wondering the same thing
(44) Hal: I guess remittance?
(45) Anne: When she says no potatoes, no night shade...... ..no grains with the
           meat, is she comparing her lifestyle with the "traditional" american
           meal?

Several elements are noteworthy in this discussion. First, there is the
well-chosen prompt by Joan (1). Rather than just asking students' general opinion on the story of the section, she instead asked a very focused
question that got them probing into the story's meaning. Joan's request
for short comments also yielded the intended result of a lot of
back-and-forth interaction.

Also noteworthy is the balanced nature of the discussion, with all
seven students participating in the discussion (and everyone but Gerald
and Aki taking between four and seven turns). The interactive and sup-
portive nature of the discussion is evident too, with students responding
well to each other and with several students making efforts to compli-
ment others' points.

Most fascinating are the content of the discussion and the way that
different participants contributed to it. Gerald is friendly and enjoys
working in groups, and it's not surprising that he started off the discussion (2) and took the most turns. Anne is vocal and articulate. Again, it is
not surprising that she put out the first idea, that perhaps the author
"feels like she lives in a box" (4). Soon the students were actively throw-
ing out other ideas and asking each other about them. Yoshi astutely observed that the author has left her memories in her old boxes (10). Gerald
(11, 12) built off of this to bring up the point that the author appears to be
searching for herself, which Yoshi agreed with (13). Then, Gerald asked a
key question, whether anyone understood the line "like bars passing the
panther in the cage" (16), a question he later reraised (23). Yoshi responded to Gerald with perhaps the crucial observation of the discussion, that the author "means she cannot get away from her lifestyle" (25).
Joan then steered the group by focusing on an important issue, whether
the bars are passing the animal or vice versa (26), which led to further

discussion by the group, including another interesting exchange between Gerald and Yoshi (33, 35, 36). Later, when Joan tried to move the discussion to another section (41), Gerald was once again the first to pick up on it (43), and Anne was first again to contribute an idea.

Essentially, the students worked together to dig at the meaning of this passage. Gerald and Yoshi, who were keenly involved in this dialogue, both had had trouble with other classroom environments. Gerald was a very poor student who had been suspended from Bay College for low grades. He complained to me about the lecture system, whereby teachers talked at students without giving them a chance to participate. Yoshi, who was from Japan, had left there a number of years ago and didn't want to go back because he felt Japan's educational system stifled creativity. He was a good student in the United States, but he seldom spoke in classes due to language and cultural barriers. In this particular situation, though Gerald and Yoshi were able to work together to help produce interesting insights into the article.

Two interrelated issues emerge from this exchange: the role of Daedalus in promoting democratization and more equal participation and the role in promoting social construction of knowledge. Before looking at those two issues, I briefly illustrate for comparison's sake a face-to-face discussion that took place later in the semester, when Joan was trying to get the students to analyze Web page design. The dynamics of this discussion were typical of the few face-to-face discussions that occurred in this semester and follow the same IRF pattern (teacher initiation, student response, teacher follow-up) that was observed in Luz's class:

Joan:	What are you finding about these pages? What's good about these pictures? The photographs are nice. What about that one? Should it be used that often? What else is good?
Daisy:	Informative
Joan:	Looking at specific pages, how could they be improved?
Daisy:	The English
Joan:	That's probably always going to be true. This is student work. What else, in terms of page design? How long did it take for that large photograph to come down? Quite a long time. It's too large for a background. When you use a background you should use something smaller. What about readability of that page? Can you read it? Is the color of the text readable?
Daisy:	I don't like it.

Joan: That's another problem with using a color like that. You can read it with one part of the photograph, but you can't read it with other parts. So with this photo, if you go over where the sun is shining, you can't read it at all. The students that put that together didn't take that into account. There's another page, with the names. What order are they in? How can you find which person your looking for? Do they all have navigational buttons at the bottom that make it easy for you to get back and forth within the page? Any other comments that you would like to make about these pages, positive or negative?

In this particular discussion, only one student participated, a White woman from California. She was one of only three or four students who participated in these face-to-face discussions. As seen from this transcript, which is typical, even that participation was very limited.

Equality of Participation

In the whole class face-to-face discussions that took place, I never heard a student from Asia speak up once, even though Asian students constituted the majority of the class. In fact, in the small group face-to-face discussions thast occasionally took place, I noticed the same phenomenon. Either Asian immigrant students formed their own separate groups, or, if they were grouped together with American students, they were virtually silent. The relative silence of Japanese and Chinese students has been well documented in American college life, but it has also been shown to be ameliorated by electronic discussion (Warschauer, 1996). Weibing, a student from China, explained to me her thoughts; her views were similar to those expressed by a number of the Asian students:

> Last semester I took another English class with American students, and we did a lot of talk, but I didn't participate that much, because sometimes I want to say but I don't know how to say. When I talk I'm afraid that I'll make mistakes, so I don't like to talk in front of my class. I don't like that kind of pressure.
>
> In Daedalus, I do participate, I'm not shy about that. Sometime I just double-check before I send it. At least I have time, I can think before I write or when I write I can think, not like the way of talk, you just don't have time to think. In this class we do a lot of [Interchange], and to help you to understand what we read, sometimes we have assignments, so it helps. Because you can get from other students, views or opinions from other students. Like when we read those textbooks, that essay is hard to read, I mean it's hard to understand so when we talk, I mean when we write, it helps to understand and get more. I like to sit there and write the opinion, not just talk, because I think that is easier for me to participate. I'm not afraid that I will make mistakes when I talk, that's the reason so I like this class.

> I know American students like to participate, they like to ask questions, answer questions, but not for Chinese students, because we were trained differently, we were trained to listen, just listen.

The American students also recognized the benefit of greater participation. Anne, who was one of the most vocal students in the class in face-to-face discussion, had this to say about Interchange:

> I like the Interchanges, when we like talk to each other over computer. I think that's kind of neat, 'cause I think that some opinions or people might be too shy to actually talk if we were all just talking as a class.

The democratic nature of the online discussions was clearly an important feature of Joan's class. Though Luz's and Kapili's classes also included shy students who were reticent in face-to-face discussion, only Joan's class contained a combination of native and nonnative speakers. In her class, face-to-face discussion left fully two thirds of the students effectively shut out from participating. In a discipline such as writing, which is based so much on finding one's voice, this situation is far from ideal. It perhaps explains in part why relatively few immigrant and international students from Asia choose careers in the social sciences and humanities, deciding instead to pursue majors in science, engineering, and accounting where fewer demands are put on their English. Yet the Interchange sessions in Joan's class, such as the one transcribed here, show that the nonnative speakers had a lot to contribute to the class when given the opportunity to participate in a way more comfortable to them. Using computer-assisted discussion, Joan was able to turn the cultural and linguistic diversity of the students in the class from a potential dividing point into a real strength.

Social Construction of Knowledge

Equally or more important to the democratization of the discussion is the content. What's important is not only that students are able to converse but that they work together to say something meaningful.

The Daedalus discussion presented previously took place at about the same time as a whole class discussion on what metaphors and similes were. That face-to-face discussion was fairly rote, with Joan asking for general definitions and a couple of outspoken students supplying them. Joan then wrote the definitions on the board. The Daedalus discussion appeared to be a much more powerful process to help students think about what metaphors are and socially construct an understanding of how they were used to make the authors' points. DiMatteo (1990) explained how networked communication helps contribute to a new understanding of how text interpretation takes place in the writing class:

> A viable theory of learning must account for several features of the synchronous writing classroom. My students, divided into groups of talk-writers, face the otherness of language directly. No longer working in just a medium of self-expression, they project a self whose power resides not in separation from others but in an ability to collaborate with them. This empowerment of the individual within an enabling group demands a reorientation of thinking about the conventional definitions of the writer and his or her audience. The group unit, emerging from the erasure of the isolated self, must write to converse, a collective activity. The writing of such interactive selves requires a different evaluation by the teacher who now must consider the work for its effectiveness as a vehicle of group discovery. How well students integrate themselves within a polyscripted group, not how well they stand out, becomes the focus. (p. 77)

Shortly after this discussion, students wrote their own autobiographical essays. Some essays included thoughtful discussion of how students had grown and changed due to events in their lives. Yoshi, for example, wrote a lengthy essay called "A Turning Point of My Life," which focused on his coming to the United States as a high school student. He noted that "Learning English and being educated in America are different aspects" and then discussed the many challenges he faced as a young Japanese in a new culture. The essay ended as follows:

> In conclusion, I think that the whole idea of my life is learning, but not studying. I happened to learn to look for my own ideas and I learned to be independent, always rely on my action and thoughts. I feel sorry for my parents to tell that studying English was not a big deal, but learning about life and changing myself through ideas is the most important. I had learned many things through life in Hawaii, and I had much profit out of it. Being independent is not easy, as I see so many adult living in Japan not independent. I still do not think that I can do everything by myself; therefore, I would like to search for more about "self."

Although the grammar is not polished, the ideas are interesting: Yoshi put forth his own understanding of some of the differences between Japanese and American culture—not regarding aspects such as food and clothing but rather the way people think and live—and how these differences have affected his life.

Other essays were straightforward accounts of personal experiences. For example, Gerald wrote an uninspired report of a cross-country trip; the flavor of his essay is well-captured in its final two paragraphs:

The rest of the drive got to be pretty boring. We no longer saw the ocean and much of the land was just plain flat and boring. We did, however, stop at the Grand Canyon in Flagstaff, Arizona, where both of us were in awe as we saw it for the first time. It was an awesome sight, and pictures just can't reveal the beauty and power of it. We also made stops in Fort Worth, Texas and New Orleans, Louisiana.

    I'm really thankful that my sister decided to drive from Seattle to St. Petersburg and I'm also glad that I got to accompany her. Her decision to drive cross-country was a decision that took courage and I know that I would never have gotten to see all those things if it were not for the independence of her.

The essay is mechanically correct at the sentence level and is reasonably coherent and organized, but there is little else to say for it. Unlike Yoshi, Gerald did not dig beyond the surface level to discuss, metaphorically or otherwise, the broader meaning of the events he described.

The range of essays written by students made it difficult to draw any direct connections between the Daedalus discussions and the subsequent writing. It would be nice to think that the collaborative interpretive discussion that took place over Daedalus encouraged students to be more reflective in their writing, yet there is insufficient evidence that this was the case. It could also be the case that students who wrote more reflective papers, such as Yoshi, would have done so anyway.

SERVICE LEARNING PROJECTS

The first half of the semester was mostly filled with Daedalus discussion and the writing of two traditional essays, one autobiographical and one biographical. Following completion of these two essays, the writing assignments and overall class organization changed dramatically.

    Assignment three was a service learning publication based on authentic writing for a community organization. A number of different models have been put forward for implementing service learning in the composition class (for an overview, see Heilker, 1997). These models include having students write narratives about their community service experience (e.g., "my experience at a homeless shelter") or incorporate aspects of their service into research papers (e.g., "homelessness in Hawai'i"). Joan chose a third model, which involves having students complete a writing assignment needed by a community organization.

    Joan presented to the students a list of organizations that needed assistance with writing and producing documents. The list included community agencies such as Leahi Hospital (which requested a newsletter), the

Honolulu Alzheimer's Clinic (a Web site), and the Waikiki Lifelong Learning Center (a newspaper article), and campus organizations such as the Hawai'i Writing Project (a Web site), the Hawai'i Arts Council (a brochure), the Writing Across the Curriculum office (a Web site), and the Service Learning Center (a Web site). She then presented this list to the class, together with the number of students each agency required, and allowed students to select the organization they wanted to work with. After selecting their particular organization, students had to contact its representatives in order to learn more of the details of their writing assignment and had to work together with those representatives through the completion of the assignment.

Just as the writing assignment changed, so did the class organization. Once students had completed their biographical essays and got fully involved in their service learning projects, Joan stopped posting messages on Daedalus, and students no longer interacted on Interchange. Class time was occasionally used for small-group or class discussion of projects, but most classes were not structured at all. Rather, students found their groupmates and worked at their own pace on their projects.

This mode of work continued throughout the rest of the semester, both on the third assignment and the fourth one. The fourth assignment, although not formally deemed service learning, was somewhat similar in structure and goals to the third one. Students worked in groups to create Web pages that would be put on Bay College's server. They were told to choose topics that they were personally interested in and that filled gaps in the Bay College Web site. Topics chosen by student groups included a review of local restaurants, a description of "local grinds" (i.e., foods popular in Hawai'i), volcanoes in Hawai'i, water sports at nearby Diamond Head beach, the local Diamond Head Theater, and the neighborhood Koko Head Fire Station.

This second half of the semester thus differed in several ways from a traditional English class. Students were writing not for the teacher but according to the demands and needs of service organizations. They were not writing essays but were authoring multimedia documents that included varying amounts of text. They organized their time in class according to the collective work they were carrying out on projects rather than to the demands of some preordained structure supplied by the teacher, and they were making connections not only with each other but with outside agencies on campus and in the community. I now explore in more depth the four main themes: (1) real-world purpose; (2) different genres, different media; (3) decentered classroom; and (4) connection to the community.

Real-World Purpose

The main motivation for service learning among many composition teachers, including Joan, is the necessity to provide real-world writing opportunities. The necessity for more real-world writing was well-stated by Heilker (1997):

> Composition students have suffered for too long in courses and classrooms that are palpably *unreal* rhetorical situations. Their audiences are not real audiences; their purposes not real purposes. In most cases, students are writing to the teacher, to an audience of one, who is required and paid to read the text at hand, who is almost always both a better writer *and* more knowledgeable about the subject matter than the writers, and who is reading primarily to find error and grade the formal attributes of the text. Sometimes students are instructed to write to their classmates as their audience, a group homogenous in strange, manufactured ways, and who almost never get a chance to actually read the *finished* versions of the texts supposedly intended for them. And sometimes students are asked to work within completely hypothetical scenarios and to simulate the kinds of writing they might need to compose outside of the composition class, whether in other courses in the university or "out there in the real world." In this case, a student writer needs to *imagine* an entire rhetorical world, to conjure up an appropriate audience, subject matter, and *ethos* out of thin air. In addition to these unreal audiences, students are almost always writing with an ultimately unreal rhetorical purpose, seeking not to persuade or inform or entertain but to complete an assignment in a required course. Given these conditions, it seems little wonder that so many students are convinced that writing has nothing to do with the "real world." They desperately need *real* rhetorical situations, real audiences and purposes to work with, real people to become in writing (p. 71, emphases in original).

In the past, Joan had attempted to get around the problem of lack of authentic purpose or audience by having her students submit their work for publication in various campus magazines and journals. However, she eventually turned to service learning as a better alternative:

> I wanted to give the students real world writing experiences that were not necessarily publication experiences. I've done that in the past, but there's a limit to what you can do to getting students published in paper. So I tried to figure out what we could do that would have them doing some writing, and they'd see what it was like also to gather information. Either to use already printed information and combine that into something that they've got, or write it from scratch, but all factual rather than creative. The other thing that they get from that, in addition to what it's like to write for the real world, is to write for a different kind of audience. And they have to figure out who their audience is probably before they start writing, or if they don't then they have to do a massive rewrite to make it fit. And of course it's a totally different kind of audience than writing for the teacher which is what they would have done in the past.

Although giving students a real-world writing experience is certainly an admirable goal in theory, it can be quite complicated to arrange in practice. Do basic writers have the skills needed to offer real service to community organizations? If they have the writing skills, do they have the necessary background knowledge? As Nora Bacon, who pioneered Community Service Writing projects at both Stanford and San Francisco State, pointed out, "Recognizing, even insisting, that texts are embedded in their social contexts, how can we introduce students to a community agency one week and expect them to write in its voice the next?" (Bacon, 1997, p. 47).

Bacon suggested two possible solutions for dealing with this problem: extending students' relationships with the community organizations beyond the limits of the academic quarter or choosing writing tasks that minimize the expert knowledge required about the agency's work. Joan chose the latter solution, opting for writing tasks that seemed relatively simple and self-contained.

Did Joan reach her goal? Did students actually perceive that they were completing a real-world writing task and adjust their writing processes and product accordingly? For the most part, yes.

One excellent example is the work done by Anne, Aki, and Asako in creating a Web site for the Hawai'i Writing Project. Anne is a 31-year-old single mother of two from Alaska. She was returning to school to become a nurse after 14 years of raising two children through housekeeping and odd jobs. Aki and Asako were both from Japan and in their early 20s. Anne and Asako had little previous experience working with computers; Aki had some experience with computers but had never made a Web site.

The group worked extremely hard to build an elaborate site with 12 separate pages. Some pages included material supplied by the Hawai'i Writing Project director (such as the group's newsletter), and other pages were written by Anne, Aki, and Asako based on interviews they conducted and information they gathered. Throughout the entire process, they indicated keen awareness of the image of the Hawai'i Writing Project, the concerns of its staff and participants, and the interests of the readers of the Web site. For example, part of the Web site included profiles of the project's staff and board members. These profiles had been obtained through e-mail interviews. (Aki and Asako explained that it was much easier for them to do interviews via e-mail than face to face because of their limited speaking and listening abilities in English.) I observed the group while they were editing these profiles and putting them on the Web. Some of the issues they dealt with included:

- *Formality.* What level of formality was both appropriate for the Hawaiʻi Writing Project and of interest to the readers?
- *Consistency.* How could they achieve a level of consistency among the individual profiles without straying too far from what individuals had stated in their interviews?
- *Organizational Integrity.* How could they organize and present the information so that it projected a coherent image of the organization overall and the proper relationship between its various constituents?
- *Readability.* How could they edit and present the information so that it was most accessible to the readers?

They worked closely with the director of the Hawaiʻi Writing Project throughout this effort, showing him various drafts of the pages and making changes based on his suggestions. The end project was a sophisticated multipage Web site that included background information on the organization and its leaders, reports on upcoming conferences and events, an online copy of the group's newsletter, and links to affiliated organizations. Anne, Aki, and Asako were tired from the long hours they put in but very pleased to create an authentic site that an organization (a writing organization, no less) would put on the Web. Anne shared her comments with me about the service learning project, comparing it to the first two assignments:

> The first two were pretty typical, biography and autobiography assignment, but as far as all the public service, yeah, I feel that's a great way to go though, I mean you're still learning how to write, but you're learning how to write like in the real world. You know when you go out in the business world or something, it's the same kind of thing, what we've been working on, for me anyway, making the pages and everything. Your audience is broad. You know what I mean. You have a broad audience, just like if you're working a job. You feel more responsibility, than if it was just like a paper about John F. Kennedy or something [laughs]. Where's the responsibility in that? But for me I feel a responsibility to the Hawaiʻi Writing Project, you know, 'cause that's a public service and if what I do doesn't look good then the Hawaiʻi Writing Project doesn't look good. So it's a lot more responsibility than the regular English writing assignment. I think the responsibility of it makes you do even better work. Plus the fact that you're gonna have an audience. If you don't write well and clearly, you're gonna look like a fool, and you don't wanna look like a fool, so you're gonna do the best job you can, right?

Although many other students had similarly positive experiences, some did not. How much attention students devoted to their writing and language seemed to depend on whether they perceived it as a real assignment. For example, Weibing worked together with Charlene on developing a brochure for the Career Placement Center. Like the students working on the Hawaiʻi Writing Project Web Site, she had to take the writing purpose and audience into consideration. "Sandra [the Center Director] explained to me that I had to write things from a students' point of view. So I asked questions and got answers that a student would be interested in." In contrast to the other students, Weibing put much less effort into the project. She didn't work carefully with her partner Charlene or with the Center Director to see that it was well edited. She just wrote her part and passed it on to Charlene to write her own part, format it, and turn it in. When I asked her why she didn't put more effort into it, she explained:

> I didn't think this is a real thing, because when I talked to Sandra and she said some students did a brochure before and we just leave it here and not use it, so that I realized, oh, it's not that important ... I think because she knew that I'm a foreign student she probably didn't want to pressure me. It's like, just do your best, and no matter what kind of things will come out, we'll accept it. We will accept it, but it doesn't mean we'll use it. I don't know if they will use our brochure or not.

Thus, in Weibing's case, her lack of confidence in the authenticity of the task seemed to undermine her motivation to do excellent work.

Different Genres, Different Media

Another of Joan's goals was to expose her students to writing in new genres and in new media. Talking about her previous service learning assignments, she told me with pride:

> And it's different *kinds* of writing too. Last semester one of the students was writing 30-second blurbs, PR blurbs, for the institute of human services. I mean that's a very different kind of writing than writing an essay. And actually so was the Palolo Pride, the newsletter that they write, is very different, the stories they write for that newsletter are very different, in focus in audience, then what they've written before in essay kinds of writing.

She was especially interested in teaching her students how to write for the World Wide Web, based on her view that this would be especially relevant for students' lives. She told me, again with pride, about how one of her earlier Japanese students had barely finished her class when she started earning money right away by making Web pages for business people from Japan.

I indicated earlier that most of the second half of the semester was devoted to group work on projects, with very few class discussions. The discussions that did take place were centered on hypertext and the World Wide Web. In one session, Joan had her students read a piece of hypertext fiction and note carefully, and then discuss, the paths they pursued. In another session (briefly excerpted earlier), students looked at World Wide Web pages created by Joan's previous students and critiqued their form and function. In these discussions, Joan called attention not only to textual matters but to a broad range of issues including graphics, icons, and links.

Students clearly learned a great deal about writing in new media. Most students in the class learned technical skills, such as how to scan photos, place photos or graphics on pages, or find and use various background patterns and images. More important, they learned rhetorical skills, that is, how and why to combine certain elements to make an effective presentation. For example, in the Hawai'i Writing Project group, there was discussion about the background colors that would appear the most professional and would show up well on a variety of browsers, how to divide information among different pages so that it would be most accessible and readable, and the size that would be most appropriate for photos on personal profile pages.

Consideration of design issues seemed to be heightened by the real-world purposes of the writing. Students learned to take audience into account not only in terms of the text but also in the formatting and the graphics. An interesting example was seen in the page for the Alzheimer's Association, made by Wolfgang (a student from Germany). In an early version of the page, Wolfgang put a spinning graphic at the top, but in the final version he removed the graphic. When Joan asked him what happened to it, he replied, "Oh, I sat there looking at that page, thinking about who was going to be reading it, and I could see these old people's eyes going around and around and around. So I decided to take it out."

Yoshi explained to me some things he had in mind while working on the Web page for Diamond Head Theater, which included a lot of graphics interspersed with the text:

> I think it's different because many people will see it, so you can't do any kind of stuff, you gotta make it so anybody can read, easy to read. Like sometimes when I open the book, or when I open one of the Web pages, I don't wanna read, because it's all small letters and dah-dah-dah-dah, the whole page filled up with single spaced-words. Sometimes I don't feel that it's worth reading, so I'm not trying to do that.

For a number of the students, learning how to create in new media was a major benefit of the course. Both Yoshi and Aki, for example, had academic interests in computer graphics and were thrilled with the opportunity to start learning about Web-based design. Anne asked about the software and hardware she would need to start her own home-based Web page design business; she was about to give birth to her third child and thought it would be a great way to make money from home. Several students were amateur photographers; at least three took their own pictures for their Web projects and enjoyed combining their photographic and writing interests.

The focus on the overall design did however have several effects on the production of text itself, which could be considered negative: the portions of text were often smaller than in traditional writing assignments, students' sometimes paid greater attention to graphical elements than to the texts they wrote, and students sometimes used others' texts rather than writing their own. The Diamond Head Theater page, for example, was well designed but didn't have substantial amounts of text for a group project of four people in a writing-intensive class. Joan didn't see this as a particular problem. She felt they had fulfilled their assignment well by going out and interviewing people, gathering information, and boiling it down to exactly what was needed for that kind of page:

> This kind of page doesn't have to be—in fact I think it's better if it isn't very verbal, because nobody's gonna read it anyway. You know you go to a page like that to find little snippets of information, not to sit down to read the whole page.

The Web site for the Bay College Service Learning Center created by Don, John, and Sung Hae, had problems associated with its content. Two of the three students had extensive computer experience, and they decided to make a very fancy site involving frames and Java scripting. The site was impressive and contained a lot of information. However, partly due to their rush to complete the graphical work on the project, parts of the page were poorly edited and lacked basic required information. After I pointed out some of the problems, the students did further editing.

Another Web site, created by Don, John, and Meilu about volcanoes in Hawai'i, contained virtually no original text at all but rather had passages that had been copied verbatim from books. Joan told me that this was a problem and that the students should have written their own passages, even if they were summarized from the same books. However, she was proud of this group for finding and using a very original and appropriate background image for the page. For Joan, writing the text was only one aspect of Web page authoring, and the other aspects were also important.

Both the advantages and disadvantages of writing in different genres and media are seen in the work of Patsy. A 42-year-old working mother, Patsy had little experience with computers when the semester started. Even by the middle of the semester, she was still struggling with opening folders and finding files. Patsy, who was majoring in art, worked by herself to make a brochure for the Hawaiian Arts Council. The brochure was an attractive three-fold page with pictures of art pieces and descriptions that Patsy wrote. The text passages were fairly short, but they were well written. Patsy was able to finish writing the copy early and had worked out issues of basic design, but then she spent several weeks working with the software to try to place the pictures correctly. A number of problems arose due to the limited memory on the computers and the large size of her file, which included numerous color photos. Patsy was assisted by Gerald, and both learned a good deal about desktop publishing. Eventually, the brochure turned out beautifully, and the Arts Council printed it. Patsy was beaming with pride to have produced a real work of writing and design that was going to be used for a public purpose. The project, however, took so much time that Patsy had little time to work on her fourth project, a review of local restaurants. Patsy worked together with another student who was from China. Patsy's passages were again well written, but she did not have the time to work together with the other student to combine their work in a coherent, well-written page.

At the end of the semester, Patsy was satisfied with what she had learned in the class. As an art major, she felt the work that she had done in producing the brochure was quite valuable to her. She also was quite happy with everything she had learned about computers; she often bragged to me about how much better she was doing with computers at the retail store where she worked in the afternoons. However, at the end of the class, she also said that

> We didn't really do a lot of writing.... I don't feel like I really wrote a lot except for the two papers [autobiography and biography], and those two papers were ones we didn't really have a lot of feedback on.... Those other two projects we spent a lot more time on, but I hardly did any writing on it. It was more trying to move stuff around and find stuff.

Patsy's situation was more extreme than some of the others in that she had spent a great deal of time trying to format the brochure precisely for the Arts Council. A number of other students also felt that they did not write as much as might be expected in a writing-intensive class, and although this may have been due in part to the particular standards of the teacher (number of assignments, etc.), it was undoubtedly influenced by the fact that they spent a good deal of time learning about working with other media such as graphics.

Joan recognized this contradiction. She told me once that there should really be a separate document design class offered by the college, but there wasn't such a class, and even if there were, "students wouldn't take it anyway." Instead, she did the best she could to incorporate document design within her English 215 class, and students appreciated it and felt it was relevant to their careers. As Wolfgang, the German student, told me:

> What I like about this class is that she seems to keep really updated. I mean not too much into her agenda that she has been teaching forever, and you know she's really flexible. She adjusts her classes to what's up, the Internet thing and the Web page thing, she's flexible with that. I'm glad that I can learn about the Web, like making a Web page, in my English writing intensive class, so I I'm not stuck with some kind of a literature stuff which I'm not interested in ... I want to do my MBA in marketing. Especially for marketing the Internet is gonna be important in the future, I'm positive, so it's a good start.

Decentered Organization

New ways of writing were reflected in new forms of class organization. As mentioned before, the second half of the semester was almost entirely devoted to group project work, with only an occasional session devoted to related discussions such as critiquing Web pages. By the last few weeks, students came in and were given no instructions whatsoever. They knew they were supposed to work on their projects and proceeded to do so. On a typical day, one group was be back at the scanner working on images, another group was be surfing the Web for information, another group was working together to transcribe interviews, and a couple of students were trying to figure out how to format brochures.

Learning by Doing.   Students in Joan's class learned through doing. Joan handled the contradiction between teaching writing and teaching technology by hardly teaching technology at all. She just put students in situations in which they needed to learn technology and provided resources—computers, programs, and peers—to help them learn. Her just in time approach to teaching technology—with students learning just what they needed when they needed it—corresponded to the same just-in-time methods becoming prevalent in industry (as discussed in chapter 1; see Castells, 1993).[2]

This approach seemed to work well. Students who were just beginning to work with computers were able to learn from their classmates. Patsy often sought help from Gerald, Anne, and others. Students at more advanced levels learned from experimentation or consulting with friends. Wolfgang had never made Web pages before but taught himself quite a bit about many as-

---

[2]This is an example of a more general convergence of business and pedagogical practices as noted by the New London Group (1996) and Lemke (in press).

pects, including image scanning, editing, and page design. Don and John, who had some basic knowledge of the Web, worked hard to develop more advanced skills, such as making and using frames.

Yoshi explained how learning by doing suited him:

> I learn the whole thing as one, many things as one whole application.... Before I took this class, I didn't know that much, I couldn't use Adobe Photoshop, but I've been working hard for the English class, so that I could edit some of the stuff on the photos I took. For example, there was a lady in the way in one photo, so I could actually erase her. I got pictures from the Internet and shareware too.
>
> She didn't teach any of these things, I just learned from the experience. Learning is like, for me, learning is like, learning and doing is occurring at the same time. You actually use and learn at the same time. Before I didn't have any chance to use, that's why I didn't know how to use such stuff or to make a home page.

Cooperative Relationships.   Another positive element was the cooperative relationships that formed among students. Students contributed their various skills and taught each other, both within and across groups. Gerald, a 26-year-old local student (third-generation Japanese) who held two part-time jobs bussing tables and stocking shelves, had been in and out of community college for 8 years, almost always doing poorly. He was even put on probation and suspended for bad grades. He criticized some of his earlier classes:

> I really don't like classes where you go in and the teacher just reads straight from the book. I hate those classes. That was my chem class. That's really what I hate, I really don't like. That's not really teaching, I mean you can just go home, read it, don't have to come back to class.

Yet he thrived in this class, participating actively and with great interest. Almost every day in the second half of the semester he was helping other students, especially with graphic work. He showed them how to scan photos, edit them, place them on pages, and do other kinds of page formatting. He also put a great deal of time and effort into his own projects, working with others to produce a brochure that was used by a local hospital and a Web site about a local fire station. By the end of the semester, he didn't have the attitude of a perpetual community college failure. Rather, he talked optimistically with me about pursuing further studies in education or maybe even educational technology.

Downtime.   The collaborative, project-oriented structure of the class had its down sides as well. With students finishing projects at different times and with the amount of computer equipment limited (e.g., only one scanner, only a few copies of certain programs), students sometimes had little to do while waiting for either their group partners or equipment to become available. Students were also given a lot of leeway in how much work to take on. Some groups, such as the Hawai'i Writing Project group, overdid it with extremely ambitious projects, but other groups chose more minimal tasks and seemed to learn less. Several students told me that they might have gotten more out of the class if it had been more demanding.

Joan's role in class was principally that of a facilitator. She devoted time to getting students started with projects and helping them with problems that arose, but otherwise she stood aside. She did not, for example, formally critique the drafts of their papers or projects, nor did she grade or otherwise respond to their final projects. Students knew how they stood in the class only when they received their final mark. She did give students informal feedback on their work in progress on many occasions, and students benefited from that. However the kind of intense student–teacher relationship that existed in the Luz's, Kapili's, or Mary's class—where students knew they were expected to do top-notch writing and that the teacher would work with them carefully until they achieved it—was missing.

Joan explained to me that her attitude toward commenting on students' drafts and final papers was determined partly by her philosophy and partly by practical matters at her institution. As for her philosophy, she felt that students learned best by doing and writing, not by responding to teacher correction, and she was thus wary of spending much time and effort in this direction. As for practical matters, with the normal teaching load at this college of five 3-credit courses per semester, she had to prioritize her efforts. The great amount of time she spent creating learning opportunities for her students (by engaging in efforts such as planning her courses and setting up service learning opportunities) meant that she had to cut back somewhere, and she chose to cut back on teacher response. As she explained:

> All of the research indicates that, and my own experience indicates that, the kinds of comments and the kinds of grades that you give to students on essays don't improve the final product anyway, and there's not time for it, so I don't do it. It's just one of those things that I've had to cut back. You can make all kinds of comments about comma splices in this particular essay, but it doesn't change anything that the student writes in printed essays. But instead what I think improves their writing is the online stuff that they do, the Interchanges. They're using the writing for communicative reason, that's what improves their writing. The accuracy comes in their desire to be accurate. And having, also having something that's interesting to them to talk about, and that usually happens in the things that they write. And more and more of us, still not large numbers, are going that route.

To me this is one more example of the impact of social context on learning and teaching. The support within the college toward teaching with technology, service learning, and writing across the curriculum provides important backing for Joan to teach in new and creative ways, but the broader organization of the state of Hawai'i (and U.S.) educational system—which mandates a large teaching load for community college professors—meant that she had to cut corners somewhere in order to fulfill her teaching goals. Like Mary, Luz, and Kapili, Joan made choices within the constraints of her situation and guided by her own teaching beliefs, beliefs that in her case prioritize providing students a communicative writing environment rather than giving intense individual feedback.

Connection to the Community

At the heart of service learning is the idea of connecting the school to the community. The purpose of this is not only to provide authentic writing experiences, but also to make students "more curious and motivated to learn," strengthen students' "ethic of social and civic responsibility," teach students to "respect other cultures more," and help students "realize that their lives can make a difference" (from a statement by 77 U.S. national and regional organizations, reported in Kendall, 1977, pp. 38–39).

Connecting to the community is often portrayed as privileged students descending from the ivory tower. However, this was hardly the case in Joan's class, where none of the students was privileged and most lived in working-class minority neighborhoods. For Joan's students, connecting to the community sometimes meant the opposite: building from their own connections they already had to the community and making those connections relevant in their college writing. For example, for the final project Gerald made a Web site about the Kaimuki Fire Station, where a friend of his worked as a fire fighter. Gerald spent several afternoons there gathering information, taking pictures, and checking copy with his friend. For his service learning project, he also chose a community agency, the Leahi hospital. He didn't know anybody at the hospital before he started, but he related well to the workers, spent many afternoons there, and seemed to relish the task.

Connecting to the community took on another meaning for the immigrant students in the class, many of whom lacked contacts and information about life in Hawai'i. Weibing told me that she chose to write the brochure for the Career Placement Center because she wanted to find more information about graduation requirements and career placement. She said that she didn't even know about the center before engaging in the service learning project but ended up getting very helpful information from them (although as mentioned previously, this interest did not appear to translate into a highly motivating writing assignment).

For some students, the connection to their organization was quite vague, especially for those working with some of the campus agencies. Liang Li, a Chinese student, seemed nonplused to be working on behalf of the Writing Across the Curriculum office. She told me that the assignment seemed less like real service than her service learning assignment in a previous class (also taught by Joan) when she tutored elementary school students:

> For this one, I actually don't know what is the purpose for the service learning. The last time I go to be a tutor in the elementary school, but this time, I think it's the same as doing project in the class, I don't know what's the difference between service learning and other projects.

Critical Awareness.   In spite of the successful experiences of a number of the students in making a personal connection to community and campus organizations, these connections fell short of the goals put forth by some proponents of experiential learning. For example, David Thornton Moore (1990) commented that "Experiential learning offers as good an opportunity as we have in higher education to create a critical pedagogy, a form of discourse in which teachers and students conduct an unfettered investigation of social institutions, power, relations and value commitments" (p. 281). Henry Giroux (1983) put it this way:

> If citizenship education is to be emancipatory, it must begin with the assumption that its major aim is not "to fit" students into existing society; instead, its primary purpose must be to stimulate their passions, imaginations, and intellects so that they will be moved to challenge the social, political, and economic forces that weigh so heavily upon their lives. (p. 201)

Thus, if a commonly expressed goal of many service learning proponents is to help students gain a deeper understanding and critique of underlying social relations why hadn't Joan selected a broader array of organizations, included those more closely tied to issues related to class, poverty, gender, or ethnicity?

Joan explained to me that neither political awareness, nor even charity, were her primary goals for this assignment:

> [Fostering social or political awareness] is the underlying motive behind service learning in general, but my motive for this class is to provide them a real-world writing assignment, it's not to help the agency. That's secondary. It's to provide a real-world

writing assignment for them apart from the canned kinds of assignments that they've used in the past that really aren't legitimate kinds of writing assignments. You never set out to write a descriptive essay, for example. You don't even set out to write an interview, you only do an interview because there's a reason for doing the interview. There are all kinds of assignments like that, that are not legitimate in terms of motivation, the reason behind them. That was *my* reason for doing this assignment.... So I selected all of the organizations that had indicated they needed brochures or newsletters or something written. Then in addition I made contacts with the people here at Bay College that I knew had those kinds of needs.

Joan seemed successful in her goal: Many students had experienced a real-world writing need and had responded accordingly. They appeared to pay closer attention to their texts (and their design) to try to create a useful product for their service learning organization. This attention forced them to think about audience in ways that they had not necessarily done before. However, comparing to Kapili's class, Joan's class did not have the same level of student engagement in the process. Perhaps this difference also explains in part why some students didn't feel they got as much out of the class as they might have. In one sense the comparison is unfair: inspiring a passionate social purpose in a heterogeneous class of many nationalities is different than doing so in a class of Native Hawaiian students whose very act of studying a language can be seen as an act of linguistic and cultural resistance. Nevertheless, other educators have put forward approaches for critically involving culturally and linguistically diverse students and such an approach lends itself well to service learning.[3]

There are of course numerous organizational constraints against such an approach. Cultivating relations with community organizations that need authentic writing assignments could take an enormous amount of time on the part of both teacher and students. In a situation in which a teacher has a 15-credit work load and students are almost all working part-time jobs, developing those relations is quite difficult to carry out. Students must not only form relations with organizations but must also develop the expertise necessary to carry out meaningful writing. For this reason, some universities are experimenting with two-quarter or two-semester courses in which students intern with an organization one term and begin to write for it the second (Bacon, 1997).

---

[3]For critical approaches to working with ESL students, see Auerbach (1995); with minority students, see Cummins (1989). For the relation between critical approaches and new technologies, see Cummins and Sayers (1995). For critical approaches of using service learning, see Bacon (1997), Herzberg (1997), and Moore (1990).

WRITING FOR THE FUTURE

In conclusion, Joan has gone further than any of the other teachers I worked with in trying to provide new and alternative writing experiences for her students. The course emphasized writing that was collaborative and practical, bringing to mind a new conception of literacy as described by Myron Tuman (1992):

> It is only the modern age that has so closely associated the intellectual with literacy, making the writer and the intellectual practically synonymous. In the pre-modern age, no one confused the lowly scribe with philosopher or the statesmen. The literate of the future will be neither the dutiful but unimaginative scribe, nor the powerful but at times heedless intellectual; the computer will support a new literate, someone committed to working with others, indeed, inextricably linked with them, both literally through computer networks and metaphorically through common causes.... Whether such a new self guarantees a better, more just society, as it seems to do, is a matter yet to be considered; what it does guarantee is that all experiences, scientific or literary, not directly connected to our common concerns will be perceived as less important, having less to do with literacy. Online literacy, in other words, will be more practical, less theoretical, and new literates themselves valued to the extent that they are team players, not traditional intellectuals. (p. 123)

Current practices in business, government, and even education seem to confirm Tuman's description of the kinds of practical, collaborative writing that are increasingly valued (Dautermann, 1996; Henderson, 1996; Sims, 1996). As Joan works in a 2-year community college, which serves a vocational as well as an academic purpose, it is perhaps not surprising that she has gone further in promoting practical literacies.

Joan's beliefs center on helping students practice the genres (such as informational Web pages), reporting skills (such as conducting and editing interviews), and writing experiences (such as communicating to a real audience) that she thinks will benefit them in the future. By combining technology and service learning, she has found a potent formula for implementing her beliefs. As seen in this class, technology is well suited to carry out the types of writing required by service learning; generally organizations desire brochures, Web pages, and other multimedia products, not essays. The question of who we write for—the teacher alone or for an authentic audience—and the medium we write in are thus related. Technology and service learning are a good match for promoting the kinds of writing that will be increasingly demanded by community agencies and businesses in the 21st century.

However, the kinds of multimedia informational writing Joan's students engaged in seemed at odds with the standard print essay favored in many

English classrooms. The question can legitimately be raised as to whether it should be the duty of colleges, even community colleges, to teach students the types of writing valued in the business world rather than academic genres. In this class, Joan tried to have it both ways, by assigning two traditional essays in the beginning of the semester and two informational multimedia projects at the end. This seemed to me a nice metaphor for the kind of uneasy truce that may exist between the literacy of the page and the literacy of the screen in the late age of print.

6

Conclusion: Striving Toward Multiliteracies

ॐ•ॐ

Clearly, issues of culture, education, and technology merge at the crossroads of the twenty-first century. Do we plan for the common good by enabling all students to navigate difference, develop intellectually and academically, and gain expertise in employing technology for enhancing democratic participation, or do we curtail the development of these social, intellectual, and technological skills in order to restrict potential challenges to the current distribution of power and resources in our society.
—Jim Cummins and Dennis Sayers (1995, p. 176)

At a recent conference on computers and writing, an audience member asked if there was any proof that computer-based teaching is superior to traditional teaching in getting students to improve their writing. Peg Syverson, Associate Director of the Computer Writing and Research Labs at the University of Texas, Austin, replied:

> Can I prove that online writing courses improve students' ability to write traditional essays? No, I can't. I also can't prove that driver's ed courses improve students' equestrian ability.... What we're doing is preparing students for the kinds of writing they need in the future.

When I first heard Syverson's answer, it struck a responsive chord. In the four classes reported in this book, a major benefit of teaching with multimedia networked computers was to introduce students to new types of reading and writing practices that they couldn't get otherwise.

After further reflection, though, I realized applying Syverson's comment to the classes in this study would be a bit too facile. The students in these four classes were all coping to varying degrees with learning both print and electronic literacies; their academic careers, job opportunities, and personal lives depended on developing interpretive and communicative ability in a variety of media. Nor were the teachers in any of these classes willing to forsake issues of traditional literacies in favor of new ones. Thus, while there are important distinctions between electronic and print literacies—distinctions discussed later in the chapter—for students in these classes these literacies intermingled as part of a broader set of academic literacies.

In analyzing the experiences of these classes, it seems more useful to use the concept of *multiliteracies*, a term put forth by a group of specialists in education, critical literacy, and discourse analysis (New London Group, 1996). This approach stresses the importance of understanding the nature of communication in a variety of media, both older and newer. It also stresses the importance of taking into account the culturally and linguistically appropriate ways of communicating in an increasingly global world. The term *multiliteracies* encompasses not only a variety of media but also a variety of forms, dialects, genres, and, in some cases, languages. As the authors explain:

> Literacy pedagogy has traditionally meant teaching and learning to read and write in page-bound, official, standard forms of the national language.... We attempt to broaden this understanding of literacy and literacy teaching and learning to include negotiating a multiplicity of discourses ... We want to extend the idea and scope of literacy pedagogy to account for the context of our culturally and linguistically diverse and increasingly globalized societies, for the multifarious cultures that interrelate and the plurality of texts that circulate. Second we argue that literacy pedagogy now must account for the burgeoning variety of text forms associated with information and multimedia technologies. This includes understanding and competent control of representational forms that are becoming increasingly significant in the overall communications environment, such as visual images and their relationship to the written word-for instance, visual design in desktop publishing or the interface of visual and linguistic meaning in multimedia. Indeed, this second point relates closely back to the first; the proliferation of communications channels and media supports and extends cultural and subcultural diversity. (p. 60)

This link between cultural–linguistic pluralism and media diversity seems especially important for the students in this study, almost all of whom were simultaneously learning to communicate in new languages and dialects as well as in new media. From the New London Group's perspective, this link is important for all students, in that the very nature of online networking means that students will encounter new cultures and communication patterns more than ever before.

With this perspective in mind, I revisit the three issues introduced in chapter 1 of this volume: the nature of electronic literacies, educational practices and reform, and the relation of electronic literacies to (in)equality.

THE NATURE OF ELECTRONIC LITERACIES

The two main new technologies that students used in these classes were computer-mediated communication and hypertext. Both technologies have been purported to have either good or bad effects on literacy development, from different points of view. For the optimist, computer-mediated communication "helps develop a sense of audience" in writing (Susser, 1992, p. 69), "encourages critical awareness about how communication" occurs (DiMatteo, 1991, p. 9), and enhances students' understanding of writing as a social and collaborative act (Barker & Kemp, 1990). Critics worry that electronic communication may foment talk-show type "chat" rather than the "sustained engagement" with written language necessary for knowing the world (Truman, 1996, n.p.).

The controversy over hypertext and the World Wide Web is even more pronounced. Searching through and reading hypertextual information is seen to foster the cognitive flexibility necessary for interpreting information and constructing knowledge from a broad range of sources (Burbules & Callister, 1996; Spiro, Feltovich, Jacobson, & Coulson, 1991); however, critics say the Web drowns students in a sea of unreliable information and encourage mindless net-surfing, equivalent to television channel-surfing (Oppenheimer, 1997).

With these positions as a background, what then were the experiences of the students in using these technologies for reading and writing?

Computer-Mediated Communication

Computer-mediated communication—which was used for teacher-student exchange, long-distance e-mail partnerships, and synchronous classroom discussion—appeared to benefit students in several ways. First, students achieved more written fluency through the greater practice of computer-based writing; this was especially important for the students who were writing in a second language or who were unfamiliar with keyboarding. Students also benefited from focusing on linguistic structures that written communication provided.

Perhaps more importantly, though, I believe that it provided students important additional opportunities for expression and reflection. In Kapili's class, computer-assisted discussion provided a chance to experience using Hawaiian for real communication, rather than for classroom tasks. In Luz's and Joan's class, students were able to collectively reflect on the nature of particular writings and of academic discourse; the results seemed similar to those found in another class by Colomb and Simutis (1996, p. 204): "Students encountered the disciplinary demands of academic writing less as a purely external imposition than as an internal dynamic of a developing 'proto-disciplinary' community of inquiry" (p. 204). At the same time, they learned important lessons about electronic cross-cultural communication, either across continents (as in the case of Zhong), or across classrooms. In these situations they could compare attitudes toward topics such as plagiarism, stereotypes, and Hawaiian life and culture. In Luz's class, e-mail provided students increased opportunity to raise issues and concerns with the teacher and thus further explore both their own writings as well as more general issues of academic discourse.

The electronic medium does have its own characteristics, and the use of electronic communication seemed most effective when these charactersitics were taken into account. In the beginning of the semester, Luz encouraged long comments on Daedalus to attempt to facilitate critical thinking. The actual result though was to discourage interaction, as students were so busy writing that they had little time to read what others had said. Joan, in contrast, encouraged short comments (as are found naturally in most synchronous forums), and though this could potentially be seen as "chatty," it actually served to get the students working together to collectively probe the meaning of texts.

When the special characteristics of the medium were altogether ignored, the results seemed least benificial, and the practice was most strongly resisted by the students. When Mary, for example, insisting on students' submitting their e-mail keypal letters for prior correction—as if they were polished essays rather than a means of informal inquiry—students became disheartened and discouraged. Later, when Mary allowed students the opportunity for more natural communication, their attitudes improved greatly.

Hypertext Reading

Hypertext reading is quite different in nature than reading in a print medium. As Tuman explained:

> The online text is nothing but a database out of which new readers construct paths to meet their specific needs-it is akin to a board game, a place where many individual pieces are connected by the rules for play. Meanwhile the author of online text is nothing but the source ... responsible for establishing and maintaining the rules for operating that database. There is no longer any basis for the central notion of print literacy, that literate exchange involves the comprehension of the unity of knowledge or vision represented by structures in either the distant author or the present (and seemingly stable) text. (p. 64)

However, as noted by many (e.g., Bolter, 1991; Landow, 1992; Slatin, 1990a), the lessening of importance of the author is balanced by an increased importance given to the reader. Reading the Web means intelligently finding, evaluating, and making uses of a great variety of sources of information.

Reading the Web was explicitly taught to some degree in all the classes. Students learned various navigation strategies, such as selecting among various search engines, refining searches using Boolean operators or other special syntax, skimming through the results of a search in order to evaluate the best possibilities for follow-up, and choosing navigation strategies within and across sites. They also worked together to analyze their own navigation paths and to evaluate particular Web pages and design features critically.

Once again, the medium worked best when the natural strengths of the environment were exploited rather than resisted. A main strength of the Web is that it allows individuals to pursue their own interests. Thus, when Joan directed students to a somewhat confusing literary hypertext of her own choosing or when Mary had students go directly to a grammar quiz, students appeared disinterested and disoriented. Yet when allowed to pursue topics of their own interest, they did so with great rigor and attention.

Web reading and print reading are clearly different processes—not principally because of the difference in psycholinguistic processes of reading from a screen rather than on paper (although those exist) but more because of the roles the Web and the book are playing in society and the way information is stored and accessed in these media. Students in these classes, who had little prior experience with the Web, gained a valuable type of electronic literacy that they will likely need in the future. Nevertheless, the overlapping relation between print and electronic literacy was also evident. Academic writing, as currently constructed, frequently relies on print documents for references and citations more than on Internet citations, but academic writers can make extensive use of the Web for background material, current articles and essays, and information on key individuals and events. I observed students immediately putting into practice what they learned about the Web for their own academic research, for example, by seeking background information on topics they were writing about. Alhough insufficient time was spent on developing Web-based searching skills, especially in the area of critical interpretation, the time that was spent seemed very well used.

Hypertext Writing

When language and composition teachers first gained access to Web servers, they saw in the Web a vehicle for student publication (see examples in Warschauer, 1995b). The purported goal was to allow students the opportunity to share their papers with distant readers. But the Web is not just a distribution vehicle; it is a communications medium in its own right. What people receive on the other end are not papers at all but on-screen presentations. This format encourages writers to attempt to achieve a rhetorical presentation that is appropriate to the medium, and especially one that includes graphics.

Skeptics such as Birkerts (1994) stress that tinkering with traditional approaches to writing leads to erosion of language and loss of deep thinking, yet others defend instruction of new rhetorical means as necessary to meet the emerging standards of business, academia, and government. Lanham (1993) made a convincing case that there is a foregrounding of images over words occurring in virtually all aspects of society, especially business and government. Faigley (1977), based in part on his research of workplace writing (Faigley & Miller, 1982), projected these trends into academia, suggesting that the academic essay may lose center stage in the next decade and be replaced by multimedia forms. Slatin (1990b) emphasized that what is key about hypertext is not only the inclusion of different media but also the associative structure of hypertext, which radically differs from the linear structure of print text.

The teachers in this study used a variety of approaches to involve their students in writing hypertexts. Mary's class at Miller College wrote straight text essays, which Mary then placed on the Web. Kapili's Hawaiian class began with text essays but then modified them in various ways to try to make them more appropriate for the medium. Luz's class of international graduate students designed personal home pages directly for the Web medium, and Joan's community college class first pasted two print essays onto the Web and then spent much more time creating original Web pages or brochures for community organizations and then additional Web pages for the Bay College Web site.

One key difference thus had to do with *rhetorical structure*. Some of the assignments were linear text essays merely posted on the Web, whereas others were hypermedia documents specifically designed (either from the beginning or as part of the process) for the Web environment. Obviously, if a goal is to teach students about particular ways of expressing meaning in this new medium, then designing documents specifically for the Web medium is necessary. Students who created hypermedia documents for the Web of course spent time on graphical design, but from my own observations (and perspective) this did not appear to be a waste of time. As indicated throughout this volume, this work involved learning both technical and rhetorical skills, ranging from photo editing to evaluating effective ways to combine images and text to communicate a message. If there was a weakness at all to carry out this work, it was that it was done in a rather ad hoc fashion. Both Kapili's students and Joan's students got so involved in their projects that there was little time to analyze rhetorical strategies collectively. Part of this problem stems from the basic structure of college: With learning divided into 3-credit, semester-long classes, it is by nature difficult to carry out and analyze sophisticated projects in a single medium, let alone using a combination of media.

In spite of this weakness, it seemed to me that students learned a great deal, not only about writing the Web but also about reading it. For example, in Joan's class, students who had already completed one Web project were able to evaluate more critically the design features of other Web pages. This is in line with an observation by Faigley (1997):

> For the first time I am devoting a significant part of a writing course to graphic design, and I am discovering that after years of attempting to teach students to analyze images, they learn much more quickly when they create images on their own. Active learners can think reflectively about any human symbolic activity whatever the medium. (p. 40)

However, perhaps even more important than the rhetorical structure in affecting students' learning experience was the sense of purpose they brought to the task of creating texts and hypertexts. In this light, it's interesting to compare the work done by Luz's and Kapili's classes. Luz's students were instructed on making personal home pages. Luz and I spent a fair amount of time assisting them with the software and also helping them evaluate and critique other graduate students' and faculty home pages. Yet even though we ourselves had a purpose in mind—to help students create an academic presence for themselves on the Internet—the students for the most part had little interest in this purpose. They didn't feel that creating a personal home page was particularly relevant to themselves or to society. Although students fulfilled the assignment, they did so cursorily and without any special interest or attention. In contrast, when they found technology to be consistent with their purpose—by, for example, giving them a chance to discuss their confusions about academic discourse—they participated with greater engagement and seemed to get more out of it.[1]

In Kapili's class, students worked throughout the semester to write papers on topics of their own choosing on aspects of Hawaiian culture. Most had a deep interest in their topics for personal, cultural, familial, or spiritual reasons. The students also had a sense that by putting this material on the Web they were making an original and important contribution by sharing their own labor of love with the broader Hawaiian community and at the same time helping establish a foothold for Hawaiian language and culture on the Internet. This feeling of pride motivated them to pay close attention to both the text and the overall design and layout of their pages, fostering an intensive and rewarding learning experience.

---

[1]See Heath (1986, 1992) for discussion of the importance of meeting students' own purposes in writing assignments.

The experiences of Joan's and Mary's students seem to confirm the same phenomenon. Joan attempted to provide an authentic purpose through the use of service learning. The results were mostly positive but depended in large measure on how individual students or groups internalized the service learning goals. In cases where students felt a personal connection and responsibility for their service learning agency, as in the case of Anne's commitment to the Hawai'i Writing Project, the same kind of deep learning experience occurred as in Kapili's class. In situations in which students were unable to feel a connection—for example, for Weibing, who doubted that the Career Placement Center would even use her brochure—the effort, and corresponding results, were minimal.

Finally, in Mary's class, students' sense of purpose seemed to shift somewhat as the semester went on. In the beginning, the overriding purpose presented by the teacher was for students to learn the structure of essays, paragraphs, and sentences. Students responded with resentment and resistance. Later, when students were given more opportunity to creatively explore their own interpretation of culture, both in a video and in their final paper, students engaged more readily and gained more opportunities to develop their rhetorical strategies.

In summary then, it seemed that the key issue was not the shift to new media per se but rather the goals to which this shift was put, a point that has been made by Mryon Tuman (1992):

> Taking the image of television seriously, we should not be too hasty in confusing the power to project an image—clearly a strength of multimedia computing—with the power to imagine, or create, that image in the first place, and, more importantly, the power to connect that image to the realization of actual goals.... Where computers, like television seem to excel is in extending geometrically our ability to transform the world, especially through the playful transformations of simulation. The same computer power that readily allows us to preview how our writing will appear if printed in Times Roman or Helvetica allows us to reshape and recombine the world at large, cutting-and-pasting, as it were, through all human experience, creating realistic graphic representations of any imaginable combination of human experience. But if this power is to be any more constructive than the power to fashion our own television shows by channel-switching via remote control, it must have a direct connection with our acting in the world, our choosing one thing over another, as individuals and, more importantly, in conjunction with others. If online literacy is to rise above the level of the bells and whistles of high-powered Nintendo games, it must be in support of the same collective task of human transformation that has characterized our experience of print literacy. (p.p. 132–133)

Judging from the experiences of the students in these classes, human transformation and the realization of actual goals demand a plurality of literacies. Students must understand how communication varies across media and how different grammars—whether the grammar of text or the grammar of visual design (Kress & van Leeuwen, 1996)—combine to express meaning. They have to learn various types of electronic literacy (such as Web research and computer-mediated collaboration) in support of print literacy (such as writing essays), and they have to learn various types of print literacy (such as scanning books for information) in support of electronic literacies (such as authoring Web pages). They have to learn the types of genres and rhetorical structures that are used in particular media, and they have to learn enough about cultural and dialectical differences to choose the right communication strategies for the particular audiences that they are likely to encounter in a new medium. Most important—and here there is continuity from the practice of print literacy—students need to have a clear and meaningful purpose for the reading and writing activities they undertake.

EDUCATIONAL PRACTICES AND REFORM

If students work best with new media when such learning is connected to the realization of meaningful goals, then what types of pedagogical approaches are necessary to bring about such results? Is there a teaching approach that matches particularly well with uses of new media in the classroom?

The first point worth noting is the well-recognized axiom that a medium does not constitute an approach or method. Technology can be used to serve many different approaches, as was evident in this study. Each teacher molded the use of technology to match her own beliefs about teaching and learning languages and writing. Mary viewed learning how to write as mastering structures, Luz viewed it as becoming familiar with new discourse communities, Joan viewed it as immersion in authentic, communicative writing practice, and Kapili viewed the learning of Hawaiian as a socially and politically significant act involving both meaningful construction of knowledge and consideration of one's relation to the culture and community. Each of these four teachers found ways to use technology to serve a broader agenda.

The question, then, is whether particular uses of technology work better than others. This is difficult to answer in the abstract because there is no single agreed-on standard for good writing or good teaching. Each of the teachers was generally pleased with the results, even though she saw room for improvement. However, Mary's class, particularly in the first half of the semester, seemed to exhibit the greatest gap between pedagogical approach and student expectations and a correspondingly high level of student resistance. This is congruent with results found in a longitudinal workplace study conducted by Soshana Zuboff (1988). Zuboff investigated the way that implementation of new information technologies affected organizational behavior in eight compa-

nies over 5 years. She found that technology served not only to automate but
also to *informate*—to make information and communications available to a
much broader grouping of people—and that once this process had begun companies no longer functioned effectively if they didn't also divest more power to
broader groups of employees. Indeed, the workers themselves demanded it.[2] As
Zuboff summarized, "The informating process sets knowledge and authority on
a collision course" (p. 310).

Similar results were found in a 10-year study conducted by Sandholtz,
Ringstaff, and Dwyer (1997) on uses of computers in five U.S. public schools.
They found that once students got used to working with computers, they began to challenge traditional assumptions about classroom organization.
Teachers who were able to adjust by devolving more power and control to students achieved excellent results. Teachers who had difficulty abandoning traditional teacher-centered methods got frustrated and engendered resistance
from their students.

A similar situation seemed to occur in Mary's class. Once students saw the
potential of the Internet for authentic communication with their classmates
and long-distance partners, they became dissatisfied with using computers for
more drill-like work. Later, when Mary's students were given more control over
their learning, they began to engage in activities with more enthusiasm and motivation. Similarly, the other classes worked well when students were working
on learner-centered projects. This finding is further confirmation of the view
that new technologies match well with more decentralized, learner-centered
pedagogical approaches (Mehlinger, 1996).

Lemke (in press) makes a contrast between what he called a curricular paradigm that currently dominates schools and universities and an interactive
learning paradigm, which is prevalent in libraries and research centers. The latter, he believed, is more suitable to the era of information and post-Fordism,
which he refered to as fast-capitalism:

> The curricular paradigm assumes that someone else will decide what you need to
> know, and will arrange for you to learn it all in a fixed order and on a fixed timetable.
> This is the educational paradigm of industrial capitalism and factory-based mass pro-
> duction. It developed simultaneously with them, in close philosophical concord, feeds
> into their wider networks of employment and careers, and resembles them in its au-
> thoritarianism, top-down planning, rigidity, economies of scale, and general unsuit-
> ability to the new information-based "fast-capitalist" world.

---

[2]One mill worker explained it thus: "If you don't let people grow and develop and make more decisions, it's a waste of human life -a waste of human potential. If you don't use your knowledge and skill, it's
a waste of life. Using the technology to its full potential means using the man [sic] to his full potential"
(Zuboff, 1988, P. 414).

> The interactive paradigm ... assumes that people determine what they need to know based on their participation in activities where such needs arise, and in consultation with knowledgeable specialists; that they learn in the order that suits them, at a comfortable pace, and just in time to make use of what they learn. This is the learning paradigm of the people who created the Internet and cyberspace. It is the paradigm of access to information, rather than imposition of learning. It is the paradigm of how people with power and resources choose to learn. Its end results are generally satisfying to the learner, and usually useful for business or scholarship. (n.p.)

Although the teachers in this study to varying degrees tried to implement an interactive paradigm, full implementation of such a paradigm would necessitate broader changes in how schooling is structured and is thus beyond the scope of any individual teacher. Both Joan and Kapili, for example, often expressed frustration at trying to carry out interesting project-based work within the confines of a 4-month, 3-hour-a-week class.

Finally, an interactive paradigm needn't imply a hands-off teacher. Tuman (1992, 1996) made a good case that sustained teacher–student dialogue ought to be a part of the innovative classroom. In all four of these particular classes, active teacher engagement—whether it was Mary working with students to improve the texts on their Web pages, Joan intervening in Daedalus discussions, Luz corresponding with students about the nature of American academic discourse, or Kapili talking with students about the sociopolitical context of Hawaiian language use—contributed positively to student learning. The electronic medium sometimes provides an effective additional environment for carrying out this kind of teacher–student engagement.

Teachers intervened in a variety of ways, ranging from assisting students with language form to helping them gain critical awareness of the context of their work. As Cummins and Sayers (1995) pointed out, the latter is too often neglected, even in progressive classrooms. If this study is any indication, such critical analysis plays an important role, as revealed in both Kapili's success in getting her students to think more about the context of Hawaiian language use and Luz's success in engaging students in cross-cultural analysis of discourse issues.

The New London Group suggested a pedagogical model that accounts for the need for interactive learning and both types of teacher intervention, focusing on language form and adding a critical perspective, in the multimedia classroom and serves as an alternative to the functional and cultural literacy models presented in the first chapter. Other such models have been put forward (e.g., Bayer, 1990; Wells & Chang-Wells, 1992), but this is one of the first that explicitly addresses issues of new media literacies. The group's "pedagogy of multiliteracies" (p. 82) is based on the concept of *design*. In their approach, learners become familiar with *available designs* (i.e., the grammars and resources of various semiotic systems, including language but also film, photography, and other media), they engage in their own *designing* (i.e. making meaning and constructing knowledge with available designs), and they critically analyze the *redesigned* (i.e. the resources that are reproduced and transformed through the designing process). The pedagogy of multiliteracies is carried out with four features: (1) *situated practice,* immersion in meaningful practices within a community of learners; (2) *overt instruction* active intervention on the part of the teacher to scaffold learner activities; (3) *critical framing,* attention to the historical, social, cultural, political, ideological, and value-centered relations of systems of knowledge and social practice; and (4) *transformed practice,* applying the knowledge gained from previous practice, instruction, and critical reflection to work in other contexts or cultural sites.

This model seems consistent with the best of what occurred in the four classes in this study. When teachers were able to combine situated practice, overt instruction, and critical framing, they were able to create classroom environments in which students were engaged, motivated, and attentive to the language, purpose, and audience of their writing. When any one of these elements became the only goal, at the expense of inclusion of the others, the learning environment seemed to suffer as students' writing became less purposeful, less authentic, or less sophisticated in rhetorical and linguistic features.

Finally, although none of the classes in the study could be said to truly have included transformed practice, such a result can be hard to achieve in a one-semester 3-credit course and might entail broader issues of educational reform. At the very least, it might include total reorganization of a course, with an entire semester devoted to working on and analyzing projects, rather than just part of a semester as was done in these classes. Some colleges have begun to experiment with approaches that break away from the traditional one-semester course, either by creating clusters of interdisciplinary courses that are taken the same semester (e.g., a history, English, and art class focusing on a common theme) or by extending courses across semesters (e.g., a two-semester research and writing course; see discussion in Bacon, 1997).

Cummins and Sayers suggested a model of multimedia educational reform that they believe can result in transformative practice at the K–12 level. They suggested that the teaching of isolated skills or cultural knowledge be replaced with a process of collaborative critical inquiry, in which part of the curriculum is devoted to long-distance partnerships for collaborative research, intercultural exploration, and student publishing. Interdisciplinary Internet-based projects, based on important themes in the lives of students and their communities, can be the basis for students' achieving more active mastery over a broad range of technologies while developing skills of analysis, cross-cultural interpretation, and writing. Teachers can interject form-focused instruction within the overall process of creating new knowledge, and long-distance partnerships may be ideal for injecting a critical perspective, as learners are forced to reconsider their values in response to the questions and concerns of a distant audience. The result can be "for all grade levels ... a rigorous pursuit of knowledge that is typically required among university graduate students" (p. 143).

Even if some agreement can be reached about what types of educational reform are needed for effective use of new media in the schools, there is still the question of how to get from here to there. Will the introduction of technology itself start to foster change, or, if not, what else is required?

The notion that technology itself can bring about some change, or at least create a climate for it, is not completely implausible. As discussed earlier, whether in the workplace or the school, the introduction of new technologies and the increased communications and information opportunities that accompany them have created rising expectations for democratization as well as increased means to bring it about (Zuboff, 1988). The democratizing potential of interactive technologies is also the reason that oppressive governments around the world fear allowing their citizens unfettered access to the Internet.

However, whether in countries or in classrooms, the powers that be can generally find a way to bend technology to their own interests, and the Internet can be used for spying on citizens as readily as for empowering them (Janangelo, 1991). The experiences of teachers and students in this study suggest that the use of interactive technologies such as the Internet can be one more element creating pressure for institutional change but that whether and how changes are implemented will depend on many other broader contextual factors.

What else then does help bring about reform? The previously mentioned 10-year study of computers in education (Sandholtz et al., 1997) provides some important clues. Factors supporting reform include support from administrators and peers, access to technical assistance, and opportunities for collaborative planning and teaching. Yet these factors influence how technology is implemented in large part through shaping teacher beliefs and attitudes. When teachers are able to change their beliefs about the nature of education, new technologies can be implemented in ways that better tap their potential for aiding student-centered learning. In a sense, then, teachers are not only objects of societal and institutional influences but also agents for transforming their own teaching and their institutions (Giroux, 1988). We see, for example, while Joan benefited from institutional support, but her own efforts over a number of years—not only for innovative uses of technology but also for programs like writing across the curriculum and service learning—which helped create that favorable institutional context. As reported in the epilogue of this volume, Mary, Luz, and Kapili are all now working to bring about broader changes within their own institutions.

ELECTRONIC LITERACIES AND (IN)EQUALITY

Perhaps the most important issue addressed in this book is the impact of the Internet on (in)equality. I look at this question from several vantage points: technological access, language and discourse access, and cultural appropriation.

Technological Access

Although informational capitalism is creating vast amounts of new wealth, it is doing so on a highly unequal basis. Within the United States, income inequality has worsened dramatically in recent years, as an economic elite reaps the profits of the informational economy while the poorer tiers of the population suffer the consequences of deindustrialization and loss of low-skill manufacturing jobs. From 1983 to 1992, the richest 1% of U.S. households saw their wealth increase by 28.3%, whereas the bottom 40% of U.S. families saw their assets decline by 49.7% (Castells, 1998). Such polarization is magnified in the international arena, with Latin America, Eastern Europe, and Africa all dropping both absolutely and relatively in gross domestic product since 1973 compared to the United States, Western Europe, and East Asia (Castells, 1998). In the developing countries, vast amounts of people, especially in sub-Saharan Africa, are being relegated to a "Fourth World of need, hunger, and ... hopelessness" (Cardoso, 1993, p. 155).

The "black holes of informational capitalism" (Castells, 1998, p. 161) increasingly overlap with people and locales that are disconnected from the so-called information superhighway. The ability to participate in the global economy increasingly depends on having the tools and the training to exchange, analyze, and interpret information. In the United States, the children of the economic elite pick up these skills readily, through technology-enhanced project work at schools and further practice on computers at home. In contrast, the children of the poor lack home access to computers, the Internet , and in many cases phones, and at schools they have less access to technology or they use it in a more remedial fashion. A massive commitment of intervention and investment in our schools, not only to provide equal access to hardware but also to provide support for the teacher training, curriculum reform, and research required to use technologies well, is necessary to ensure that the informational economy is accessible to all.

Students in the four classes reported in this book, most of whom were either international students from developing countries or local students from low socioeconomic status neighborhoods, had little previous experience with computers. Those who had used computers in school had not learned to take full advantage of their interactive or multimedia potential. These students enthusiastically threw themselves into the task of learning to write in new media, in spite of or perhaps because of difficulties caused by lack of home access, weak keyboarding skills, and language difficulties, and they achieved impressive results.

Critics of technology in the schools, such as Neil Postman (1995), have suggested that there are no educational problems that can be solved with computers that cannot be solved without computers, implying that what is most important is good teaching, rather than use of computers. That is certainly hard to argue with, yet I contend in response that good teaching with computers is far better for students than good teaching without computers—especially for students who do not come from privileged backgrounds. Students from wealthy American families may have many opportunities to learn to use new technologies at home. That is certainly not the case for most students in the United States, let alone other countries, and the failure to provide access to new technologies in school will thus perpetuate unequal opportunity.

Computer technology is not the answer to all the problems in U.S. education, nor in U.S. society. Yet, as discussed earlier, when educators make technology part of a broader reform process, in order to promote collaborative, critical inquiry and the development of multiliteracies, a substantial impact can be achieved. Failure to move aggressively in this direction will likely result in another generation of "savage inequalities" (Kozol, 1991, p. iii) in U.S. education and society.

Language and Discourse Access

The Internet has served to strengthen the already existing trend of English becoming the dominant language of international business, entertainment, and scholarship (The Coming Global Tongue, 1996), thus further privileging those who speak the language and disadvantaging those who don't. An increasing number of people around the world face the same situation discussed by the Cambodian student Prasit in Luz's class at the University of Hawai'i, who said that "if you ask for a job ... , the first thing they ask is computer skills and English-speaking." Similar linguistic obstacles to success also face speakers of different dialects of English, as seen by the struggles of Donald, who spoke Hawaiian Creole English but who failed his English class in part due to his relative unfamiliarity with Standard American English. Even students who are or who become familiar with English or with its standard spoken dialects may be unfamiliar with the written genres and discourses needed for powerful communication in academic and economic arenas. Thus the contradiction: The Internet extends possibilities for international communication but may reinforce unequal opportunities to have a real voice, as most of the world's people find themselves lacking access to the particular language, dialects, genres, or discourses privileged in Western society.

Two approaches have been put forwarding for dealing with such unequal access. One approach emphasizes that students must be taught the languages, dialects, genres, and discourses of power so that they have better chances to achieve material success and political influence in the world (Cope & Kalantszis, 1993; Delpit, 1998). Another approach emphasizes that students should be supported in finding their own modes of expression—in minority languages, nonstandard dialects, and alternative genres and discourses—in order to challenge language and cultural hegemony (Barrs, 1994; Phillipson & Skutnabb-Kangas, 1996). Elsa Auerbach (1997) referred to these competing views as the power of voice and the voices of power approaches.

In the particular context of the higher education students in this volume, it seems that a combination of the two approaches is necessary. Students who have entered U.S. higher education deserve to become familiar with both dominant and alternative uses of language, dialect, genre, and discourse and to learn how to make decisions as to which language modes to use in different circumstances. To give students such a choice means to invite them into a dialogic process of interaction, reflection, and problem solving. Computer-mediated communication worked best in these four classes when it was used to assist students in expressing their own voices and critically choosing among new genres and discourses. In contrast, as a means of unilaterally imposing a certain structure of language and communication, computer-mediated communication met resistance.

Combining the two approaches does not necessarily mean finding a happy medium. Rather, it means using one approach to help accomplish the other-in other words, teaching students the voices of power to help them express more powerfully their own voices or encouraging them to use their own voices to reflect critically on the voices of power (Auerbach, 1997).

The electronic medium, which provides ample opportunities for combining interaction and reflection, appears quite useful for such an integrative approach. This was seen, for example, in Luz's class, where free-flowing, uncorrected synchronous communication was used to reflect critically on the discourses of power, such as the particular interpretations of plagiarism in Western academic discourse. Another example was seen in Kapili's class, where new media were appropriated (when necessary in English, for example, by searching for information on English-language web pages) in order to help students better express their voices in their own indigenous language.

Beyond the question of how language is dealt with in the classroom is the larger issue of linguistic diversity in cyberspace. The Internet was launched and is dominated by Americans. It is based on the ASCII (American Standard Code for Information Exchange) character system, which complicates written exchange in anything other than the Roman alphabet, and this has served to normalize the use of English. The use of English as a weapon of unequal power relations online was seen in the case of the Japanese student, Atsuko, who was harassed by a self-appointed guardian of "correct" English after she dared venture on an international e-mail list.

At the same time, with the decreased importance of the nation state, language has become a critical terrain for defining identity in the postmodern age. It is thus likely that the dominance of English, or of certain standard Englishes, will be increasingly challenged in cyberspace. The struggle for language online will take place on many levels, from the individual student who asserts the right to communicate in his or her own dialect to the indigenous groups that work to establish an online presence for their native languages to the international organizations that seek replacement of ASCII with a new character-representation system that better expresses the world's languages. The multiplicity of communication channels allowed by the Internet can be well exploited on behalf of linguistic diversity in both the classroom and society.

Cultural Appropriation

This final point, cultural appropriation, contains an intentional ambiguity: are culturally diverse learners able to appropriate new media for their ends, or, in doing so, is their own culture appropriated and absorbed into a homogenous whole?

Bowers (1988), in his book on the cultural non-neutrality of educational computing, warned that non-Western cultures are threatened not by lack of access to computers, but rather by access, because the new forms of knowledge and technology they encounter may often lead to unanticipated consequences. He asserted:

> Traditional practices, beliefs, technologies, and architectural forms that have evolved over time may simply be replaced by a new technology that is disconnected from context, including implicit forms of knowledge that sustain both the everyday lives of people and a sense of historical continuity. In effect, the technicist mind-set privileges experiment over substantive traditions, abstract and theoretical ways of thinking over implicit forms of understanding, the autonomous individual over the collective memory and interdependence of the cultural group, and a reductionist materialistic view of reality that denigrates the forms of spiritual discipline necessary for living harmoniously with other forms of life. (p. 9)

Although the book was published in 1988, when the Internet had already started to emerge, Bowers did not discuss the Internet per se but rather more general uses of computers. He emphasized, for example, that commercial software packages are based on a particular way of organizing and presenting information that may be in contradiction to patterns of communication and education in non-Western cultures.

Some might claim that the Internet voids Bowers's assertion, because the Net is based to a large extent on user-defined content rather than on commercial software. What's more, many writers have claimed that network-based digital technologies are particularly congruent with many non-Western and oral cultures. They have pointed out that new technologies are restoring an attention to imagery and visual communication that pre-dates the print era (Bolter, 1996) and that is prominent in many non-Western cultures (Lemke, in press). They have also stressed that the structure of computer-mediated texts harkens back to features of oral communication. For example, Fowler (1994) contended that both hypertext and primary orality are (1) flexible and dynamic (with information continually updated rather than expressed permanently as in print); (2) aggregative and associative (based on piecing together texts or formulaic language, rather than analytic and hierarchical, as is text); (3) interactive (with the audience able to respond more actively than in the print medium); (4) empathetic and participatory (by bringing people into a community rather than separating an idealized author from a distant reader); and (5) close to life (based on hands-on apprenticeship learning rather than distancing and objectification).[3] It was clear from my own study that many Hawaiian students and teachers feel that online communication is congruent with non-Western ways of learning and communicating.

Yet this study also indicated the challenges expressed in achieving cultural expression in a new medium. First, the technology of network-based communication, based on the ASCII system, did not allow use of Hawaiian diacritical marks without resorting to cumbersome software patches. Second, when the Hawaiian students first started to explore the Web they found a lot of information about Hawai'i, but most of it was written by hotel owners and other tourist promoters. Third, they found racist and sexist stereotypes about Hawaiians (such as the comment about "girls in grass skirts") put forth by the American males who dominate the Internet.

The Hawaiian students were then able to make use of the medium to put forward their own views and in their own language about what it means to be Hawaiian and thus in a small way reshape the net as they engaged it. Yet even in doing this, they faced contradictions between traditional and electronic ways of communicating. This was seen most clearly in the case of Kamahele, who put a sound recording of himself performing a Hawaiian chant on the Web. Kamahele explained to me that he had been somewhat hesitant to do so, as he was afraid of criticism from Hawaiian elders. He was concerned they might not look kindly on the idea of putting a Hawaiian chant—which is usually shared in an intimate oral setting—up on the Internet for anyone in the world to access. In the end, he decided to put up the chant anyway.

Indeed, Hawaiian history is filled with examples of the conflictive impact of new technologies. U.S. missionaries introduced literacy and printing presses to Hawai'i in order to spread the English language and Christianity (Schütz, 1994), steps that undermined Hawaiian ways of life as the introduction of literacy and Western-style education helped create inroads for American colonialists who eventually overthrew the Hawaiian monarchy. Yet Hawaiians printed not only Bibles but also Hawaiian-language newspapers, epics, and literature. These 19th-century Hawaiian language documents, many still available on microfiche, are an important resource today for revitalization of the language.

---

[3]See Lanham (1993) and Bolter (1991) for similar arguments.

At root in this discussion is a conflict between *substantive* and *instrumental* views of technology (also called *determinist* and *neutralist* views, respectively; see Ebersole, 1995). The substantive view "argues that technology constitutes a new type of cultural system that restructures the entire social world as an object of control" (Pacey, 1992, p. 7). Many proponents of this view point out what they view to be the negative consequences for cultural pluralism, with diverse cultures and languages destroyed in the wake of the inexorable march of technology (Ellul, 1990; Heidegger, 1977). In contrast, the instrumental view considers technology to be devoid of any particular content or values and thus "indifferent to the variety of ends it can be employed to achieve" (Feenberg, 1991, p. 5). In this view, it is not technology per se that creates problems or solutions but rather how technologies are put to use.

Feenberg (1991) put forward a third perspective that helps to bridge these contradictory views and also helps to explain the phenomena in this study. Feenberg's *critical theory of technology* views technology as neither completely deterministic nor as completely neutral, but rather "ambivalent" (p. 14). The ambivalence of technology is distinguished from neutrality "by the role it attributes to value in the *design*, not merely the *use*, of technical systems" (p. 14, emphasis added). Yet the values inherent in particular technologies do not mean that their impact is predetermined; technology is "not a destiny but a scene of struggle" (p. 14).

In the area of literacy—which both makes use of technology and can be considered a technology in its own right (Bigum & Green, 1992)—Brian Street (1984, 1993) adopted a similar perspective. Street criticized what he called *autonomous* models of literacy, which he portrayed as being deterministic. In response he put forward an *ideological model of literacy*. According to this model, "literacy practices are aspects not only of 'culture' but also of power structures" (1993, p. 7), involving "fundamental aspects of epistemology, power, and politics" (p. 9). The acquisition of literacy involves "challenges to dominant discourses, shifts in what constitutes the agenda of proper literacy, and struggles for power and position" (p. 9).

Applying a similar outlook to electronic literacy practices, Kaplan (1995) argued:

> The proclivities of electronic texts—at least to the extent that we can determine what they are—manifest themselves only as fully as human beings and their institutions allow, that they are in fact sites of struggle among competing interests and ideological forces. Or, to put the matter another way, social, political, and economic elites try to shape the technologies we have so as to preserve, insofar as possible, their own social, political, and economic status. They try to suppress or seek

to control those elements of electronic technologies uncongenial to that purpose. The degree to which they are successful in controlling the development and use of electronic texts will define the nature and the problems of literacy in the future (p. 28).

These types of critical perspectives are essential for understanding twhat occurred in the four classes discussed in this study. The technologies that students encountered could not be considered neutral; rather, they were shaped by their historical designs and uses. The Internet, for example, privileges those who use the English alphabet compared to other alphabets or writing systems, those who have keyboarding skills compared to those who don't, and those who have money to purchase computers compared to those who are poor. Although these values shape the way the Internet is used in society and schools, they do not determine it. Students and teachers of a variety of backgrounds and cultures can struggle to appropriate technologies for their own ends.

Of course, as they do so, cultures themselves change. Inherent in a critical perspective of technology or literacy is the view that culture is not a permanent trait of a community or individual but a set of values that is constantly in the process of being reshaped and redefined (Spicer, 1980). Cultural groups that are able to survive are ones in which the community and its members continually find new ways to recreate their identity, even as technologies and circumstances change. In this study, and in particular in Kapili's class, students made use of the Internet not merely toerspective of technology or literacy is the view that culture is not a permanent trait of a community or individual but a set of values that is constantly in the process of being reshaped and redefined (Spicer, 1980). Cultural groups that are able to survive are ones in which the community and its members continually find new ways to recreate their identity, even as technologies and circumstances change. In this study, and in particular in Kapili's class, students made use of the Internet not merely to express their culture, as if culture were an unchanging internal characteristic, but rather to explore and shape their cultural identity. They made use of a combination of media and rhetorical structures to find forms of expression and content congruent with their evolving cultural and social identity. This finding is consistant with Turkle's (1995) research; she found the Internet a powerful medium for encouraging exploration of identity. However, whereas Turkle's interviewees often used anonymous chat lines to explore fantasy selves, students in these classes seemed to be changing their notion of their "real" self (cf. Tobin & Tobin, 1997) in some cases making important life decisions based on these evolving identities.

In not all circumstances was this same result achieved. For example, Paulo, whose cultural and social identity as a Brazilian was tied up to his own critique of economic inequality in his country felt that he'd better avoid such a topic in his paper and instead stuck to the class assignment of discussing his nation's tourist sites. The less than durable results—at least from Paulo's perspective, if not the conservative college he attended—reflect an explanation from the New London Group (1996):

> The use of diversity in tokenistic ways—by creating ethnic or culturally differenti-ated commodities in order to exploit specialized niche markets or by adding fes-tive, ethnic color to classrooms—must not paper over real conflicts of power and interest. Only by dealing with them can we create out of diversity and history a new, vigorous, and equitable public realm. (p. 69)

In the same vein, Sleeter and Grant (1988) critiqued "human rela-tionships" (p. 75) approaches in multicultural education, which reduce multiculturalism to building ties of understanding and tolerance across cultures, and stressed instead that multicultural education is most em-powering when it prepares students to work actively for cultural diversity and social equality. This explanation seems to be congruent with the ex-periences in these classes. When students were encouraged to explore is-sues of cultural and social significance to their lives and were provided with opportunities and skills to fully exploit a variety of media in doing so, the learning experiences seemed to be the most profound.

CONCLUSION

In summary, I return briefly to the interrelation among new electronic literacies, educational practices and reform, and struggles for social and cultural equality. A new network society is emerging based on an infor-mation revolution that has transferred almost all spheres of life. Tele-communications will be as central to life in the network society as print has been in the *Gutenberg Galaxy* (McLuhan, 1962). The age of print is far from over; rather, we are entering a transitional period in which print literacies and electronic literacies coexist as prerequisites for economic and academic success. Print and electronic literacies both overlap and conflict. In their best sense, they both involve making use of semiotic sys-tems to interpret critically and construct knowledge. They emply differ-ent media and rhetorical strategies to do so. Becoming fully literate in today's society, at least in the industrialized world, means gaining competent control of representational forms in a variety of media and learning how those forms best combine in a variety of genres and discourses.

Technologies themselves do to imply a particular teaching method or approach, and computers are used for a variety of pedagogical purposes depending on sociocultural context. However, not all teaching approaches are equally useful for the new media. New technologies provide the opportunities for more democratic and self-directed learning; when those opportunities are thwarted, frustration and resistance is likely to follow. Although approaches to teaching with new media are shaped in part by institutional and societal expectations, teachers have the capacity to make changes based on their own beliefs about learning and teaching, and students also have the power to affect change by struggling for full participation in the classroom.

The internet and multimedia build on trends of the last few decades in media diversification and social stratification. In some ways the internet is one of the most top-down media, as its use requires the income to purchase a computer and the education to use it. In the future, commercial use interests are expected to try to implement even more top-down control of the Net. On the other hand, the Internet is also potentially the most democratic medium in that it allows individual users a great deal of latitude as to what information is accessed as well as a revolutionary new capacity to publish their own texts and communicate directly with other users around the world.

These dynamic and interactive capabilities of the Internet make it potentially more subject to control from below than other mass media such as television, film, or the press. At least in the industrialized countries, the Internet creates possibilities for more people than ever before to have a voice in society, but there is a difference between a medium and a voice. For students of diverse cultural, linguistic, and class backgrounds to have a voice, they need more than an Internet account. Rather, they need knowledge of the languages and discourses of power and opportunities to reflect critically on whether, when, and how to use them as well as opportunities to develop and use their own dialects and languages as they wish. They need access to and mastery of a variety of media and understanding of the ways that rhetorical structure and media interact, and they need chances to read, write, and think about issues of cultural and social relevance for their lives, as they work together with others near and far to tackle authentic complex problems collaboratively. If we as educators join with our students to help create these opportunites, together we can strive for a digital era that is more free, more just, and more equal than the print era we may one day leave behind.

Epilogue

ॐ•ॐ

After the courses reported on in this book ended, I stayed in touch with all four teachers through e-mail, telephone calls, personal visits, and occasional observations of their classes. All four had deepened their commitment to using new technologies in the classroom and were trying to improve their teaching based on the experiences they had in the semester I was working with them. Each teacher's efforts continued to be shaped by the sociocultural context of their institution, and all the teachers were actively involved in shaping that context by working to promote the use of technology in their departments and colleges.

MARY

Although Mary's course schedule changed, she continued to integrate new technologies into the various courses she taught. Following the study, she taught a Western humanities course. As part of the course material, she used information that she had found on the Internet about art, architecture, music, and other topics. She then had students search themselves for information on the same topics from their own home countries. As she explained:

> We had a student from Sri Lanka, a student from Indonesia, they found wonderful information on poetry and art and music. So we had them put up their favorite papers and find another site on the Web that related, but in their own cultures, so they would have a little comparison paper, and they could make a link to illustrate their own culture's humanities aspect, art or music or whatever it was, and the person reading their paper could see what their art looks like in comparison to Western Art.

She later taught an intermediate grammar course in which students "wrote about themselves and their cultures to apply their grammar." After students revised and developed their papers all semester, Mary put the students' papers on the Web together with their photos.

In spite of what Mary felt had been successful teaching experiences, it had been a difficult year for her. The stress of working so many hours had taken a toll on her health, and she had had to take some time off from her job. Then, soon after she returned to work, she found out that she had been denied an application for promotion. According to Mary, it was a fairly standard promotion, and she hadn't anticipated any difficulties, but it turned out that her own department had spoken out against her in the promotion committee. As she explained to me:

> They told me a couple of months after my illness that your promotion won't go through because you've been too involved in the language center and you've been working with computers with your students, you're not supposed to be doing that. You have to go back to the traditional classroom if you want to be an effective teacher. These people, they don't know all that's happening, how exciting it is, and how fun the students find it, communicative opportunities, and opportunities to show their work off.... I don't know what else they expect, but I felt like I sacrificed my whole being to their program. But they just don't see things from the same light. It was so depressing.

Mary thought that the problems were due to the different approaches she was starting to apply in her classes: "I had never had problems with the school before, but in the last couple of years, I started to change my outlook on teaching, tried to do some different things, and that's when the problems surfaced." Mary told me that she felt she had to choose between doing what she believed was right and what would help her advance her career:

> If I stay out of the language center and away from computers, I can go up for promotion again, but I don't know, it seems so political.... I thought, shall I choose between a promotion or should I choose between what I enjoy and know what's fun and exciting? And I decided to go, just choosing what's fun and exciting, enjoy life and not worrying about a big title in front of my name [laughs]. Titles I guess kind of come and go.

Mary decided to forge ahead and continue trying to integrate technology into her teaching. Recently, she persuaded one ally in the department that the Methods and Materials course for future ESL teachers should also include technology. The course thus expanded from two units to three units, and Mary was allowed to teach the technology unit. I visited the class one day while she was teaching. In the first part of the class, the students were discussing various aspects of using e-mail discussion lists. In the second part, Mary took students to the computer lab where she taught them how to use sound editing software to record and analyze speech. The students enjoyed the experience quite a bit, and it seemed to make concepts such as frequency, pitch, and intonation real to them.

Mary explained to me how the course was organized. From her comments, it seemed like she was trying to use a more student-centered approach:

The course is going well. I really de-emphasize exams and quizzes and emphasize projects, so there are three or four students together in a project … Mini-group projects, they had choice: tutoring the ELP students by e-mail; helping a group produce a video, a cultural presentation of the school; another group is making pronunciation exercises for students; another is doing a review of *Virtual Connections*[1]; another is reviewing eight favorite sites from the Internet, another is laminating pictures for Samoa.

I've even thought about making a proposal at TESOL [Teachers of English to Speakers of Other Languages] conference on how to set up a technological course.

It's been a really rough year. But this has been a highlight. This is kind of keeping the sunshine there, shining around the clouds. I just kind of backed away from it all except for this.

In my most recent discussion with her, Mary explained to me that she still hoped to change the general atmosphere in her college. She told me that "I want to write a letter to the vice-president of the university, explaining to him that we're really falling behind technologically. I hope he'll do something to try to change things."

LUZ

Both Luz and the English Language Institute director were so satisfied with the results of the ELI 83 class that in the following semester it was decided to institutionalize the changes in all sections of the course. ELI 83 would now be conceived and taught as a course that included a focus on technology, and all the sections would meet regularly in the lab.

Three sections of ELI 83 were offered the next semester, each of them meeting part of the week in the computer lab. Luz taught one of the sections, and she was very pleased with the way it turned out. Even though she was on her own, without a coteacher to help her with the technology, she was now more self-confident. As she explained:

I can handle the teaching of some basic technology without freaking out, and I know how to present things now, how to go from simple to complicated in gradual steps depending on the kind of students I have. I started class by showing students' comments from last semester and explaining very up front what the goals and possibilities are and how students can make the most out of taking the class. I think knowing that this is a technology-based writing class makes me feel convinced, and convincing to others, that the class is useful and justifiable, that we're doing something for the students and offering something that they really need in graduate school.

---

[1]*Virtual Connections* (Warschauer, 1995b) is an edited collection of teachers' articles about how they use the Internet in the language classroom.

Based on her previous experience, Luz could now make more informed decisions on how to implement technology. For example, in the previous semester students had gotten confused by the lesson on making Web pages because the software was complex and because they hadn't yet acquired a good sense of what the Web was. The next semester, Luz explained:

> I did Web browsing a whole period in the lab before I asked them to start thinking of their own homepage. I asked them to take notes about things they liked and didn't like from the homepage samples that they saw. And then we spent almost another whole period in class talking about their notes, comparing Web pages to CVs and resumes, and planning the content and format of their pages. After that, we did the one first session on [Web page design], and I went on with it in a very relaxed manner: I just gave them time to work on the page and circulated around offering help when they got stuck. At the point we did the pictures, most of them had pretty nice pages with links to their home universities, etc.

As a result of some of the changes she made, Luz found it to be "a very nice class, more relaxed for everyone than last semester, and with more writing in it. Technology was less the center of the class and more the taken for granted medium of the class, for them and for me."

Luz was less certain about how the other two sections of ELI 83 (taught by other teachers) had gone. Although they were taught part of the time in the computer lab, she was concerned that they were just using word processing rather than taking advantage of the networked computers. She told me:

> I think it will take a more serious effort to make the curriculum be a real writing and technology one. Teachers will need some training and some convincing that this is worthwhile and different from just teaching how to use software.... Kate [ELI Director] and Kenny [Assistant Director] are really into having our [ELI] 83 curriculum changed and establishing clear guidelines for technology and writing instruction.

Toward the end of the semester, when the teachers were preparing for the next year's courses, a minicrisis ensued. The lab that they were using was the only computer lab shared by all the language classes in the college for both class and individual use. As it was getting increasingly popular, new rules were announced restricting any one class from using the lab more than five times per semester. This rule would mean the end of the ELI's experiment in having its writing classes taught regularly in a networked environment.

Luz decided to dedicate part of a summer vacation to seeking outside funding so that the ELI could establish its own networked computer writing class. In one of her recent e-mail messages, she explained her grant-writing plans:

```
Date:Thu, 8 May 1997 18:04:32 -1000
From:Luz Santos luz@hawaii.edu>
To: Mark Warschauer rkw@hawaii.edu>
Subject: re: Merci!!!
```

I told Kate and Kenny we ought to be planning for the long-term future how to establish a serious writing & technology curriculum, and I think we won't be able to do that until we have autonomy from the LLL facilities (because they are shared by so many and controlled by 'others'; the ELI ought to have its own lab, in the best of worlds). So I offered to put some time into grant writing to see if we could come up with the money for a writing lab. This of course could only be done if we have a research (teacher development, very likely) project for which the equipment would be needed.... So, me and Kenny will be looking at possible sources of money and try to write a grant or two. So far, we've identified a couple of calls for grants but haven't done much more. We're planning on doing the big thinking and writing during the summer (e.g., in July). So, this is another manifestation of the big impact that your study had on teacher development (my development :)) and perhaps on curriculum and program development- but we'll see about that.
L.

KAPILI

The semester following the study reported in this volume, Kapili taught Hawaiian 202. The size of her class had increased from 15 to 20 students, indicating the popularity of Kapili's multimedia approach. Kapili included many of the same elements as the semester before. Students used Daedalus Interchange for discussion in Hawaiian, and they worked throughout the semester to make Web projects. Kapili and Susan (the teacher from Pearl College) had been planning to continue an improved version of the e-mail exchange, but Susan was not rehired, so that plan was dropped.

Kapili made a number of important changes in how the computer work was organized. First, she started teaching computer-based vocabulary early to help ensure that more of the interaction was done in Hawaiian. Kapili told me:

I kind of stepped backwards and we put together a vocabulary list and we gave them diagrams of the parts of the computer, and so that when we talked about the functions and the uses of the computer, we did it from the vocabulary building on up, which we should have done last semester. But it needs to continue, to develop, whether it's tutorials or even one-page sheets that students can refer back to, I think those kinds of things would help to keep it *pa'a* [fixed] on the language.

Also, the students got started on their projects earlier in the semester. This change gave them more time to think about and work on their projects and to develop the necessary technological skills to do them well. Because half of the 20 students in the class had returned from the previous semester, they could assist the new students. As Kapili explained:

> I think the momentum that we started with last semester is kind of carrying through. Those who were with me from last semester really are mentoring, there's a lot of peer interaction and expertise of ideas, which created a bond that we saw last semester, students working on something that was exciting to them. So, I think again it's really been successful, the things that they're learning, their processes of writing and their skills, are all being strengthened through what we're able to do.

I visited the class the last day of the semester when students were showing off their projects. The projects were more sophisticated than the previous semesters work, even for those students who hadn't been in Kapili's class before. This was partly because their Hawaiian language ability was more advanced (level 202 vs. 201), but also, from a design point of view, the pages were more sophisticated hypertexts. In the previous semester, students had started by writing papers that they eventually transferred onto Web pages. They had then worked with these pages to make them more appropriate for the medium—by adding graphics or adding links to additional material—but at root they were still "papers" transferred to the Web. In this second semester, students were cognizant right from the beginning that they were producing not papers but hypermedia documents. They thus incorporated hypertextual elements, such as splitting up the information into many different pages, from the start of their projects. For example, one student's Web site on Hawaiian music encompassed 10 different pages that were linked together.

Once again, Kapili was very content with the students' work:

> And again I'm really happy with the level of language that they're using as well as their ideas, and they're being very creative. And I can appreciate the amount of work that goes into it. It's not just writing a research paper. They're having to look at the multimedia dimension of it and the delivery of it. And I think that's where their reward comes in too, they're very proud of what they're able to produce.
>
> I think our students feel really privileged, they feel that they've been given something, you know, an extra tool from last semester and continuing this semester. Just technology gives them a little extra, I don't know what it is, empowerment. They're able to do something and it's not just Hawaiian language, I think they've been able to do it in all their other courses. They feel a little bit more sophisticated and competent and communicative, all these really important things I think that being a univer-

sity-level student we would assume that they're getting somewhere out there. And because they're doing it in Hawaiian, and I think they just feel good about that. I don't think they came in to Hawaiian thinking they're gonna become techies or get those kinds of skills, incorporating it into their course work. It just seems positive all the way around.

Like Luz, Kapili was concerned about the future of the program. Her second-year classes were in danger of facing the same restrictions of access to the college's computing lab as Luz's classes. Beyond this, she wanted to expand the computer-mediated program to include third-year students as well. She didn't want the students finishing her class to have no other choices but taking third-year classes focusing on grammar and translation. As she explained:

I think that's important that there is some kind of continuum, and looking long range, because if we really think that technology is gonna play a crucial part in both education and for us with language revitalization, that we need to keep developing our own expertise and resources to make it all come together. So, projects and things in second year are kind of just like a stepping stone of what can happen out there in the real world.

To help make her vision a reality, Kapili, like Luz, had turned to grants. Interestingly, she followed Joan's path and got involved in a service learning grant. Together with two University of Hawai'i professors of English, she had prepared and submitted a large grant proposal for a project called "Going to Class, Getting On-Line, and Giving Back: University of Hawai'i Students Building Community Learning and Information Networks." The aim of this grant was "to combine communication technology infrastructure with service-learning education so that students at the University of Hawai'i can develop their technology skills by bringing technology training and resources to underserved communities in Hawai'i."[2] The plan called for the purchase of computers to equip not only a lab for the Hawaiian department at the University of Hawai'i but also four Hawaiian institutions in the community: two immersion preschools and family centers, a K–12 immersion school, and a community-based Hawaiian language organization. As part of this plan, Kapili also proposed to her department a new course, Hawaiian 316: *Kekeka'a'ike Lolouila* (Computer-Mediated Communication). According to her course description, students in Hawaiian 316 would "become familiar with on-line composition and communication, ... develop multi-media technological tutorials and resources in the Hawaiian language, and ...

---

[2]Quoted from the grant proposal.

plan, develop, and deliver computer-mediated communication and information technology to the community."

It was an uphill battle for Kapili to get the course approved by her department. Some people in the department were concerned that the focus on technology would be at odds with a focus on Hawaiian literature and culture. Kapili had been discouraged by the opposition, but eventually she made some minor adjustments to the proposal and was able to get it approved as a 2-year experimental course. Another proposal will have to be put forward later to make it a permanent course.

The last time I saw Kapili, she was teaching in a month-long summer workshop for K–12 (and preschool) Hawaiian immersion teachers. The entire computer lab was decorated with posters of Hawaiian language vocabulary for hardware, software, and computer operations, and immersion teachers from throughout the state were learning both the technical and pedagogical aspects of Hawaiian language computing.

JOAN

After the semester ended, Joan immediately started teaching the English 215 course again, this time trying to squeeze a whole semester's worth of papers and projects into a 5-week summer session. Other than adjusting the schedule, she didn't make any major changes in the course, as she felt the previous semester had gone well and she wanted to stick with a good thing. Her one concern was streamlining the service learning project so that it didn't become so all-encompassing that it prevented students from working well in the fourth assignment. That same summer, Joan also taught a 2-week technology training course for high school teachers throughout the state of Hawai'i organized by the Hawai'i Education and Resource Institute (HERN).

More recently, Joan, too, has been working on another service learning grant, this one to pair her ESL students with an ESL program at a local elementary school. As she told me:

> I just keep finding new things that the students could do, my students can do. That's what brought me into the Ala Wai school. That was actually a HERN connection. The teacher I met, he came to one of the HERN training sessions that I did a long time ago, the summer of '95. But when this happens, if they get this grant, my students will go down there—well, until they get equipment their students may still come up here, but my students will be assisting other ESL students at Ala Wai and their parents with learning to use the computer facilities ... Students start tutoring, they're scared, and these are ESL students and they think their English is not good enough to talk to any-

body, let alone to tutor somebody. And so they go into it very apprehensive, but they get there and they learn differently, they just learn a lot.

In my most recent conversation with her, Joan talked to me about some changes she could make in her English 215 class to make it better for the students:

> In terms of evaluation, and maybe I'll get that worked around is for them to do a self-evaluation of the third and the fourth project in particular, I think that's more worthwhile than for me to give it an evaluation. For them to put their own grade on it. And then the other thing I'd like to do more of is to work in somehow for the third project, for them to do more reporting on what they've done, to show what they've created, for the rest of the class. That worked better this time, but still wasn't like I'd like it to be. And I don't know how to do it, I haven't figured that out, because the nature of, you saw, you turn 'em loose, they stay loose [laughs]. It's harder to get them back in and centered again. And I don't necessarily want it to, I don't wanna change that, I like that, I like that aspect of the way that the class works. But in order for that sharing to happen, there needs to be a time to pull 'em back together again, somehow. But I haven't worked that out. We'll see.

Joan's last comments focused on the patterns of relationships among students and teachers in the technology-enhanced classroom. This issue raises the questions of how class evaluation changes, who should be responsible for it, how students can best be brought together to teach and learn from each other while also given full reign to pursue their own interests, and what is the appropriate relationship between student initiative and teacher control, between group collaboration and individual autonomy, in the multimedia networked classroom? These questions are being grappled with not just by Joan but also by Mary, Luz, Kapili, and thousands of other educators around the world, as we work together to redefine the nature of education in the digital era.

Appendix:
Researching the Online
Classroom

ॐ•ॐ

Believing, with Max Weber, that man is an animal suspended in webs of significance he himself has spun, I take culture to be those webs, and the analysis of it to be therefore not an experimental science in search of law but an interpretive one in search of meaning.
—Clifford Geertz (1973, P. 5)

Behind every research method lies a belief, and behind every belief lies a person. Before discussing the research methodology I used for this study, I first introduce the person and beliefs behind the method.

I was raised in a middle-class suburb of Los Angeles and spent much of my adult life in the San Francisco Bay Area. I have been involved in education for nearly 20 years, as a high school Spanish bilingual teacher, an adult school teacher of English as a second language and GED (high school diploma equivalency) preparation courses, and a teacher trainer at universities in Russia, the Czech Republic, and the United States. My academic interests—nurtured by a bachelor's degree in psychology, graduate degrees in English and in second language acquisition, and several years as a full-time and part-time community organizer on issues ranging from bilingual education to farmworkers' rights to international labor solidarity—include social psychology, educational anthropology, multicultural education, composition pedagogy, and educational technology.

In recent years, these issues have converged in my focus on the development of electronic literacies among culturally and linguistically diverse learners. I have researched this topic since 1993 at the University of Hawai'i. In this research, I have struggled with many insider–outsider contradictions. I began as a *malihini* (i.e., newcomer to Hawai'i) and started to become a *kama'aina* (i.e., long-term resident) with emerging ties to local communities. I am a *haole* (i.e., white) who speaks "standard" American English in a state where 70% of the people are of Asian and Pacific origin and the majority of the people speak Hawaiian Creole English. I've carried out this research in a department of English as a second language, while my own interests have broadened to include more general issues issues of language and literacy development. I've tried to be an insider in Hawaiian language classes of mostly 19- to 20- year-old students, but I myself am on the other side of 40. I've been viewed by many people as an expert on computers, but I've struggled to find the time to keep up with rapid changes in online technologies.

Wearing numerous (and at times contradictory) hats, I have carried out a number of research projects related to the uses of new technologies for language and literacy development. The first study I did on computer-mediated interaction made use of a controlled experiment (Warschauer, 1996). Although I felt that the study had value, I also felt that the experimental method of the study served to exclude the very contextual factors that were most important. I began to seek other approaches that were based on understanding learning in context rather than attempting to shut out context, and I eventually found a home in ethnography.

Ethnography and other interpretive qualitative approaches are based on the theory that human experience is holistic, complex, and perspectival (Denzin, 1989; Diesing, 1972; Guba & Lincoln, 1994; Lincoln & Guba, 1985). In other words, the boundaries within any social system are arbitrary, and knowledge thus requires engagement within a system in its environment and context (Schwartz & Ogilvy, 1979). Furthermore, there is no single neutral vantage point for understanding human experience, but rather its interpretation depends on the perspectives of particular sociocultural groups that are shaped by social, political, cultural, economic, ethnic, and gender values (Lincoln & Guba, 1985).

Because reality has particular meanings within particular contexts and cultures, it is necessary to participate within a culture to understand how participants interpret reality and construct meaning within that particular sociocultural context (Davis, 1995; Diesing, 1972; Erickson, 1986). The qualitative researcher seeks to determine "the *immediate and local meanings of actions*, as defined from the actors' point of view" (Erickson, 1986, p. 119, emphasis in original).

This interpretation of culture is achieved in part through *thick description* (Geertz, 1973), which seeks to describe and interpret not just human behavior but also purposeful action. This interpretation is contrasted with *rich description*, which may employ much narrative detail but fails to take into account the socioculturally influenced meanings invested in actions by the actors.[1] Findings are created through the interaction of researcher and participants rather than by the researcher "standing behind a one-way mirror, viewing natural phenomena as they happen and recording them objectively" (Guba & Lincoln, 1994, p. 107).

Due in part to my activist background and my critique of unequal power relations in society, I was sympathetic to critical perspectives within the qualitative research paradigm . These perspectives emphasize that educational and literacy practices "are aspects not only of 'culture' but also of power structures" (Street, 1993, p. 7). I felt that power relations are especially important to consider when dealing with new technologies, which can be used as either gatekeepers or bridges. I therefore sought to practice a critical ethnography that would seek to explore and understand the various power relations involved.[2]

Critical ethnographers believe that it is important not only to understand reality but also to work to change it. As Whyte, Greenwood, and Lazes (1991) suggested, "it is possible to pursue both the truth and solutions to concrete problems simultaneously" (p. 21). For this pursuit to take place in any sort of serious way required that I collaborate closely with the classroom teachers involved, for only in that way could any change be long-lasting and meaningful. My research approach was thus influenced by perspectives on collaborative action research as well (e.g., Wells, 1994; Wells & Chang-Wells, 1992).

There are of course many potential dangers in attempting to do critical, collaborative ethnography. Ethnography is an admittedly subjective research process.[3] The point is not to carry out a value-neutral study—all research is based on values—but rather to be cognizant of and to reflect on the values that one brings to research. This emphasis is particularly important for critical ethnography, which by its nature is based on a more explicit social or political framework. In my case, some of the values that have influenced me in this study are my beliefs that indigenous peoples have a right to

---

[1]Geertz (1973) illustrated the difference nicely with the example of twitches and winks. Rich description is sufficient to take note of and record the examples of people twitching their eyes, but thick description is necessary to understand the significance of the action, that is, whether it is just a twitch or whether it is a wink (and what that might mean for the actors involved within the particular culture), or whether it is even a parody of a wink (and what that might mean for the actors involved within the particular culture).

[2]For an overview of critical ethnography, see Kincheloe (1994), Thomas (1993), Carspecken (1992), and Quantz (1992). For discussion of literacy and power structures, see Lankshear (1994), Shor (1992), McLaren (1988), and Freire (1970/1994, 1985, 1991).

[3]Ethnographers would claim that all research is subjective; see discussion in Guba and Lincoln (1994).

control their own destinies and speak their own languages, that language minority students deserve access to dominant discourses as well as the opportunity to shape those discourses to their own needs, and that individual teachers or students are not in complete control of their destinies but are influenced by broader situational contexts, such as class, race, ethnic, and gender divisions in society. With this background in mind, the following is a specific description of the methods and techniques I used for carrying out this study.

PREPARING FOR THE STUDY

Selection of Sites

The purpose of the study was to look at the development of electronic literacies in college writing classes for students from a variety of cultural and linguistic backgrounds. Within this framework, I sought out a wide variety of research sites in order to provide possible cross-site comparisons. I consciously chose various types of institutions (i.e., community college, public university, and private college) and various levels of students (i.e., undergraduate and graduate). I also sought to work with classes in both Hawaiian and English, the two official languages of the state of Hawai'i, and to include students of a wide range of ethnicities and language backgrounds.

The particular teachers were chosen through personal contact. I selected teachers that I knew to be using computer networks in their classes and who were open to having me work in their classes. It was important that I chose teachers who were willing to have an intense working relationship with me over a period of an entire semester.

Negotiation of Entry

I met with each teacher several times before the semester started to discuss the research project. I explained that I would be carrying out a broad study that was designed to look at the experiences of students in computer-intensive language and writing classes. I reviewed the various ways I would be collecting data (i.e., observation notes, access to texts, interviews, occasional tapings) and received the teachers' permission to do so.

During my first visit to class, I explained to the students what my role would be. Then, either that first day or another day early in the semester, I passed out consent forms to students to get their formal permission to be included in the study. I ensured them that all students would be included anonymously. I also provided my phone number and e-mail address for students in case they had any questions.

GATHERING DATA

Participant Observation

Participant observation is one of the central tenets of ethnography, based on the notion that only by delving into a community can a researcher come to know it (Glesne & Peshkin, 1992; Lincoln & Guba, 1985; Spradley, 1980).

The exact nature of my participation varied according to particular circumstances of the four courses. In Mary Sanderson's class (chapter 2), my participation included helping students with their questions (whether about technology or about writing) and meeting with Mary to discuss suggestions about how the course might be structured. In Luz Santos' class (chapter 3), my participation was as a co-teacher, with particular responsibility for helping with tasks related to technology. In Kapili Manaole's class (chapter 4), I participated as a learner of Hawaiian, as a collaborator with Kapili providing advice and suggestions about the integration of technology, and as an assistant teacher helping provide technology instruction to the students. In Joan Conners' class (chapter 5), I occasionally offered ideas or suggestions about the course, but my main participation was by helping students with technology and writing, both inside and outside of class.

In all four courses, in addition to attending classes, I participated in electronic discussion lists, maintained individual e-mail contact with students and teachers, joined organized social activities, and informally socialized with students and teachers in the cafeteria and elsewhere. I spent additional time wandering around the campuses, in bookstores, libraries, and lounges, to try to get a feel for what life was like on the campus.

Whether in class or outside of class, I took extensive field notes about what I observed. If I was not able to take notes in class due to other activities (e.g., when I was helping students), I wrote the notes after the class ended. My notes were generally descriptive in nature.

Interviews

The other main staple of ethnographic research is the personal interview. Near the beginning of each semester, I interviewed all students who were willing to be interviewed (a total of five students in the four classes chose not to be interviewed). I conducted interviews in a variety of locations, including campus offices, empty classrooms, outside benches, and cafeterias. Interviews were usually conducted on a one-to-one basis, but on a number of occasions I interviewed students in pairs and on rare occasions in groups of three.

I used a semistructured approach to the interviews, as suggested by Glesne and Peshkin (1992). I wrote interview protocols ahead of time to help me focus on the general areas I wanted to cover but encouraged tangential discussion to learn about the issues considered important by the students. I tape recorded these interviews, in all cases with the knowledge and permission of the students, turning off the recorder if the person wanted to make an off-the-record comment. Interviews lasted anywhere from 10 minutes to 90 minutes.

I continued to interview students throughout the semester, seeking if possible a minimum of three interviews at different times of the semester. I put the greatest priority on arranging interviews with those students who either had a lot of interesting things to say or who had life experiences that I found especially relevant to the goals of the study. For example, in Kapili Manaole's class, I especially sought students who seemed to have a deep personal connection to Hawaiian traditions and culture.

I spoke with students informally in the classroom before, during, and after class as well as in the cafeteria or elsewhere on campus. Occasionally, if students were making especially interesting spontaneous comments, I would take out my tape recorder and ask if they would mind being taped. In addition, I corresponded by e-mail with many students. In Luz Santos's class (see chapter 3), this correspondence often took the form of formal dialogue journals. In other classes, I sometimes informally wrote to individual students asking them their thoughts on certain issues. I also occasionally wrote to an e-mail list of the whole class asking for comments. Finally, I conducted several taped interviews with each of the four teachers involved, in addition to the almost constant contact I had with them in class and by e-mail.

Taping Class Sessions

I occasionally audiotaped class sessions. Audiotaping was done with the knowledge and permission of all participants. I also occasionally audiotaped, and on one occasion videotaped, sessions when I was assisting students in working with the computer outside of class, again with their explicit knowledge and permission.

Student and Teacher Texts

I was given access, with the permission of students and teachers, to a broad range of electronic and print texts, including transcripts of com-puter-assisted discussions, e-mail messages sent by the teacher and students to the class and to small-group lists, e-mail messages sent between students and the teacher, and of course e-mail messages sent between students (or teacher) and me. In addition, I received electronic or hard copies of papers written by students, and I had access to the Web pages produced by students and teachers.

Background Documents

I gathered a number of background documents related to education on the various campuses, including course catalogues, schedules of classes, institu-tional policy statements, and departmental publications.

ANALYSIS OF DATA

I transcribed all interviews as soon as possible after conducting them. I also wrote many field notes on the computer to provide easier access.

Analysis was an ongoing process that started from the very beginning of the study. As each course proceeded, I thought about what main themes and issues were emerging. I developed my thoughts by reflection, reviewing notes, and bouncing ideas off participants. This iterative analysis allowed me to refine my data collection as I went along, focusing my observations and my interview questions on issues that seemed particularly important. It also allowed me to start doing additional outside reading to explore what other theorists and researchers had to say about those issues.[4]

Usually, about halfway through the semester, I developed some ideas about the key issues emerging in the class. I then studied my notes and tran-scripts again to look for further evidence related to these issues, and I began to code sections of interviews according to themes. I followed these issues

---

[4]Ongoing, iterative analysis is considered an essential feature of qualitative research. Leaving analy-sis until the end of a study rules out the possibility of collecting new data to fill in gaps or to test new hy-potheses that emerge during analysis. It discourages the formulation of 'rival hypotheses' that question a field-worker's routine assumptions and biases. And it makes analysis into a giant, sometimes overwhelm-ing, task, that demotivates the researcher and reduces the quality of the work produced. (Huberman & Miles, 1994, p. 50)

further by tailoring my interviews with students and teachers, and I reflected more on these issues by writing about them in private notes. I also sought additional writings on these issues by other researchers.

This iterative process occurred both within each class and within the broader study. For example, at Miller College, I noticed early that Mary seemed to shape the uses of technology according to her own belief system, as reinforced by her institutional context. In the rest of the study, I paid more attention to how this process might be occurring, not only at Miller College but at other institutions as well.

As I continued to analyze data, I made sure to triangulate data—that is, to compare data across a variety of sources (e.g., notes, interviews, texts)—to seek out and confirm regularities. I also checked all my hypotheses and conclusions by explicitly looking for negative evidence, carefully considering rival explanations, and seeking additional feedback from teachers and students.

GROUNDED THEORY

In order to draw conclusions within each study and across studies, I used the principle of *grounded theory*. Glaser and Strauss (1967) defined grounded theory as theory generated from a qualitative study that will

> fit the situation being researched, and work when put into use. By "fit" we mean that the categories must be readily (not forcibly) applicable to and indicated by the data under study; by "work" we mean that they must be meaningfully relevant to explain the behavior under study. (p. 3)

Although grounded theory can be used in individual studies, it is also a good approach for cross-case studies, because it allows a framework to be built inductively and then tested and refined with further comparison groups (Huberman & Miles, 1994). For example, I started in the first study to develop some conclusions about the relations between teachers' belief systems and the implementation of technology, which I then explored further in the other classes. As the study progressed, I began to develop additional conclusions related to the relations between technology and literacy, technology and education, and technology and culture, which I examined in each class. Using what has been termed an *interactive synthesis* (Huberman & Miles, 1994, p. 436), I looked for themes that emerged across the studies, then cycled back to the individual cases to see how these themes were manifested in each case.

DEPENDABILITY AND CREDIBILITY

I believe it is incumbent on all researchers to demonstrate the steps they have taken to ensure the dependability of their data and the credibility of their interpretations (Lincoln & Guba, 1985). I have attempted to ensure the credibility and dependability by recommended steps (Erickson, 1986; Lincoln & Guba, 1985) such as *prolonged engagement* (i.e., observing the classes through their entire cycle), *triangulation of data*, and *member checks* (i.e., checking interpretations with participants). I have also attempted to seek and present disconfirming data to the general patterns I have noticed or interpretations I have made.

One possible threat to the credibility of the study is the particular influence that I had, through both my actions and my biases. As discussed earlier, scientific neutrality is not a goal of the ethnographer. It is inevitable that a research project such as this one is influenced by the values, ideals, and practices of the researcher. The point is not to purge values or ideals but rather to recognize the role they may have played. This is tied to the more general point of the observer's paradox: A phenomenon is inevitably shaped by the influence of the observer, so how can one really know reality?

In this particular study, it is necessary to consider how my outlook and participation helped shape the outcome. As mentioned before, it was a goal of mine to affect the outcome—to help bring about change as I studied it—so I certainly hope that I had some effect. One natural question, however, is whether results achieved are solely or principally due to my involvement.

It is likely that the extra assistance I provided, especially in Luz's and Kapili's class, allowed those teachers to organize and implement new projects involving technology that might not have been possible otherwise. That influence should of course be kept in mind when evaluating what took place in their courses. What is significant to me is that both of these teachers were able to make a successful transition to carrying out the same types of projects on their own in the following semesters. In fact, from what I was able to observe, the uses of technology were smoother and more effective the following semester (without outside assistance but with the benefit of experience) than during the first semester (when I was participating in the class). Thus, my assistance may or may not have been critical in helping introduce certain changes, but the teachers were able to continue and improve on curricular changes without my participation.

GENERALIZABILITY

The final issue is that of generalizability. What does this study say about other online classes? Naturalistic research, which revels in context rather than denying it, does not claim to be generalizable in the same way that experimental research can claim to be. Instead, qualitative research helps us "see generic processes; our generalizations are not to 'all kindergartens,' but to existing or new theories" (Miles & Huberman, 1994, p. 27). It is then up to the reader to consider how those theories might shed light on other situations.[5]

The conclusions that I reached in this 2-year study are steeped in the local circumstances relating to the nature of the institutions involved, the backgrounds and personalities of the particular teachers and students, my own personal role as an active participant, and the social and political history of Hawai'i. As Geertz (1973) pointed out:

> The whole point of a semiotic approach to culture is ... to aid us in gaining access to the conceptual world in which our subjects live so that we can, in some extended sense of the term, converse with them. The tension between the pull of this need to penetrate an unfamiliar universe of symbolic action and the requirements of technical advance in the theory of culture, between the need to grasp and the need to analyze, is, as a result, both necessarily great and essentially irremovable. Indeed, the further theoretical development goes, the deeper the tension gets. This is the first condition for cultural theory: it is not its own master. As it is unseverable from the immediacies thick description presents, its freedom to shape itself in terms of its internal logic is rather limited. What generality it contrives to achieve grows out of the delicacy of its distinctions, not the sweep of its abstractions. (pp. 24–25)

Thus the purpose of this study can be compared to the purposes many of us invest in network-based teaching: not to provide a single definitive answer but rather to open new forms of conversation and to encourage the process of reflecting on them.

---

[5]To make this point further, some reject the use of the term *generalizability* in qualitative research, suggesting an alternate term of *transferability*; see discussion in Lincoln and Guba (1985).

References

ॐ•ॐ

Agre, P. (1997). Networking on the network . Retrieved July 18, 1997, from the World Wide Web: at http://communication.ucsd.edu/pagre/network.html

Anderson, D. (1994). Not maimed but malted: Nodes, text and graphics in freshmen compositions. *CWRL* [Electronic journal], *1*(1), Retrieved July 1, 1997, from the World Wide Web at http://www.cwrl.utexas.edu/~cwrl/v1n1/article1/notmaimedbutmalted.html

Atkinson, D., & Ramanathan, V. (1995). Cultures of writing: An ethnographic comparison of L1 and L2 university writing/language programs. *TESOL Quarterly, 29*, 539–568.

Au, K. (1980a). Participation structures in a reading lesson with Hawaiian children: Analysis of a culturally appropriate instructional event. *Anthropology and Education Quarterly, 11*, 91–116.

Au, K. (1980b). Principles for research on the early education of Hawaiian children. Los Angeles, CA: Asian American Studies Center, UCLA.

Auerbach, E. (1997, August). *The power of voice and the voices of power.* Paper presented at the Literacy for Change: Community-Based Approaches conference, Honolulu, HI.

Auerbach, E. R. (1995). The politics of the ESL classroom: Issues of power in pedagogical choices. In J. W. Tollefson (Ed.), *Power and inequality in language education* (pp. 9–33). Cambridge, England: Cambridge University Press.

Bacon, N. (1997). Community service writing: Problems, challenges, questions. In L. Adler-Kassner, R. Crooks, & A. Watters (Eds.), *Writing the community: Concepts and models for service-learning in composition* (pp. 39–55). Urbana, IL:AAHE/NCTE.

Bakhtin, M. M. (1986). *Speech genres & other late essays.* Austin, TX: University of Texas Press.

Barker, T., & Kemp, F. (1990). Network theory: A postmodern pedagogy for the written classroom. In C. Handa (Ed.), *Computers and community: Teaching composition in the twenty-first century* (pp. 1–27). Portsmouth, NH: Heinemann.

Barringer, H. (1995, May). *The educational, occupational and economic status of native Hawaiians.* Paper presented at the Conference on Socioeconomic Issues in Hawai'i, Honolulu, HI.

Barrs, M. (1994). Genre theory: What's it all about? In B. Stierer & J. Maybin (Eds.), *Language, literacy and learning in educational practice* (pp. 248–257). Clevedon, UK: Multilingual Matters.

Bartholomae, D. (1986). Inventing the university. *Journal of Basic Writing, 5*(1), 4–23.

Bartholomae, D. (1995). Writing with teachers: A conversation with Peter Elbow. College Composition and Communication, 46(1), 62–71.

Bayer, A. (1990). *Collaborative-apprenticeship learning: Language and thinking across the curriculum, K-12.* Mountain View, CA: Mayfield.

Benton, R. (1996). Making the medium the message: Using an electronic bulletin board system for promoting and revitalizing M_ori. In M. Warschauer (Ed.), *Telecollaboration in foreign language learning* (pp. 187–285). Honolulu, HI: Second Language Teaching & Curriculum Center, University of Hawai'i.

Bernard, H. R. (1992). Preserving language diversity: Computers can be a tool for making the survival of languages possible. *Cultural Survival Quarterly, Fall 1992.*

Bickerton, D., & Wilson, W. H. (1987). Pidgin Hawaiian. In G. Gilbert (Ed.), *Pidgin & Creole languages* (pp. 61–76). Honolulu, HI: University of Hawai'i Press.

Bigum, C., & Green, B. (1992). Technologizing literacy: The dark side of the dream. *Discourse: The Australian journal of educational studies, 12*(2), 4–28.

Birkerts, S. (1994). *The Gutenberg elegies: The fate of reading in an electronic age.* Boston: Faber and Faber.

Bizzel, P. (1992). *Academic discourse and critical consciousness*. Pittsburgh, PA: University of Pittsburgh Press.

Boggs, S. (1985). *Speaking, relating, and learning: A study of Hawaiian children at home & at school*. Norwood, NJ: Ablex.

Bolander, M. (1989). Prefabs, patterns and rules in interaction? Formulaic speech in adult learners' L2 Swedish. In K. Hyltenstam & L. Obler (Eds.), *Bilingualism across the lifespan: Aspects of acquisition, maturity and loss* (p. 73–86). Cambridge: Cambridge University Press.

Bolter, J. D. (1991). *Writing space: The computer, hypertext, and the history of writing*. Hillsdale, NJ: Lawrence Erlbaum Associates.

Bolter, J. D. (1996). Ekphrasis, virtual reality, and the future of writing. In G. Nunberg (Ed.), *The future of the book* (pp. 253–272). Berkeley: University of California Press.

Bordieu, P. (1977). The economics of linguistic exchanges. *Social Science Information, 16*, 645–668.

Bowers, C. A. (1988). *The cultural dimensions of educational computing: Understanding the non-neutrality of technology*. New York: Teachers College Press.

Bridwell-Bowles, L. (1997). Service-learning: Help for higher education in a new millennium? In L. Adler-Kassner, R. Crooks, & A. Watters (Eds.), *Writing the community: Concepts and models for service-learning in composition* (pp. 19–28). Urbana, I/: AAHE/NCTE.

Briggs, K. (1996). Geography lessons for researchers: A look into the research space for humanity lost or gained. *Anthropology & Education Quarterly, 27*(1), 5–19.

Brown, J. S., Collins, A., & Duguid, P. (1989). Situated cognition and the culture of learning. *Educational Researcher, 18*(1), 32–42.

Bruner, J. S. (1972). *The relevance of education*. Middlesex, UK: Hardmonsworth.

Burbules, N. C., & Callister, T. A. (1996). Knowledge at the crossroads: Some alternative futures of hypertext learning environments. *Educational Theory, 46*(1), 23–50.

Bush, V. (1945). As we may think. *Atlantic Monthly, 176*(July), 101–108.

Cardoso, F. H. (1993). North–South relations in the present context: A new dependency. In M. Carnoy, M. Castells, S. S. Cohen, & F. H. Cardoso (eds.), *The new global economy in the information age* (pp. 149–159). University Park, PA: The Pennsylvania State University Press.

Carnoy, M., Castells, M., Cohen, S. S., & Cardoso, F. H. (1993). *The new global economy in the information age: Reflections on our changing world*. University Park, PA: The Pennsylvania State University Press.

Carspecken, P. F., & Apple, M. (1992). Critical qualitative research: Theory, methodology, and practice. In M. D. LeCompte, W. L. Millroy, & J. Preissle (Eds.), *The handbook of qualitative research in education* (pp. 507–554). San Diego, CA: Academic Press.

Castells, M. (1993). The informational economy and the new international division of labor. In M. Carnoy, M. Castells, S. S. Cohen, & F. H. Cardoso (eds.), *The new global economy in the information age: Reflections on our changing world* (pp. 15–43). University Park, Pennsylvania: The Pennsylvania State University Press.

Castells, M. (1996). *The rise of the network society*. Malden, MA: Blackwell.

Castells, M. (1998). *End of Millenium*. Malden, MA: Blackwell.

Cazden, C. (1988). *Classroom discourse: The language of teaching and learning*. Portsmouth, N. H: Heinemann.

Chun, D. (1992). Beyond form-based drill and practice: Meaning-enhancing CALL on the Macintosh. *Foreign Language Annals, 25*(3), 255–267.

Coles, N. (1988, March). *Raymond Williams: Writing across borders*. Conference on College Composition and Communication, St. Louis, MO.

Colomb, G. G., & Simutis, J. A. (1996). Visible conversation and academic inquiry. In S. C. Herring (Ed.), *Computer-mediated communication* (pp. 203–222). Amsterdam: John Benjamins.

Cope, B., & Kalantszis, M. (Eds.). (1993). *The powers of literacy*. London: Falmer Press.

Craver, K. W. (1997). *Teaching electronic literacy: A concepts-based approach for school library media specialists*. Westport, CT: Greenwood.

Crookes, G. (1989). Planning and interlanguage variation. *Studies in Second Language Acquisition, 11*, 367–387.

Cuban, L. (1986). *Teachers and machines: The classroom use of technology since 1920.* New York: Teachers College Press.

Cuban, L. (1993). *How teachers taught: Constancy and change in American classrooms 1890–1980* (2nd ed.). New York: Longman.

Cummins, J. (1989). *Empowering minority students.* Sacramento, CA: California Association for Bilingual Education.

Cummins, J., & Sayers, D. (1995). *Brave new schools: Challenging cultural illiteracy through global learning networks.* New York: St. Martin's Press.

Cyberspeech (1997, June 23). Cyberspeech. *Time,* p. 23.

D'Amato, J. D. (1988). "Acting": Hawaiian children's resistance to teachers. *The Elementary School Journal, 88,* 529–542.

Daedalus Inc. (1989). *Daedalus Integrated Writing Environment.* Austin, TX: The Daedalus Group.

Dautermann, J. (1996). Writing with electronic tools in Midwestern businesses. In P. Sullivan & J. Dautermann (Eds.), *Electronic literacies in the workplace: Technologies of writing* (pp. 3–22). Urbana, IL: National Council of Teachers of English.

Davis, K. A. (1995). Qualitative theory and methods in applied linguistics research. *TESOL Quarterly, 29,* 427–453.

de Castell, S., & Luke, A. (1986). Models of literacy in North American schools: Social and historical conditions and consequences. In S. de Castell, A. Luke, & K. Egan (Eds.), *Literacy, society, and schooling* (pp. 87–109). New York: Cambridge University Press.

Delpit, L. (1988). The silenced dialogue: Power and pedagogy in educating other people's children. *Harvard Educational Review, 58,* 280–298.

Denzin, N. K. (1989). *Interpretive interactionism.* Newbury Park, CA: Sage.

Dewey, J. (1938). *Experience and education.* New York: Macmillan.

Dierckins, T. (1994). Macintosh versus IBM in composition instruction: Does a significant difference exist. *Computers and Composition, 11,* 151–164.

Diesing, P. (1972). *Patterns of discovery in the social sciences.* London: Routledge & Kegan Paul.

DiMatteo, A. (1990). Under erasure: A theory for interactive writing in real time. *Computers and Composition, 7*(S.I.), 71–84.

DiMatteo, A. (1991). Communication, writing, learning: An anti-instrumentalist view of network writing. *Computers and Composition, 8*(3), 5–19.

Dudley, M. (1993). *Call for Hawaiian sovereignty.* Honolulu, HI: N_ K_ne O Ka Malo Press.

Ebersole, S. (1995). *Media determinism in cyberspace* [online essay]. Retrieved September 5, 1997, from the World Wide Web at http://www.regent.edu/acad/schcom/rojc/mdic/md.html

Eisenstein, E. L. (1979a). *The printing press as an agent of change: Communications and cultural transformations in early-modern Europe* (Vol. 1). Cambridge, England: Cambridge University Press.

Eisenstein, E. L. (1979b). *The printing press as an agent of change: Communications and cultural transformations in early-modern Europe* (Vol. 2). Cambridge, England: Cambridge University Press.

Elbow, P. (1995). Being a writer vs. being an academic: A conflict in goals. *College Composition and Communication, 4f6*(1), 72–83.

Ellul, J. (1990). *The technological bluff.* Grand Rapids, MI: Eerdmans.

Erickson, F. (1986). Qualitative methods in research on teaching. In M. Wittrock (Ed.), *Handbook of research on teaching* (pp. 119–161). New York: Macmillan.

Eveland, J. D., & Bikson, T. K. (1988). Work group structures and computer support: A field experiment. *Transactions on Office Information Systems, 6,* 354–379.

Faigley, L. (1997). Literacy after the revolution. *College Composition and Communication, 48*(1), 30–43.

Faigley, L., & Miller, T. (1982). What we learn from writing on the job. *College English, 44,* 557–567.

Feenberg, A. (1991). *Critical theory of technology.* New York: Oxford University Press.

Finholt, T., Kiesler, S., & Sproull, L. (1986). *An electronic classroom.* Working paper, Carnegie Mellon University, Pittsburgh, PA.

Finholt, T., & Sproull, L. (1990). Electronic groups at work. *Organization Science, 1*(1), 41–64.

Fishman, J. (1991). *Reversing language shift.* Clevedon, UK: Multilingual Matters.

Foo, J. (1995). Endou. In J. Kincaid (Ed.), *The best American essays 1995* (pp. 93–99). Boston: Houghton Mifflin.

Foreign Relations of the United States (1894). *Affairs in Hawaii. The executive documents of the House of Representatives for the Third Session of the Fifty-Third Congress 1894–95.* Washington, DC: Government Printing Office.

Foucault, M. (1979). *Discipline and punish: The birth of the prison* (Alan Sheridan, Trans.). New York: Vintage Books.

Fowler, R. (1994). How the secondary orality of the electronic age can awaken us to the primary orality of antiquity. *Interpersonal Computing and Technology, 2*(3), 12–46.

Freire, P. (1970/1994). *Pedagogy of the oppressed* (3rd ed.). New York: Continuum.

Freire, P. (1985). Pedagogia: dialogo e conflito. *(Pedagogy: Dialogue and conflict).* Sao Paulo, Brazil: Cortez.

Freire, P. (1991). The adult literacy process as cultural action for freedom. In M. Minami & B. Kennedy (Eds.), *Language issues in literacy and bilingual/multicultural education.* (pp 248-265) Cambridge, MA: Harvard University Press.

Gee, J. P. (1996). *Social linguistics and literacies.* London: Taylor & Francis.

Gee, J. P., Hull, G., & Lankshear, C. (1996). *The new work order: Behind the language of new capitalism.* St. Leonards, Australia: Allen & Unwin.

Geertz, C. (1973). *The interpretation of cultures.* New York: Basic Books.

Gibson, S. (1996). Is all coherence gone? The role of narrative in web design. *Interpersonal Computing and Technology, 4*(2), 7–26.

Gilster, P. (1997). *Digital literacy.* New York: Wiley.

Giroux, H. (1983). *Theory & resistance in education.* New York: Bergin & Garvey.

Giroux, H. A. (1988). *Teachers as intellectuals: Toward a critical pedagogy of learning.* New York: Bergin & Garvey.

Glaser, B., & Strauss, A. (1967). *The discovery of grounded theory: Strategies for qualitative research.* Chicago: Aldine.

Glesne, C., & Peshkin, A. (1992). *Becoming qualitative researchers.* New York: Longman.

Guba, E. G., & Lincoln, Y. S. (1994). Competing paradigms in qualitative research. In N. K. Denzin & Y. S. Lincoln (Eds.), *Handbook of qualitative research* (pp. 105–117). Thousand Oaks, CA: Sage.

Hafner, K., & Lyon, M. (1996). *Where wizards stay up late: The origins of the Internet.* New York: Simon & Schuster.

Hale, C. (1995). How do you say computer in Hawaiian? *Wired, 3*(8), 90–100.

Halio, M. P. (1990). Student writing: Can the machine maim the message? *Academic Computing, 4,* 16–19, 45.

Halio, M. P. (1995 April). *Writing the future: How computers are changing writing.* Paper presented at Charles University, Prague, Czech Republic.

Halio, M. P. (1996). Multimedia narration: Constructing possible worlds. *Computers and composition, 13*(3), 343–352.

Halio, M. P. (1997, March). *Webbed writing: Helping students find a voice online in a changing world.* Paper presented at the College Conference on Composition and Communication, Phoenix, AZ.

Halliday, M. A. K. (1993). Towards a language-based theory of learning. *Linguistics and Education, 5*(2), 93–116.

Hara, K. (1992). *Fontpatchin'* [Computer software]. Tokyo: Author.

Harasim, L. (1990). Online education: An environment for collaboration and intellectual amplification. In L. Harasim (Ed.), *Online education: Perspectives on a new environment* (pp. 39–64). New York: Praeger.

Harnad, S. (1991). Post-Gutenberg galaxy: The fourth revolution in the means of production and knowledge. *Public-Access Computer Systems Review, 2*(1), 39–53.

Harris, J. (1989). The idea of community in the study of writing. *College Composition and Communication, 40*(1), 11–21.

Hartman, K., Neuwirth, C., Kiesler, S., Sproull, L., Cochran, C., Palmquist, M., & Zubrow, D. (1991). Patterns of social interaction and learning to write: Some effects of networked technologies. *Written Communication, 8*(1), 79–113.

Hawaii State Department of Health. (1990). *Statistical report.* Honolulu, HI: Hawaii State Department of Health.

Heath, S. B. (1983). *Ways with words: Language, life, and work in communities and classrooms.* Cambridge, England: Cambridge University Press.

Heath, S. B. (1986). The functions and uses of literacy. In S. de Castell, A. Luke, & K. Egan (Eds.), *Literacy, society, and schooling.* (pp. 15–26) Cambridge, England: Cambridge University Press.

Heath, S. B. (1992). Literacy skills or literate skills? Considerations for ESL/EFL learners. In D. Nunan (Ed.), *Collaborative language learning and teaching* (pp. 40–55). Cambridge, England: Cambridge University Press. Heidegger, M. (1977). *The questions concerning technology and other essays* (W. Lovitt, Trans.). New York: Harper & Row.

Heidegger, M. (1977). The question concerning Technology and other essays (W. Lovitt, trans.). New York: Harper & Row.

Heilker, P. (1997). Rhetoric made real: Civic discourse and writing beyond the curriculum. In L. Adler-Kassner, R. Crooks, & A. Watters (Eds.), *Writing the community: Concepts and models for service-learning in composition* (pp. 71–77). Urbana, IL: AAHE/NCTE.

Henderson, P. G. (1996). Writing technologies at White Sands. In P. Sullivan & J. Dautermann (Eds.), *Electronic literacies in the workplace: Technologies of writing* (pp. 65–88). Urbana, IL: National Council of Teachers of English.

Herzberg, B. (1997). Community service and critical teaching. In L. Adler-Kassner, R. Crooks, & A. Watters (Eds.), *Writing the community: Concepts and models for service-learning in composition* (pp. 57–69). Urbana, IL: AAHE/NCTE.

Hirsch, E. D. (1987). *Cultural literacy: What every American needs to know.* Boston: Houghton Mifflin.

Hornberger, N. (Ed.). (1997a). *Indigenous literacies in the Americas: Language planning from the bottom up.* New York: Mouton.

Hornberger, N. (1997b, March). *Language policy, language education, and language rights: Indigenous, immigrant, and international perspectives.* American Association for Applied Linguistics Annual Conference, Orlando, FL.

Huberman, A. M., & Miles, M. B. (1994). Data management and analysis methods. In N. K. Denzin & Y. S. Lincoln (Eds.), *Handbook of qualitative research* (pp. 428–444). Thousand Oaks, CA: Sage.

Jacoby, B. (1996). *Service-learning in higher education.* San Francisco: Jossey-Bass.

Janangelo, J. (1991). Technopower and technoppression: Some abuses of power and control in computer-assisted writing environments. *Computers and Composition, 9*(1), 47–63.

Jopson, D. (1997). *Spinning ancient tales on the modern web* [Sydney Morning Herald Online Article, August 20, 1997, Edition]. Retrieved August 20, 1997 from the World Wide Web at http://www.smh.com.au/

Jordan, C. (1985). Translating culture: From ethnographic information to educational program. *Anthropology and Education Quarterly, 16*, 105–123.

Joyce, M. (1998). New stories for new readers: Contour, coherence and constructive hypertext. In I. Snyder (Ed.), *Page to screen: Taking literacy into the electronic era.* (pp. 163–182) London: Routledge.

Judd, L. F. (1880). *Honolulu, HI: Sketches of life social, political, and religious in the Hawaiian islands.* New York: Randolph & Co.

Jungck, S. (1987). Computer literacy in practice: Curricula, contradictions, and context. In G. Spindler & L. Spindler (Eds.), *Interpretive ethnography of education: At home and abroad* (pp. 475–493). Hillsdale, NJ: Lawrence Erlbaum Associates.

Kachru, B. B., & Nelson, C. L. (1996). World Englishes. In S. L. Mckay & N. H. Hornberger (Eds.), *Sociolinguistics and language teaching* (pp. 71–102). New York: Cambridge University Press.

Kaplan, N. (1995). E-Literacies. *Computer-Mediated Communication Magazine, 2*(3), 3–35. Retrieved July 2, 1997 from the World Wide Web: http://sunsite.unc.edu/cmc/mag/1995/mar/kaplan.html

Kaplan, N., & Moulthrop, S. (1990). Other ways of seeing. *Computers and Composition, 7*(3), 89–102.

Kelly, K. (1997). New rules for the new economy. *Wired 5*(9), 140–144, 186–194.

Kendall, J. (Ed.). (1977). *Combining service and learning: A resource book for community and service learning.* Raleigh: National Society for Internships and Experiential Education.

Kern, R. (1995). Restructuring classroom interaction with networked computers: Effects on quantity and quality of language production. *Modern Language Journal, 79,* 457–476.

Kern, R. (1996). Computer-mediated communication: Using e-mail exchanges to explore personal histories in two cultures. In M. Warschauer (Ed.), *Telecollaboration in foreign language learning* (pp. 105–19). Honolulu, HI: University of Hawai'i Second Language Teaching and Curriculum Center.

Kincheloe, J. L. (1994). Rethinking critical theory and qualitative research. In N. K. Denzin & Y. S. Lincoln (Eds.), *Handbook of qualitative research.* (pp. 138–157). Thousand Oaks, CA: Sage.

Kozol, J. (1991). *Savage inequalities.* New York: Harper Collins.

Kress, G., & van Leeuwen, T. (1996). *Reading images: The grammar of visual design.* London: Routledge.

Landow, G. P. (1992). *Hypertext: The convergence of contemporary critical theory and technology.* Baltimore: John Hopkins University Press.

Lanham, R. A. (1993). *The electronic word: Democracy, technology, and the arts.* Chicago: University of Chicago Press.

Lankshear, C. (1994). *Critical literacy.* Belconnen, Australia: Australian Curriculum Studies Association.

Lankshear, C., & Knobel, M. (1995). Literacies, texts and difference in the electronic age. *Critical Forum, 4*(2), 3–33.

Lave, J., & Wenger, E. (Eds.). (1991). *Situated learning: Legitimate peripheral participation.* Cambridge, England: Cambridge University Press.

Lemke, J. (1990). *Talking science.* Norwood, NJ: Ablex.

Lemke, J. L. (in press). Metamedia literacy: Transforming meanings and media. In D. Reinking, McKenna, L. Labbo, & R. D. Kieffer (Eds.), *Handbook of literacy and Technology Transformations in a post-typographic world.* Mahwah, NJ: Lawrence Erlbaum Associates.

Levin, P. (1992). The impact of preschool on teaching and learning in Hawaiian families. *Anthropology and Education Quarterly, 23,* 59–72.

Lincoln, Y. S., & Guba, E. G. (1985). *Naturalistic inquiry.* Newbury Park, CA: Sage.

Long, M. H. (1991). Focus on form: A design feature in language teaching methodology. In K. de Bot, R. Ginsberg, & C. Kramsch (Eds.), *Foreign language research in cross-cultural perspective* (pp. 39–52). Amsterdam: John Benjamins.

Long, M. H. (1996). The role of the linguistic environment in second language acquisition. In W. C. Ritchie & T. K. Bhatia (Eds.), *Handbook of research on language acquisition. Vol. 2: Second language acquisition.* (pp. 413–468). New York: Academic Press.

Lyotard, J. F. (1984). *The postmodern condition* (G. Bennington & B. Massumi, Trans.). Minneapolis, MN: University of Minnesota Press.

Mabrito, M. (1991). Electronic mail as a vehicle for peer response: Conversations of high- and low-apprehensive writers. *Written Communication, 8,* 509–532.

Martin, D. E. (1996). *Towards an understanding of the native Hawaiian concept and manifestation of giftedness.* Unpublished doctoral dissertation, University of Georgia.

Martin, J. R., Christie, F., & Rothery, J. (1994). Social process in education: A reply to Sawyer and Watson (and others). In B. Stierer & J. Maybin (Eds.), *Language, literacy and learning in educational practice* (pp. 232–247). Clevedon, U.K.: Multilingual Matters.

Matusov, E. (1996). Intersubjectivity without agreement. *Mind, Culture and Activity, 3,* 25–45.

McLaren, P. L. (1988). Culture or canon? Critical pedagogy and the politics of literacy. *Harvard Educational Review, 58,* 213–234.

McLuhan, M. (1962). *The Gutenberg galaxy: The making of typographic man.* Toronto, Canada: University of Toronto Press.

Mehan, H. (1985). The structure of classroom discourse. In T. A. van Dijk (Ed.), *Handbook of discourse analysis* (pp. 120–131). London: Academic Press.

Mehlinger, H. D. (1996). School reform in the information age. *Phi Delta Kappan, 77*, 400–407.

Mental Health Task Force (1985). *E olu mau: The Native Hawaiian health needs study.* Honolulu, HI: Alu Like Native Hawaiian Program.

Meskill, C., & Rangelova, K. (1995). U.S. language through literature: A transatlantic research project. In M. Warschauer (Ed.), *Virtual connections: Online activities and projects for networking language learners* (pp. 134–136). Honolulu, HI: University of Hawai'i Second Language Teaching and Curriculum Center.

Miles, M. B., & Huberman, A. M. (1994). *Qualitative data analysis.* Thousand Oaks, CA: Sage.

Minh-ha, T. T. (1994, April). *Critical rhythms of borderlands and permitted boundaries.* Paper presented at Smith College, Northampton, MA.

Moore, D. T. (1990). Experiential education as critical discourse. In J. C. Kendall (Ed.), *Combining service and learning: A resource book for community and public service* (pp. 273–283). Raleigh, NC: National Society for Internships and Experiential Education.

Murray, D. E. (1995). *Knowledge machines: Language and information in a technological society.* Longman: London.

Nattinger, J. R., & DeCarrico, J. S. (1992). *Lexical phrases and language teaching.* Oxford, England: Oxford University Press.

Network Wizards. (1997). *Internet domain survey.* Retrieved August 28, 1997, from the World Wide Web at http://www.nw.com/zone/WWW/top.html

New London Group (1996). A pedagogy of multiliteracies: Designing social futures. *Harvard Educational Review, 66*, 60–92.

Newman, D. R., Johnson, C., Cochrane, C., & Webb, B. (1996). An experiment in grouptechnology: Evaluating critical thinking in face-to-face and computer supported seminars. *Interpersonal Computing and Technology, 4*(1), 57–74.

Nystrand, M., Greene, S., & Wiemelt, J. (1993). Where did composition studies come from?: An intellectual history. *Written Communication, 10*, 267–333.

Office of Technology Assessment. (1995). *Telecommunications technology and Native Americans: Opportunities and challenges* (Report No. OTA-ITC-621). Washington, DC: U.S. Government Printing Office.

Office of the Vice President for Student Affairs. (1994). *Diversity and equity at the University of Hawai'i-Manoa: A report to the board of regents.* Honolulu, HI: University of Hawai'i at Manoa, Office of the Vice President for Student Affairs.

Ogbu, J. (1978). *Minority education and caste: The American system in cross-cultural perspective.* New York: Academic Press.

Olson, D. R. (1994). *The world on paper.* Cambridge, England: Cambridge University Press.

Olson, D. R. (1996). Language and literacy: What writing does to language and mind. *Annual review of applied linguistics, 16*, 3–13.

Ong, W. (1982). *Orality and literacy: The technologizing of the word.* London: Routledge.

Oppenheimer, T. (1997, July). The computer delusion. *Atlantic Monthly,* pp. 48–62.

Pacey, A. (1992). *The culture of technology.* Cambridge, MA: MIT Press.

Panos Institute. (1995). *The Internet & the South: Superhighway or dirt track.* London: Panos Institute.

Paolilo, J. (1997, March). *Toward a sociolinguistic survey of South Asian cyberspace.* American Association for Applied Linguistics Annual Conference, Orlando, FL.

Peirce, B. N. (1993). *Language learning, social identity, and immigrant women.* Unpublished doctoral dissertation, Ontario Institute for Studies in Education,University of Toronto, Canada.

Peirce, B. N. (1995). Social identity, investment, and language learning. *TESOL Quarterly, 29*, 9–31.

Pennycook, A. (1995). English in the world/The world in English. In J. W. Tollefson (Ed.), *Power and inequality in language education* (pp. 34–58). Cambridge, England: Cambridge University Press.

Pennycook, A. (1996). Borrowing others' words: Text, ownership, memory, and plagiarism. *TESOL Quarterly, 30*, 201–230.

Penuel, W. R., & Wertsch, J. V. (1995). Vygotsky and identity formation: A sociocultural approach. *Educational psychologist, 30*(2), 83–92.

Phillipson, R., & Skutnabb-Kangas, T. (1996). English Only worldwide or language ecology. *TESOL Quarterly, 29*, 429–452.

Pica, T. (1994). Research on negotiation: What does it reveal about second-language learning conditions, processes, and outcomes? *Language Learning, 44*, 493–527.

Poole, D. (1990). Contextualizing IRE in an eighth-grade quiz review. *Linguistics and Education, 2*, 185–211.

Postman, N. (1992). *Technopoly: The surrender of culture to technology.* New York: Alfred Knopf.

Postman, N. (1995). *The end of education: Redefining the value of school.* New York: Vintage Books.

Quantz, R. A. (1992). On critical ethnography (with some postmodern considerations). In M. D. LeCompte, W. L. Millroy, & J. Preissle (Eds.), *The handbook of qualitative research in education* (pp. 447–506). San Diego, CA: Academic Press.

Quarterman, J. S. (1996). *Sizes of the Internet in 1995, from the Third MIDS Internet demographic survey* [online article]. Retrieved August 28, 1997, from the World Wide Web at http://www3.mids.org/mn/601/demo9510.html

Reich, R. (1991). *The work of nations: Preparing ourselves for 21st century capitalism.* New York: Knopf.

Reinecke, J. E. (1936). The competition of languages in Hawai'i. *Social Process in Hawai'i, 2*, 7–10.

Reinecke, J. E. (1969). *Language and dialect in Hawai'i.* Honolulu, HI: University of Hawai'i Press.

Rich, P., & De Los Reyes, G. (1995). An electronic library for a department of international relations and history in Mexico. In M. Warschauer (Ed.), *Virtual connections: Online activities and projects for networking language learners* (pp. 287–288). Honolulu, HI: University of Hawai'i, Second Language Teaching and Curriculum Center.

Rifkin, J. (1995). *The end of work.* New York: Tarcher/Putnam.

Roberts, J. M. (1991). *Language in Hawaii in the nineteenth century and its relation to Hawaiian Pidgin English.* Unpublished manuscript, University of Hawai'i, Honolulu.

Roberts, J. M. (1995). Pidgin Hawaiian, a sociohistorical study. *Journal of pidgin and creole languages, 10*(1), 1–56.

Rosaldo, R. (1989). *Culture and truth: The remaking of social analysis.* Boston: Beacon Press.

Roszak, T. (1994). *The cult of information: A neo-Luddite treatise on high-tech, artificial intelligence, and the true art of thinking* (2nd ed.). Berkeley, CA: University of California Press.

Sandholtz, J. H., Ringstaff, C., & Dwyer, D. C. (1997). *Teaching with technology: Creating student-centered classrooms.* New York: Teachers College Press.

Sato, C. (1985). Linguistic inequality in Hawaii: The post-creole dilemma. In N. Wolfson & J. Manes (Eds.), *Language of inequality* (pp. 255–272). Berlin: Moutin Publishers.

Sato, C. (1991). Sociolinguistic variation and language attitudes in Hawaii. In J. Cheshire (Ed.), *English around the world: Sociolinguistic perspectives* (pp. 647–663). Cambridge, England: Cambridge University Press.

Sayers, D. (1993). Distance team teaching and computer learning networks. *TESOL Journal, 3*(1), 19–23.

Schiller, H. I. (1996). *Information inequality: The deepening social crisis in America.* New York: Routledge.

Schmidt, R. (1983). Interaction, acculturation, and the acquisition of communicative competence: A case study. In N. Wolfson & E. Judd (Eds.), *Sociolinguistics and Language Acquisition* (pp. 137–174). Rowley, MA: Newbury House.

Schmidt, R. (1993). Awareness and second language acquisition. *Annual Review of Applied Linguistics, 13*, 206–226.

Schütz, A. J. (1994). *The voices of Eden.* Honolulu, HI: University of Hawai'i Press.

Schütz, A. J. (1995). *All about Hawaiian.* Honolulu, HI: University of Hawai'i Press.

Schwartz, P., & Ogilvy, J. (1979). *The emergent paradigm: Changing patterns of thought and belief* (Analytical Report No. 7). Melo Park, CA: SRI International.

Senge, P. (1991). *The fifth discipline: The art and practice of the learning organization.* New York: Doubleday.

Shor, I. (1992). *Empowering education.* Chicago: University of Chicago Press.

Sims, B. R. (1996). Electronic mail in two corporate workplaces. In P. Sullivan & J. Dautermann (Eds.), *Electronic literacies in the workplace: Technologies of writing* (pp. 41–64). Urbana, IL: National Council of Teachers of English.

Sing, D. K. (1986). *Raising the achievement level of native Hawaiians in the college classroom through the matching of teaching strategies with student characteristics.* Unpublished doctoral dissertation, Claremont Graduate School, CA.

Slatin, J. (1990a). Computer teachers respond to Halio. *Computers and Composition, 7*(3), 73–79.

Slatin, J. (1990b). Reading hypertext: Order and coherence in a new medium. *College English, 52,* 870–883.

Sleeter, C. E., & Grant, C. A. (1988). *Making choices for multicultural education: Five approaches to race, class, and gender.* Columbus, OH: Merrill.

Soh, B.-L., & Soon, Y. P. (1991). English by e-mail: creating a global classroom via the medium of computer technology. *ELT Journal, 45,* 287–292.

Spicer, E. H. (1980). *The Yaquis: A cultural history.* Tucson, AZ: Tucson Arizona Press.

Spiro, R. J., Feltovich, P. J., Jacobson, M. J., & Coulson, R. L. (1991). Cognitive flexibility, constructivism, and hypertext: Random access instruction for advanced knowledge acquisition in ill-structured domains. *Educational Technology, 31*(5), 24–33.

Spradley, J. P. (1980). *Participant observation.* New York: Holt, Rinehart & Winston.

Sproull, L., & Kiesler, S. (1986). Reducing social context clues: Electronic mail in organizational communication. *Management Science, 32,* 1492–1512.

Sproull, L., & Kiesler, S. (1991). *Connections: New ways of working in the networked organization.* Cambridge, MA: MIT Press.

Stoll, C. (1995). *Silicone snake oil: Second thoughts on the Information Highway.* New York: Anchor Books.

Street, B. (1993). Introduction: The new literacy studies. In B. V. Street (Ed.), *Cross-cultural approaches to literacy* (pp. 1–21). Cambridge, England: Cambridge University Press.

Street, B. V. (1984). *Literacy in theory and practice.* Cambridge, U.K.: Cambridge University Press.

Sullivan, N., & Pratt, E. (1996). A comparative study of two ESL writing environments: A computer-assisted classroom and a traditional oral classroom. *System, 24,* 491–501.

Susser, B. (1992). ESL/EFL process writing with computers. *CAELL, 4*(2), 16–22.

Takenaka, C. (1995). *A perspective on Hawaiians.* Honolulu, HI: Hawai'i Community Foundation Diversity Project.

Takeuchi, D. T., Agbayani, A., & Kuniyoshi, L. (1990). Higher education in Hawai'i: A comparison of graduation rates among Asian and Pacific Americans. In R. Endo, V. Chattergy, S. Chou, & N. Tsuchida (Eds.), *Contemporary perspectives on Asian and Pacific American education* (pp. 78–95). South El Monte, CA: Pacific Asia Press.

Talbott, S. L. (1995). *The future does not compute: Transcending the machines in our midst.* Sebastopol, CA: O'Reilly & Associates.

Tharp, R. G., & Gallimore, R. (1988). *Rousing minds to life: Teaching, learning, and schooling in social context.* New York: Cambridge University Press.

The Coming Global Tongue. (1996, December 21). The coming global tongue. *Economist,* pp. 75–77.

Thomas, J. (1993). *Doing critical ethnography.* Newbury Park, CA: Sage.

Tobin, J., & Tobin, L. (1997, July). *Case studies of an adolescent girl's and an adolescent boy's lives on the Internet.* Computers & Writing Conference, Honolulu, HI.

Trask, H. K. (1993). *From a native daughter : Colonialism and sovereignty in Hawai'i.* Honolulu, HI: Common Courage Press.

Tuman, M. (1992). *Word perfect: Literacy in the computer age.* Pittsburgh, PA: University of Pittsburgh Press.

Tuman, M. C. (1996). *Prof. Tuman responds* [Essay]. Retrieved July 2, 1997, from the World Wide Web at http://raven.ubalt.edu/staff/kaplan/lit/Tuman_responds.html

Turkle, S. (1995). *Life on the screen: Identity in the age of the Internet.* New York: Simon & Schuster.

Volosinov, V. N. (1973). *Marxism and the philosophy of language* (L. Matejka, & I. R. Titunik, Trans.). New York: Seminar Press.

Wang, Y. M. (1993). *E-mail dialogue journaling in an ESL reading and writing classroom*. Unpublished doctoral dissertation, University of Oregon, Eugene.

Warner, S. L. (1996). *I ola ka 'ōlelo i nā keiki: Ka 'apo 'ia 'ana o ka 'ōlelo Hawai'i e nā keiki ma ke kula kaiapuni*. Unpublished doctoral dissertation, University of Hawai'i.

Warschauer, M. (1995a). *E-mail for English teaching*. Alexandria, VA: TESOL Publications.

Warschauer, M. (Ed.) (1995b). *Virtual connections: Online activities and projects for networking language learners*. Honolulu, HI: University of Hawai'i, Second Language Teaching and Curriculum Center.

Warschauer, M. (1996). Comparing face-to-face and electronic communication in the second language classroom. *CALICO Journal, 13*(2), 7–26.

Warschauer, M. (1997). Computer-mediated collaborative learning: Theory and practice. *Modern Language Journal, 81*, 470–481.

Warschauer, M., & Donaghy, K. (1997). Léokī: A powerful voice of Hawaiian language revitalization. *Computer Assisted Language Learning, 10*, 349–362.

Weedon, C. (1987). *Feminist practice and poststructuralist theory*. London: Blackwell.

Weinert, R. (1995). The role of formulaic language in second language acquisition. *Applied Linguistics, 16*, 180–205.

Weisband, S. P. (1992). Group discussion and first advocacy effects in computer-mediated and face-to-face decision making groups. *Organizational Behavior and Human Decision Processes, 53*, 352–380.

Wells, G. (Ed.). (1994). *Changing schools from within: Creating communities of inquiry*. Portsmouth, NH: Heinemann.

Wells, G., & Chang-Wells, G. L. (1992). *Constructing knowledge together*. Portsmouth, NH: Heinemann.

Wertsch, J., & Bivens, J. A. (1992). The social origins of individual mental functioning: Alternatives and perspectives. *The quarterly newsletter of the laboratory of comparative human cognition, 14*(2), 35–44.

Whitney, S. (1987). "I would always take care of my net": Self-esteem and the assumptive world of local youth. *The Journal of the Hawaii Community Education Association, 1*(1), 7–13.

Whyte, W. F., Greenwood, D. J., & Lazes, P. (1991). Participatory action research: Through practice to science in social research. In W. F. Whyte (Ed.), *Participatory Action Research* (pp. 19–55). Newbury Park, CA: Sage.

Williams, R. (1977). *Marxism and literature*. New York: Oxford University Press.

Wilson, W. H. (in press). *International Journal of the Sociology of Language*.

Wilson, W. H. (in press). I ka '-ēlelo Hawai'i Ke ola, "Life is found in the Hawaiian language." *International Journal of the Sociology of Language*.

Wong-Fillmore, L. (1976). *The second time around: Cognitive and social strategies in second language acquisition*. Unpublished doctoral dissertation, Stanford University, Stanford, CA.

Wresch, W. (1996). *Disconnected: Haves and have-nots in the information age*. New Brunswick, NJ: Rutgers University Press.

Youra, S. (1990). Computers and composition: Maiming the Macintosh (a response). *Computers and Composition, 7*(3), 81–88.

Zamel, V. (1995). Strangers in academia: The experiences of faculty and ESL students across the curriculum. *College Composition and Communication, 46*, 506–521.

Ziman, J. (1968). *Public knowledge: The social dimension of science*. Cambridge, England: Cambridge University Press.

Zuboff, S. (1988). *In the age of the smart machine: The future of work and power*. New York: Basic Books.

Author Index

Subject Index

A

Aboriginal groups on the Internet, 20
Academic listservs, *see* Mailing lists
Alphabet, English, 175
Alphabetic literacy, 106
Apprenticeship learning, 47–60
Archiving indigenous languages, 19
ASCII (American Standard Code for Information Exchange), 171, 173
Asian students, preference of electronic over face-to-face discussion, 135–136
Assembly line, 4n.1
Assignments, e-mail, 24–25, 71
Assimilation, 94–97
Asynchronous computer-communication, 6
Audience, writing for an, 144, 152–153, 162
Australia, Aboriginal groups on the Internet, 20
Authenticity, 59
Authoring, collaborative, 61–62
Automobile industry, 10
Autonomous models of literacy, 174

B

Bay College, 126–128
  English 215, 128–130, 186–187
    cooperative relationships, 148
    critical awareness, 151–152

decentered organization, 147
discussions using Daedalus Interchange, 131–135
downtime, 148–150
face-to-face discussion, 134–135
home pages, *see* Service learning, web-based projects
immersion philosophy, 130–131
learning by doing, 147–148
real-world writing, 140–143, 151–152
service learning, *see* Service learning
social construction of knowledge, 136–138
World Wide Web, learning to write for, 143–147
Books, 2
Bulletin boards, 6
  Hawaiian, 20n.6, 122–123
  Maori, 20n.6

C

Campus Compact, 127, 128
Career Placement Center, service learning project for, 142–143, 150–151, 161
CD-ROMs, 8
Chat groups, 6
Chinese students, preference of electronic over face-to-face discussion, 135–136
Cognition, 5–6
Collaborative apprenticeship, 47, 60